The author Anthony (Tony) Tennaro was the son of two Italian immigrants. A High School graduate, Tony was fortunate to get into the Grocery Store business, because Tony loved working in the store, eventually being promoted to Store Manager. But Tony's greatest 'gift' was that of his affinity to the female population. For some unforeseen reason females of all ages are drawn to have sexual relations with Tony and Tony is always willing to oblige.

I want to thank all of the women that I have had the pleasure, of pleasuring. I have enjoyed it as much as you have!

Antoine Tennaro

THE SEXPERT

One man's sexual exploits
with a multitude of women

AUSTIN MACAULEY PUBLISHERS™

LONDON • CAMBRIDGE • NEW YORK • SHARJAH

Ordering Information
Quantity sales: Special discounts are available on quantity purchases by corporations, associations, and others. For details, contact the publisher at the address below.

Publisher's Cataloging-in-Publication data
Tennaro, Antoine
The Sexpert

ISBN 9798889109334 (Paperback)
ISBN 9798889109341 (Hardback)
ISBN 9798889109365 (ePub e-book)
ISBN 9798889109358 (Audiobook)

Library of Congress Control Number: 2023924223

www.austinmacauley.com/us

First Published 2024
Austin Macauley Publishers LLC
40 Wall Street, 33rd Floor, Suite 3302
New York, NY 10005
USA

mail-usa@austinmacauley.com
+1 (646) 5125767

Table of Contents

Foreword

Prepare yourself to take a sensual trip in the life of Tony Tennaro. His sexual exploits are incredible. You will see that he learns as he goes along (and so will you).

Other than Tony, there are no names—of cities or individuals. The women that Tony is intimate with are referred to by number. All of the women, men, and places are a figment of Tony's imagination, yet the realism in the story is incredibly believable.

A listing describing the variety of sexual positions and a listing of definitions describing parts of the anatomy are included at the end of the story.

Relax, enjoy, and learn as you read.

Chapter 1
In the Beginning

It was a cool evening, in the 30s, but as I walked off the porch of my house toward the sidewalk, I took in a deep breath of cool air and it felt great. I was filled with pride since this would be my first New Year's Eve that I would be away from my extremely protective parents. How I got permission to spend the night with my friends was mind-boggling. It may have a little to do with the fact that at 6'2" and with a muscular build, my folks thought that I could take care of myself, or it may be that I had a knack for staying out of trouble, or that I was a silver-tongued devil…

So, off I went, to meet up with my buddies at the local hangout spot, the ice cream shop, for 7 pm. It's not a long walk, about a half mile. Although it was cool outside, I was dressed warmly in a black leather jacket, black leather gloves and blue jeans … no hat since it would muss up my hair.

When I arrived, I could see two of my buddies standing in a corner of the parking lot. They were pleased to see me and eager for our fourth friend to arrive so that we could begin our evening's activities. After shooting the breeze for about 5 minutes, W arrived and we set off.

Our de facto leader, B, at 15 years old was a year older than the rest of us and, having had more experience, was calling the shots and we were only too happy to follow along.

We were on a search for some girls that we could party with, so we first checked out the ice cream shop, next we went down the main street to the bowling alley, then over to the pizza house, then back to the ice cream shop. We made the round trip three times over the next several hours. We ran into several friends … but no girls!

Somewhat discouraged, when it started to snow ever so lightly, our leader suggested that we head over to his house to shoot some pool and drink some beer. That sounded great since my nose and ears were freezing.

B's parents were gone for the night and they allowed B to have up to 3 friends over for the night. His parents spoke to our parents and everything was cool.

B's house was quite large, with 5 bedrooms up and a basement loaded with gaming tables and equipment; like a full-size pool table, a card table, air hockey, a ping pong table and a seating area around a TV that was hooked up to a variety of games. I loved it!

Once there, we headed directly to the basement to shed our jackets and pick teams to play pool. B went up to the kitchen and returned with four cold beers … can it get any better?

For the first several hours, we played pool, drank several beers, and told some dirty jokes. Then, when we heard a car pull into the driveway, about 11:30 pm, and B said, "She's back early!" Meaning his sister, a senior in high school and one of the hottest chicks I'd ever seen, was back from her date with some college guy. B's sister was 5'6" tall, had beautiful blond hair, usually pulled back into a ponytail, gorgeous blue eyes, cute nose, full luscious looking lips, terrific breasts, small waist, great butt and super fantastic legs, which she usually showed off by wearing short skirts. B had earlier instructed us to run upstairs and hide in the living room to watch what happened between his sister and her date when they came in. B's sister did not have a good reputation at school (she was known as a slut). So, we all ran up and took positions behind sofas and chairs to watch, what we imagined to be, some sort of sexual display.

As they came into the foyer, the sister took off her coat and tossed it over a chair, she was wearing an absolutely beautiful pink party dress (low cut, with tiny straps and it was fairly short), displaying her perfect body. Much to our dismay, she was arguing vehemently about something with a tall, muscular guy in a gray suit. I could tell that she was irritated about something, since she was doing all of the talking and in just a few minutes, she told the guy to leave. She slammed the door behind him and ran up the stairs, crying.

We were all bummed out since we thought we were going to watch the sister and her boyfriend in some sort of make-out session, or more. So, we each grabbed a beer and headed back to the basement.

My buddies decided to turn on the TV to watch the New Year's Eve ceremony at midnight, but it was a little early, so they started to play video games. I didn't play, not being into those types of games, I just drank my beer and waited for the ball to drop at midnight.

About fifteen minutes later, I was feeling tired, so I told the guys that I was headed to bed. B's older brother was away in the service and W and I were sharing his bedroom. Of course, on my way upstairs, I swung by the kitchen to get another beer. As I opened the refrigerator, B's sister came into the kitchen, looking hotter than ever in her pink baby doll PJs … WOW!

She came over to the refrigerator and said, "I came down for a bottle of champagne." Somewhat in a trance, I took a bottle from the refrigerator and handed it to her. She asked me to open it. I took the bottle over to the sink and I removed the foil and wire from the top. B's sister came over and pressed up against me to watch. This was hot, hot, hot since B's sister was not wearing any underwear. When the cork popped, she yelled and jumped up and down (rubbing her breasts against my arm).

The sister held two champagne glasses in front of me and said, "Fill them up!" I obeyed. She handed me one glass and said, "To a Happy New Year!" Then she tapped her glass against mine. We both took a drink and she smiled at me; with a glimmer in her eye, she said, "Grab the other bottle and come with me." She took the open bottle and headed out of the kitchen. Like an obedient servant, I grabbed the other bottle from the refrigerator and caught up to my new, beautiful, baby doll-clad drinking buddy as she was walking up the stairs … what a view! She led me to her bedroom, opened the door, and said, "Come in!"

As I entered her bedroom, I was amazed to see about 40 white candles burning brightly all around her room. With just the candlelight, I could see that everything in the room was pink. The sister shut off the TV and turned on some soft, slow music. She brought me over to her canopy bed and told me, "I am ready for another!" She put her glass out and I agreed and filled both of our glasses from the open bottle. She patted the bed and said, "Take a load off your feet." I sat down about a foot away from her and took a big gulp of my champagne.

The sister started to explain what a crumby night she had with her date. Evidently, they had gone to a nice restaurant for dinner, dancing, and a New Year's Eve celebration. While they were eating their dinner, the guy she was with saw his ex-girlfriend. Her date left B's sister at the table for the longest time, while he talked with this other girl. It was obvious that her date cared for the ex-girlfriend much more than her, so, the sister was miffed and when he returned to the table, the sister demanded that he bring her directly home. As she told the story, from time to time, she would stick out her glass and I would fill it up, then she would continue on with her story. I would console her at various points and she seemed to like that.

In no time at all, the first bottle was empty, so, I opened the second bottle. At that moment, I was a little buzzed from the booze and I was lying on the bed just listening to this gorgeous gal, with see-through PJs, babble on … thinking it doesn't get any better that this!

Eventually, the sister stopped, hesitated a moment, then with a sigh said, "And I was really horny too."

Immediately, without thinking, I replied, "And so am I!"

She just stared at me, then she slid over next to me, put her face near mine, and said softly, "You know, you're a great guy." As I started to smile, she lowered her face and started to kiss me very sensuously. When we started to French kiss, she put her hand on my jean-covered crotch and started to rub it around. I was stunned and couldn't move a muscle … but it didn't stop me from getting an immediate erection (I think she liked that). After a minute or two, B's sister took my hand and put it on her breast … whaaa-who!

Now, my instincts kicked in. I started to caress her breast with one hand, while the other hand caressed her back (under the nightie). She started to moan and wiggle around … I was thinking, this was good! The sister stopped kissing me for a second and said, "You're a really good kisser," then, she resumed the kiss with a little more passion. Next, she slid her knee up, to rub on my crotch, and she slipped her hand under my sweater to rub around on my chest … talk about hot! As her tongue probed the recesses of my mouth, her knee, with incredible expertise, rubbed my already engorged manhood and her hand, ever so softly (and sensuously), stroked my nipples and caressed my breasts and abs.

Learning from what she was doing to me, I softened my grip on her breast and started to more delicately caress her breasts, sort of rubbing the bottom of her breast, while lightly lifting it up … she seemed to really like what I was doing … I know I loved what she was doing to me … I was almost too hot! I slowly slid my other hand down her back, into her panty and I softly cupped and squeezed the check of her butt and I pulled her into me. She started to moan and sigh, which turned me on even more! Knowing that I could give such an experienced girl the kind of pleasure that she was giving me.

All of a sudden, she sat up and announced, "Let's get out of these clothes!" As she sat on the edge of the bed to slip off her panties, I kicked off my sneakers, stood up, pulled my sweater over my head (tossed it on the floor) and grabbed the waistbands of my jeans and boxers and pushed them off. It took me just seconds to remove all but my socks. As I turned naked back toward the bed, with a smile and a raging erection, I was proud of my body. B's sister reached into her bed stand drawer, removed a condom and placed it in my hand and said, "You better put this on."

With B's sister lying on the other side of the bed, I sat down on the edge of the bed to put the condom on. Fortunately, I knew how to put a condom on, since I had done it once before. When an older friend bought a pack of three and gave me one. Of course, I was alone when I put that one on and I was so excited that I came almost immediately from just putting it on. I hoped that wouldn't happen this time.

Then, with just my socks and the condom on, I laid on my side next to B's sister. She was lying on her back. In the soft light of the candles, her perfect breasts pointed straight up in the air, just calling for my attention! So, I lowered my mouth onto her dark, pink, stiff nipple and started to kiss and run my tongue around. My hand was caressing her other breast and B' sister pressed her chest up into my mouth, and she was moaning. This was the first time doing this, but I could tell B's sister was enjoying it!

I became more aggressive, as I was gaining confidence. So, I decided to move my hand down between her legs. Ever so softly, I dragged my hand across her body. On the trip down to her golden triangle. She was definitely a real blond! When my hand reached its destination, B's sister spread her legs. As I started to rub around, she started to grind her hips … this was starting to excite me, more and more, so, I started to suck and lick harder than before. Finally, I stuck my middle finger between the moist lips of her vulva and started to move it up and down … she moaned, "Yes!"

Then, I lifted my head off her breast and I started to kiss her aggressively. She put one hand on each side of my face, holding and caressing it so softly. All the while, my finger was working like a jackhammer between her legs. She lifted my head up, looked me in the eye and said, "Let's put it in!" WOW!

Well, all of this sexual activity had excited me to the point that I, fortunately, had the biggest erection of my life. I quickly got on my knees between her legs, which were now widely spread and I guided my shaft into her spectacular cavity (the missionary position). The first few strokes were very slow and she was very tight, which made me too hot to hold back … so I started to pump in and out faster and faster … I could feel her vagina getting more and more slippery. BANG! BANG! BANG! I have never felt anything so good in my life! BANG! BANG! BANG!

My climax came so quickly, I didn't want #1 to be left out so I just kept pumping away for a while and when I felt #1 relax, I slowed way down, lowered myself down and kissed her. #1 said, "You have a great erection!" That was the best compliment that I have ever received!

In a short time, #1 said, "Let's get up and clean up." While I hated the moment to end, I knew that she was right, When I stood up, #1 gave me a wad of tissues to put my condom in when I took it off. Once I put the condom in the tissue and wiped my penis off, #1 asked for the wad of tissues back. I handed it to her and she went to a small trash receptacle next to her bed, removed the plastic bag that was in it and deposited the wad in another plastic bag which was beneath. The bottom bag appeared to have a number of similar contributions. #1 said, "I don't want my mom finding condoms in the trash."

"Good idea!" I agreed.

I slipped back into my pants and put on my sweater and sneakers, as #1 slipped back into her nighty and panties. Then, as I turned to go, #1 came over to me, put her hands on each side of my face, gave me a short, soft, sensuous kiss and said, "Thank you for making my New Year's Eve special!"

I was stunned … my reply was, "It was completely my pleasure!" And that was the truth.

As I left her room, #1 said, "Now don't tell anyone what we did."

I replied, "Don't worry, a gentleman would never tell," She smiled and waved goodbye.

I went to the bathroom and as I walked to my room, I could hear the other guys, somewhat drunk and very loud, coming up from the basement to go to bed. Moments after shutting off the light and getting into bed, W came into the room and turned on the light. Slurring his words, he mumbled, "What a great night!" Then, he staggered to the edge of the bed, kicked off his sneakers, laid face down on the bed and fell immediately to sleep. I got up, shut off the light and laid in bed with a huge smile on my face, contemplating my accomplishment.

The following day, we were back in school. I almost always walked to and back home from school with my longtime friend, confidant and next-door neighbor (a girl). We would always return to her house to do our homework, while she watched her little brother and sister. She was the only person in the neighborhood that was my age. All the boys were 3 years older or 3 years younger. I played ball with the older guys because I was so tall … I was six feet tall at eleven years old, but I didn't have much in common with them. My neighbor-girl and I were always going through the same things, at the same time and we could discuss them together in complete confidence.

For example, we taught each other how to dance and how to kiss. We learned to dance by watching dance shows on TV and then mimicking their movements. Being such close friends, we didn't worry about screwing up in front of each other. We understood that we were both learning and we gave each other constructive criticism.

She was tall, 5'8", with a slender build. Her medium brown hair was shoulder-length, parted in the middle; she had a fairly light complexion, cute face, small breasts, tiny waist, small hips with a nice butt and long, thin legs.

As we walked along, my gal-friend asked me what I did for New Year's Eve. I said that I had hung out with my buddies … W, B, and K. She had to stay home and watch her brother and sister … it was boring.

I must have displayed some sort of emotion when she asked me what we had done, so, as we walked along, she kept asking more questions about my evening. Finally, she said, "You got lucky … didn't you?"

With a big smile, I said, "Yes!" Then she started to pry into who it was and I said emphatically, "A gentleman would never tell!" By then we had reached the school and we went our separate ways.

On the way home, my gal-friend was even more inquisitive regarding the details of what I had done. Of course, I told her how fantastically wonderful the foreplay and sex were. As we walked down our street approaching her house, she said, "You have just got to show me!"

I looked at her, befuddled, and said, "Show you what?"

"Just how great it is … the sex," she replied. "You have to teach me how to do it right, so that I will be prepared for my first time with a boyfriend." This was not out of character for us, since we had taught each other how to dance and how to kiss. We had spent hours practicing our kissing technique, telling each other what we liked, what felt good and what didn't. I must say that all of the practicing really helped and prepared me for dating. Even #1 complemented on my kissing.

Being a teenage male with hormones cursing through my body, it would have been extremely difficult for me to refuse sex of any nature. So, I agreed that we could do it. For instructional purposes only.

Once inside her house, my neighbor gal-friend took out an electronic game that she had received for Christmas and she set it up for the kids to play with. "That will keep them busy for hours," she said. Next, she went into her parent's bedroom and returned with a condom. We usually did our homework in her bedroom, so, that did not alarm her siblings. She closed and locked the bedroom door.

"Where do we start?" She asked.

I decided that we should start by kissing. She decided we should strip down to our underwear and get under the covers … which we did. I started to kiss and caress her breasts (which was what #1 had done to me). I suggested that she should rub her hand around on my crotch. WOW! She aggressively complied, but I had to instruct her to rub her hand around softly and slowly … so she wouldn't make me come too soon. Then, we went back to kissing and fondling. Next, I taught her how #1 rubbed her knee on my crotch … freeing up her hand to softly touch my face and neck, my chest and nipple and my abs (and I explained how hot it made me). Slowly I moved my hand down between her legs and rubbed around, while we were kissing. I could tell this was exciting her, but I had to tell her to spread her legs, so I could get my fingers between them. After a few minutes of slowly, softly caressing this area, she started to squirm around, as #1 had done … what I was doing must be working. Carefully, I slipped my finger under the leg band of her undies and I started to explore the moist folds beneath. She whispered, "Oh boy that feels great!" She must have been enjoying it, for she reached down and slipped off her panties. I took that as a signal that she would like me to get even more aggressive with my fondling. So, I felt around for the opening to her vagina and I slipped my finger in. She repositioned her hips/legs to allow me better access. I very gently pulled my finger out and slipped it all the way up over her clitoris untill I reached the top folds of her labia, which I gave a tug … she moaned and held her breath, so I started the decent of my finger along the same path. Each time I made my descent, I could feel her getting wetter and wetter.

Next, I tried to push her bra up over her breasts, but she sat up, unsnapped it and threw it onto the floor. When she laid back down, she grabbed my head and brought my mouth to her tiny brown nipple. I started to lick and suck on that nipple and as it became stiff in my mouth, she started groaning. I looked into her eyes and said, "Let's put it in!"

She replied, "Are you ready?"

I could not have been hotter after all of the foreplay, so I replied, "Men are always ready!"

I had to put the condom on … so, as quickly as possible I laid on my back, threw the covers off, slid my boxers off and with my erection sticking straight up into the air, I rolled on the condom.

My partner gasped when she saw the size of my manhood. "Is that going to fit inside of me?" She asked.

"I hope so." I don't think she ever saw an erection before and mine looked enormous at the moment … I was very proud!

Next, I kneeled between her legs. She was ready! As I gently pushed the head of my erection into her love canal, I started to run into an obstacle and could not penetrate any further … so, I pulled out and slipped it in again, but I just could not slide in as expected. I pushed a little harder and then I reached down and lifted her hips up, to get a better angle of entry, then, all of a sudden, the impediment opened up and I slid in all the way.

"OUCH, OUCH, OUCH!" Screamed #2. I felt really bad for hurting her, so, I pulled out. "No!" she said. "Put it back in!"

As I put it back in, I said, "I don't want to hurt you."

#2 replied, "It feels great!" Obediently, I pushed back in and began to stroke in and out, trying not to hurt her anymore, but the real passion was gone. Fairly quickly I came to a climax and continued the pumping for a while after my spasms stopped. #2 looked like she had enough, so I pulled out and as I did, I noticed blood on the sheet.

#2 explained the blood on the sheet was from her broken hymen (a membrane which partially closes the opening of the vagina and whose presence is traditionally taken to be a mark of virginity).

#2 jumped up, put on a robe and removed the sheets from the bed while I removed my condom. I rolled it up in a wad of tissues and stuffed it into my jeans pocket. "I'll put the sheets in the wash and tell my mom we spilled soda on them while we were studying," she said.

"Good thinking," I said, as I completed getting dressed. "I am sorry that I hurt you," I confided.

#2 just looked me in the eye and said, "It only hurt for a second and then I was fine."

I grabbed my books, said my goodbyes to #2 and the kids and headed home. Of course, I had to get rid of the evidence first. I went directly into the garage and hid the wad of tissues containing the used condom and love juice in a box in the trash. No one will ever find it since I was the one responsible for taking the trash out.

Then, I really had to buckle down to finish my homework before dinner.

The next day, #2 was beaming when I picked her up for our walk to school. Her thin lips had a permanent smile during out walk and all she could talk about was what a great time we had the previous afternoon. That made me feel better because I was still sorry for hurting her.

#2 said, "You really seemed like you knew what you were doing."

I replied, "Yeah … after all the experience I've had!"

"Give me a week to heal and then let's do it again and work on our technique," #2 insisted and I reluctantly agreed.

The week went by quickly and on the walk home from school, #2 asked how much homework I had?

"Not much."

"Great!" She said, "We can work on our love making technique when we get home."

Once we got to #2's house, she was hell-bent to get going. She put a movie on for her brother and sister, got a condom and a small bottle of some sort of lubricant from her parent's bedroom and turned down the covers on the bed.

"Let's start out nude this time," she announced. I took off everything but my socks and slid under the covers. #2 was down to her bra and panties and had her back toward the bed. As I watched her unfasten her bra, I noticed that she had a much more sensuous body than I had envisioned and her butt looked hot, as she removed her panties, I was getting aroused!

#2 quickly slipped under the covers and said, "Let's start with the kissing, but I want to use this lubricant when we actually do it."

"That's fine with me," I replied.

#2 smiled, turned on her side, held my face in her hands and brought her lips to mine. The kissing was sensational, with tongues darting all over. When

I placed my hand on her naked breast #2 went, "Ummm." A good response, I think. Very soon, #2 reached down and picked up my penis; she gently put her hand around it, picked it up and slid her hand downward. HOLY COW … that is hot! This was the first time, someone other than me had held my penis and it felt phenomenal! Unfortunately, if she continued to stroke me … I was going to climax! "You better stop doing that … for now," I bleeped out … "You're getting me too hot too fast!"

"Does it feel good?" asked #2.

"It feels too good," I assured her that what she was doing felt WONDERFUL!

"You really have a big penis," #2 whispered … "I like to hold it," she said as she nestled her body closer to me. I explained that direct skin contact is a bit too intense for me at this stage and it would be safer to keep the sheets between her hand and my manhood. #2 complied and now I became the aggressor, positioning my head over her nipple. I started to rub my tongue around and softly lick, while moving my hand slowly down her body … caressing her skin ever so softly with my fingers … circling her belly button and then moving to my destination … between her legs. #2 held her breath as my hand moved southward and remembering our first encounter, she spread her legs as my fingers approached. Next, I started to stroke up and down and caress the folds of her skin. "Let's try the lube," #2 urged, as she handed me the bottle.

I was thinking, 'How the heck am I going to do this'. So, I pulled back the covers, reached down with the bottle, squirted some of the magic fluid onto #2's crotch and started to rub it in. My fingers quickly parted #2's love lips and then I squirted more lube inside of them. Next, I spread some of the lube up over #2's clitoris, circling it several times. #2 relaxed and laid back on the bed, evidently enjoying what I was doing. Next, my fingers pushed some of the lube down to and into #2's love canal. That made her moan, "That feels fantastic! I love it when you circle my clit then go down into my love canal … it makes me soooo hot!" She whispered. I continued for several minutes then #2 said, "I want you to put it in me … I am wicked hot!"

I slipped on the condom she had given me and I knelt between her legs, "Try some more of that lube oil," #2 instructed me. With one hand I parted her love lips and squirted some more oil on them and I squirted some oil in her love canal, as well. Next, I put some oil on my already lubricated condom. As

I started to move inward, I slid the head of my erection up and down between her slippery folds … it felt great! When I started to push my erection into #2, she was so well lubricated that I went … wham … all the way in (the missionary position). It took #2's breath away and surprised me as well. #2 told me to. "Pull it out slowly and I will tell you when to stop." I obeyed. "Now slowly in … now slowly out," she instructed, over and over. I could feel the rim on the head of my penis rubbing against #2's G-spot, and she loved it!

As I continued my movements, I could see #2's face getting more and more serious, she reached out to the sides and grabbed a handful of the sheets with each hand and then, her whole body began to shake and spasm. As #2's vagina started to tighten and loosen, I had become so hot that I could not contain myself anymore and I started to thrust violently in and out … BANG … BANG … BANG! I was shooting my sperm into the condom as #2 arched her body for more! I continued to thrust until both of our bodies relaxed. Then I laid on my back feeling spent.

#2 turned on her side, looked me in the eye, smiled, then murmured, "That was beautiful … I never imagined that sex could be that great … WOW!"

I asked, "Did you have an orgasm?"

#2 replied, "Yes … that was my first real orgasm … and it was FANTASTIC!" She could barely get the words out, since she was out of breath.

I laid on my back, staring at the ceiling thinking how great sex was for me and how much pleasure I could give someone else … WOW! Suddenly, I was brought back to reality, feeling the 'drippage' from my condom as my erection subsided. I sat up, grabbed a wad of tissues and deposited the condom, tissues and contents in the pocket of my jeans.

When #2 sat up, she laughed … there was a great big oil stain, on the sheets, in the middle of the bed. She pulled off the sheet to put it into the wash and said, "I guess we spilled another soda."

I chuckled, and replied, "Yeah!"

After getting dressed and depositing the used condom in my trash at home, I headed to my bedroom. Lying on my back in my bed, I reflected on what we had done. How I had come to know all about sex … and how lucky I was. Little did I know then that I had discovered only the tip of the iceberg.

Chapter 2
Discovery

As I contemplate how fortunate I have been to have had sex with two considerate girls, I am coming to the realization that I was fortunate that they both had protection available. I realize that I cannot continue to rely on my partner. I need to be prepared. I will need to purchase condoms and keep them on my person at all times.

So, just how will I pull off this purchase? I can't go to the local pharmacy; the owner knows my parents by name. The next town is about 8 miles away, they have several pharmacies and I remember going into one that had a back door, which was next to the pharmaceutical counter (I was thinking that this would be advantageous, since once purchased, I could just exit the store without all of the customers watching me walk through the entire store with my loot).

With the decision made where the purchase would take place, I headed for the store. On arrival I leaned my bike against the back wall of the building, took a deep breath and entered the store. I walked in and the pharmaceutical counter was to my right. I went directly into one of the aisles so that I could look around to see who was shopping in the store (fortunately there were only a few shoppers). I checked to see if anyone was at the pharmaceutical counter (no one in the area) and what the pharmacist looked like … there was a man, in his 20's on the second level behind the counter, filling prescriptions. All indications were a "go."

As I approached the counter, sweating profusely, to try to make my first purchase of sexual protective devices, I started to think "is there an age limit to buy this stuff … hopefully not." When I finally reached the counter, a beautiful, young, blond pharmacist popped out from behind a counter display that she was filling. She had a very light complexion, with gorgeous blue eyes, bright red lipstick on her lips, wearing a crisp white smock with a gold name tag stating that she was a pharmacist. OH NO! Not a girl! How could I ever ask her for condoms? I just stood at the counter stuttering and looking around.

She smiled and very nicely asked, "Can I help you?"

Oh boy, could she! Looking down at the counter, I just couldn't look her in the eye, I mustered up the courage to say, "I would like a package of three condoms … please."

She smiled again, then she opened a drawer, looked inside and asked, "What kind?"

What kind! Do I look like a connoisseur of condoms? What kind! How the heck would I know? Then, it came to me, "Lubricated," I replied.

She reached into the drawer, took out a package, put it into a small white bag, folded the top down a few times and came back to the register. I was soooo embarrassed, I must have been 1,000 degrees, sweating and I must have been blushing bright red, but I paid for my purchase and quickly turned and walked out of the store.

Outside I got thinking that this was the hardest thing that I have ever done. I was glad that I did this at a young age, for I don't know if my heart could have taken this much pressure if I was older.

As I rode home on my bike, I thought to myself, 'now you are prepared.' But when … if ever … will I get to use my protection? It didn't matter … I was prepared.

******

One warm spring evening, I was walking by this big old church, as a gal I met through #2 was just walking out. She was wearing a pretty dress and high heels. Although she was very attractive, her best attribute was that she had the nicest breasts in the school. She had a very friendly and bubbly personality, so I didn't think twice about approaching her.

"Confessing all your sins?" I asked.

She laughed, threw her shoulder-length brown hair back and replied, "I sing in the choir."

"How are you getting home?" I asked. Knowing that she lived over a mile away.

"Walking, of course."

"I better walk with you to keep you safe." I said with conviction.

She wrapped both of her arms around my right arm and snuggled her body into my side, while looking into my eyes saying, "You are such a gentleman … I would like that!"

So, we began to walk. She was very easy to talk with and when she eventually let go of my arm, I kind of instinctively, put my arm around her shoulder and held her closely … and she did not pull away!

WOW! Here I was walking with this HOT girl and I had the guts to put my arm around her. Of course, had I thought about it beforehand, I wouldn't have been able to move my arm at all. She seemed to like me and was comfortable with me, as I pretended to be her protector.

As we walked toward her house, we decided to take a short cut though an old cemetery. Since it was dark and romantic, I thought it would be a great opportunity to try for a kiss. I knew I was taking a big chance, but this gal was very pretty, had a great figure and she had been making me hornier and hornier as we have walked along, with her rubbing up against me. What the heck … go for it!

So, I stopped … turned to face her … pulled her toward me … and I planted a nice, soft kiss on her full luscious lips. She did not pull away! After a while, I started to introduce my tongue and as I did, she pushed me away and said enthusiastically, "Let's hurry to my house, my father has a big boat stored in the backyard, and he just took the shrink wrap off … preparing it to go back into the water … I think you will like it." She took my hand and started to pull me along as she started to walk toward her house.

'ARE YOU KIDDING ME!' I was thinking. Why would I be more interested in a boat than kissing her? It really ruined the moment.

As we walked along, at a much faster pace now, she couldn't stop telling me all about the boat in her backyard.

I didn't want to break her heart by telling her that at 15, I was really into girls and definitely not into boats. So, I just let her go on and on, with her preoccupation regarding the boat.

Eventually, when we reached her house, I could see, from the light of the streetlights, this monster big motor yacht in her yard … WOW! Then, I was interested in seeing the boat.

"Be very quiet," my guide whispered, "I don't want my folks to know that we are going onto the boat."

In the limelight of the backyard, she kicked off her high heels and I took off my sneakers. We climbed up a short stepladder onto a back platform of the boat, then, another short ladder brought us to the back deck of the motor yacht. WOW, the boat was big! I was getting very interested in checking this boat out. We opened the door end entered the living room of the boat, "This is the Salon," my guide decried. It was so dark that I could hardly see anything. I was able to make out the outline of the furniture but I was unable to tell exactly what it looked like.

"Where is the light switch?" I ask.

"Oh, we can't turn on the lights or my parents will know that we are here."

I was getting a bit frustrated, since she had been harping about the details on the boat for a while and without light, I really couldn't see very much.

She took my hand and led me through the boat to the master bedroom, where she opened up a hatch to let in more light. Then, I could see a large bed, sort of built into the wall, with cabinets for storage on each side.

Next, my little choirgirl surprised me with a slow, soft, sensuous kiss. I moved my hands to her back and pressed her body close to mine. She reached down, while we were kissing, and through the material of my jeans I could feel her hand caressing my manhood! This sent me a message loud and clear that she was interested in some sort of sexual activity … and so was I!

NOW, FINALLY … I was getting the message! She wanted to bring me to the boat so we could be in private, with a bed! What a dummy I was.

Once I came to the realization that we were there for SEX and not for a tour of the boat, I lowered my hands to feel her butt and I gently introduced a little tongue … she seemed to melt in my arms.

Then, abruptly she pushed me away, turned her back toward me and said, "Pull down my zipper."

As I lowered the zipper on her dress, she untied the bow in the back, reached up and dropped the dress to the floor. "Now unhook my bra," she asked, "We don't have much time. My parents will wonder where I am."

With her back still toward me, I diligently unhooked her bra and as I brought each end around to the front, I cupped her breasts in the palms of my hands and pulled her toward me. Her breasts were large, big, round, and incredibly soft.

She allowed me to have fun for a while, then, she turned toward me and said, "Take off your pants."

I quickly removed my belt and stepped out of my pants and boxers, she pushed down her dainty panties and kneeled on the floor. When I stood straight up, I peeled my off my T-shirt as she took my semi-erect penis in her hand, she pushed the foreskin back and sucked the head into her mouth … SHAZAM!

I was rock hard in a moment and loving what she was doing, but she stopped, stood up and asked, "Do you have any condoms?"

I was sooooo happy and sooooo proud of myself to be able to reply, "Of course!"

When I bent over to get the little package, containing one lubricated condom, she jumped onto the bed and laid on her back. When I climbed onto the bed, the streetlight shined through the hatch and directly onto her body, showing her perfectly formed breasts, large dark nipples and she spread her legs, displaying her love triangle, covered in thick brown curly pubic hair.

I laid on my side next to her, put one hand on her cheek and began to kiss her. I noticed a salty taste … it must have come from my penis when she was sucking on it. It wasn't objectionable, but it was noticeable. As the kiss progressively became more aggressive, I moved my hand onto her breast. Softly caressing around her breast and her nipple. I very lightly moved my fingertip back and forth over her nipple and I could feel it hardening as her body started to tremble. She turned toward me and started to run her free hand, up and down my arm and shoulder, I positioned my hand between her legs and started to move my middle finger up and down. Immediately, it found the crease between her love lips. which was moist already … good. I gently pressed downward to get to the entrance to her love canal and then back up to circle her clitoris, around the little knob and then back down and into the hole. My partner began to grind her hips into the mattress, as she pushed her pelvis up to meet my finger, over and over.

Next, I gently moved my mouth over to her breast, kissing and sucking on her magnificent nipples. She gently held and caressed my head with both hands. I reached up to my mouth and deposited a big lump of saliva onto my fingertip, which then headed south to her love canal. This added lubricant allowed my finger to slide around much better and I noticed that this gal was getting hot!

I started to think, it's about time to go for the next step, so I asked, "Do you want me to put it in?"

"Yes ... now!"

I felt around on the sheets for the condom that I left there and I tore open the package, she reached down and started to fondle my erection, "You've got a big one," she stated, as a compliment.

I hated to move her hands to put the condom on, but as I did, I muttered, "You are going to love it!" And with that, I rose to my knees and positioned myself between her legs.

She spread her legs even farther apart and reached up to grab my face with her hands, to bring it to hers, I brought my body forward to enter her. As my mammoth erection easily slid in (the missionary position), #3 was giving me the most wonderful, wet kiss that I ever received. #3 continued to hold my face and kiss me the entire time we made love. Oh boy! Did we make love! As I pushed in and out, #3 ground her hips, around and around. With each inward thrust #3 would moan, "EWUuuuuu ... EWUuuuuu!" Then as she pulled her knees up, I could feel her body stiffen, I could feel a warm gush of #3's own body lubricant wash over my erection and her moaning became non-stop, "EWUuuuuu ... EWUuuuuu ... EWUuuuuu ... EWUuuuuu ... EWUuuuuu!" This all combined to push me over the edge, and I started to come with the strongest climax ever! BANG! BANG! BANG! BANG! BANG! My penis just kept shooting and shooting my love juice into the waiting condom. Soon I could feel #3 relax. She let go of my face.

"Tony," she said, "that was outstanding!" Sort of out of breath.

I was still lying on top of #3, I looked her in the eye and replied, "It was ... It was very, very good!"

With that said, #3 pushed me off her and said, "I have to get dressed and into the house quickly."

Realizing that I had no tissues, I grabbed my pants and used my handkerchief to wrap up my condom and its heavy load. Then, I put it back into my pocket and I got dressed in a minute. "Can I zip you up?" I asked.

"Yes ... thank you," #3 replied.

We made small talk as we both rushed out of the boat and down the ladders. When we reached her back door #3 put her hand on one side of my face and gave me a quick kiss on the cheek. Then, with a wide smile on her face she said, "Goodnight ... I enjoyed myself ... you are a great guy!"

Before I could say anything, #3 opened the door and ran into her house.

It was like I was walking on air all the way home; I kept replaying our encounter, over and over. I would pause in my mind and contemplate just how beautiful #3's naked body was. I would try to remember just how soft #3's breasts were in my hands. Finally, I would try to remember how incredibly intense the feeling was of my engorged erection, thrusting forward and back inside of her.

I must have had the biggest smile ever when I walked into my house. Because my mom said, "What are you so happy about, Tony?"

"I just met a real pretty girl, who sings in the church choir," I answered.

My mom looked very pleased with my reply. Her son dating a religious girl.

******

The next day, I didn't run into #3 until I saw her in the lunchroom. When she saw me, she got up from the table that she was sitting at, with her girlfriends and walked swiftly over to me with a scowl on her face. "I do not want to see you ever again! You have been running all over the school telling all of the guys that you have been banging me!"

"Oh no!" I said. "I would never say anything to anyone."

"That's what I have been told. Stay away!" #3 just turned and walked away.

My feelings were really hurt. I would never say anything about what we had done and I hadn't told anyone … but our relationship was over. I also noticed over time that the group of girls #3 hung with, were giving me the cold shoulder as well. What a shame!

Soon after she told me that she didn't want to see me, I heard that #3 had started to date a senior, with a car and a job.

About six months later, #3 approached me after school and told me that she had broken up with the senior, and when she did, he told her that he had made up the story about me. Since he wanted #3 to dump me for him. Which she did.

#3 apologized for believing the other guy instead of me, the damage was done. I asked her to tell all of her friends how she was wrong about me. She said that she would. But I just wasn't interested in her any longer. Maybe sometime in the future.

During our walk to school, #2 informed me that she would not be walking home with me after school because now that the days have warmed up, the high school band is going to practice marching after school. #2 was the best clarinet player in the band and she loved to march and perform. So, I will just have to walk home solo after school.

That afternoon, as I exited the school, I came across a gal I had never seen before, standing on the curb. She was cute. With very dark, brown hair pulled back into a ponytail, held by a red bow. Her red bow matched her red lipstick, skirt and shoes. She had an excellent tan for this time of year, large breasts held in by a very lacey brassiere that could be seen through the thin fabric of her white blouse, with a tiny waist and nice legs.

"The bus doesn't stop here anymore," was my smart guy comment.

"Oh," she sighed. "I am just contemplating my long walk home."

"Where do you live?" I asked.

I was amazed to find out that she lived several blocks past my house, on the same street.

"Well why don't we walk together since I live in the same neighborhood?" I offered.

With a very warm smile, she replied, "I would be delighted!"

So, we started to walk and talk. She had just moved, with her mom and dad, to my town from a city 40 miles away.

As she continued with her life story, she confided that she had just had a baby (eight weeks earlier) and her family moved here so that the 'stigma' of her having a baby at the age of 16 would not follow her.

So, she told the first person that she talked to that she had a baby. I promised her that I would never tell anyone her secret, but if I was her, I wouldn't be telling others. She laughed at me and seemed unconcerned about what others think.

Evidently, the boy that fathered the baby was just a passing fancy and the girl went to Florida to live with her grandmother while she had the baby, which she gave up to adoption. She had been incredibly bored for the past 7 months since the grandmother lived in a retirement community and there was no one her age to talk to.

Her family had moved in over the weekend and this day was her first day in school. Her mom gave her a ride to school but she had to walk home because both of her parents would not be home from work for several hours.

When we reached her house, she invited me in for a drink, which I gladly accepted. Once inside she turned on the TV, got two beers from the refrigerator and plopped down on the sofa next to me.

"I haven't been with a boy for ages," she told me. "I have been very lonely."

I put my arm around her shoulder and held her close to comfort her. She had very soft lips and was a delight to kiss. "Come with me," she asked as she stood up and offered me her hand. She led me into her bedroom and sat on the edge of her bed. Next, she stuck both of her arms out and up, to beckon me to her. As I bent over, she encircled my head with her arms and pulled me down onto the bed. She tried to suck my tongue out of its socket. I sunk down into the soft bed covers and laid on my back as I kissed and caressed her face and neck. She was really horny … and so was I … what's new?

I slid both of my hands around to her back. As one hand moved up to the back of her head, the other hand slid down to the cheek of her butt. We kissed very aggressively, I sucked her tongue into my mouth, then, she sucked my tongue into her mouth. Soon, she pushed me away, while she knelt on the bed to unbutton her blouse and remove her bra, letting her two large breasts free. What a difference between the color of her skin, which was deeply tanned and the pure white skin of her milk filled breasts. Her nipples were very dark brown, very large and stuck out like two thumbs. She seemed very proud of herself. With a big smile, she lowered her breasts onto my waiting face.

I reached up and grabbed one while my mouth devoured the nipple of the other … that was heaven, her breasts were very soft, warm and enveloped my face. I sucked on one nipple and it became even larger in my mouth. Softly, I started to lick around and around her nipple. Then, I switched to the other and as I sucked, and licked and nibbled on it, I reached up with my free hand to caress the other. She really seemed to like it when I nibbled on her one nipple and rolled the other nipple between my thumb and finger, squeezing ever so softly.

"Ummmm … Ummmm … Ummmm!" She moaned.

She reached down and tried to unbuckle my belt but she was having difficulty so I said, "Let me help you with that."

She stopped, looked me in the eye, smiled and then she stood up to remove her skirt, then her tiny panties. She had a great body but there still was a little sag to the skin on her tummy. Simultaneously, I sat on the edge of the bed, kicked off my sneakers and pushed down my jeans, When I stood up to pull my feet out from my jeans, she brushed by me and grabbed the top of the covers on the bed. She lifted them up and slid under in one movement. When I pulled back the covers, I was looking straight down on her naked body and as I slid in next to her, I noticed that she had no pubic hair, just some stubble from her hair previously being shaved and starting to grow back in … very interesting.

I laid on my side and reached over to run my fingers over her hair, along her cheek and I held her face as I leaned in for a warm, soft kiss. She reached down under the covers. Put her hand on my thigh and slid it up under my shorts to grab my erection. It caught me by surprise … it felt great for her tiny, soft hand to be stroking my manhood … almost too good! I relocated my lips to one of her nipples and slid my hand down past her navel to the stubble between her legs.

I moved my middle finger around in large circles, over and over her stubble covered lips down there. Slowly, I made the circles smaller and smaller, until I was centered between her two love lips. Then, I started to rub straight up and down, while I increased the pressure of my fingertip, it slid in between her two wet, slippery vulva lips. My finger, gently explored … as I slid my fingertip around and around her clitoris, then, down the straight path to the soft lips guarding her vagina. Around and around my finger explored, before I pushed it into her love hole. Then, while I pushed my finger in and out, I noticed that I had slobbered all over the breast that I had been kissing and sucking. I was sliding my face all over her breast in complete ecstasy, while my partner was moaning and grinding her pelvis onto my finger.

I hated to stop but I felt it was time to move to the next step. I rolled over to reach for my jeans and pulled out a condom. I pushed my shorts off, rolled my condom onto my erection and rolled back over to my waiting partner.

She knew the drill, for as I positioned myself for the entry, she spread her legs and pulled them up a little, which seemed to open up her love lips as though they were smiling at me. I centered my throbbing erection and as I started to lower my pelvis toward hers, I could feel the prickling of her stubble along my love rod. It felt bad and good, all at the same time … mostly good. Of course, after the first few strokes, I lost all consciousness of the stubble and I was completely consumed by the pleasure of my penis slipping in and out of her warm, wet cave (the missionary position). After a while, I realized that I am not coming as quickly as usual. Is it because I am becoming more experienced or is it because #4's vagina is not quite as tight as what I was used to? But it is warm, it is wet and it is inviting.

All I know is this was ecstasy … I changed the angle that I was thrusting at several times, and #4 seemed to like every angle … she was moaning and groaning (which turns me on) and gyrating her hips. Finally, I reached down and lifted her legs up in front of my chest, which seemed to tighten her vagina around my shaft and as I thrust in, it felt like I was going all the way in. That pushed me over my limit of pleasure and I started to pump quicker and quicker, while #4 yelled, "Yes … Yes … Yes!" Over and over.

My climax was incredibly strong and lasted longer than usual … "WOW was that great!" I uttered.

"I loved it … you are great!" #4 replied, as she caught her breath, #4 continued, "You were the first guy to ever use a condom to screw me … and I liked it more … because I wasn't worried about getting pregnant."

I laid next to her, holding her in my arms and glowing in the 'after climax pleasure'. We kissed occasionally … but there was no rush to get up. She caressed my body, including my semi-soft, condom covered penis. I felt like I was in another world (the world of pleasure). I was brought out of my world of pleasure by the drippage of my love juice onto my stomach, as my penis softened in my condom.

"Do you have any tissues?" I asked.

"Sure," #4 replied, and she reached over me to grab a tissue from the nightstand.

That sort of brought us back to reality and we both got up and got dressed. #4 put on a sweat suit and we went back to the couch, holding each other. We finished our beers and started to watch TV.

We made some small talk and looking toward the bedroom I told #4 how much I enjoyed the sex.

"I did too," #4 replied, with a big grin.

After a while, I said that I thought I should be leaving and #4 said that she needed to tidy up and do some homework before her parents got home. So, I gave #4 a big kiss and I left for home.

******

The next morning on our walk to school I told #2 that we had a new neighbor, just down the street. I described what she looked like, that she was 16, pretty and just moved in over the weekend. I explained that the new girl gets a ride to school by her mother but she has to walk home and that I walked her home yesterday.

All day I looked forward to the walk home and I wasn't disappointed.

As I exited the school, I saw #4 waiting for me in the same place as the day before. She was wearing pink … bow, lipstick, skirt and shoes. To me it was HOT PINK. WOW, was she hot!

"Would you like company for your walk home?" I queried.

"Would I," was her reply.

On our walk, #4 told me about the girls she was meeting and which ones she liked. She talked about the differences in our school and in her last school and she talked about the teachers.

When we arrived at her house, we both just walked in. #4 told me that we couldn't have any more beer because her mom noticed that there were several beers missing last night and chewed #4 out about it. So, she took out two sodas and led me directly to her bedroom.

"That was great yesterday," #4 informed me. "It was the first time that I have had an orgasm!"

I loved to have sex and I am somewhat uninhibited but I am very uncomfortable talking to a girl about it … maybe embarrassed. So, my humble reply was just, "Great!"

She just stood there and took off all of her clothes, as I stood there and watched. When she was completely naked (except for the bow in her hair), she told me, "Today I would like to have two or three." Then, she stepped forward, put her hands on my cheeks, gave me a small kiss and climbed into her bed.

WOW, that put a lot of pressure on me. Can I last that long? Well, I didn't need to think about it long before I decided to take up the challenge. What's the worst that can happen?

So, as she laid in her bed watching, I took off all of my clothes, except for my socks. I took out a condom and put it on the nightstand and climbed into bed next to #4.

Gosh, was her bed comfortable!

We both turned onto our side and started kissing. I slid my hand up and down #4's body, from her back, over to her butt and down her leg. I noticed that her leg seemed awfully smooth compared to the day before, but it may just be my imagination.

As we warmed up to the situation, #4 turned onto her back, and instinctively my hand made its way between her legs, which to my amazement, was perfectly smooth.

"I shaved … just for you," #4 announced.

I pushed back the covers and moved my head down to her tummy to take a look. WOW, I have never seen a vagina without hair before … it turned me on. I caressed the entire area, spending a little extra time on her love lips. I wet my finger with some saliva and watched as the tip slid between her lips, #4 moaned. I had read that some guys even put their head down there and lick. I was not interested, so, I returned my lips to #4's breasts.

I decided that my best chance to give her multiple orgasms was to bring her right to the edge before I put it in. So, I continued my prodding with my finger and sucking, nibbling and licking her nipples. It really seemed to turn her on when I stroked my finger from her clit straight down and into her love hole and then back up, so, I continued to do it. Also, I noticed that as I moved my finger past her clitoris, I got a good response. After a while I positioned my fingertip next to #4's clit and softly moved the skin forward and back, forward and back, over and over, faster and faster. It worked. I could feel her body stiffen and she tightened her grip on me, while I ferociously sucked on her nipple and stroked my finger back and forth.

"Yes … Yes … Yessssss!" #4 yelled as her body seemed to convulse. She pulled her knees up to her waist, then pushed them straight out, then back again, several times. "Oh boy is that good!" #4 proclaimed.

I was amazed, since this was the first time that I have made a girl orgasm, with my hand … and I felt great too! To be able to give someone else that type of pleasure was terrific!

#4 lifted her legs and encircled my pelvis, "I just have got to feel you inside of me," she told me.

"Don't rush it," I replied. "I'm not ready and we need to get you hot like that again."

With that said, #4 released my pelvis from the tight grip of her legs and laid back on the bed for an instant. Then, she popped onto her side and grabbed my penis in both hands and started to caress and stroke my entire groin area. It felt great and as my erection responded we began kissing again. I had to push her hands away before she got me too hot, so that I could re-start my efforts on her.

At first, as we kissed, I brought both hands up and fondled her breasts. Then, slowly one hand traveled down to her baron love nest. My finger slid easily into the still moist and slippery folds and #4 moaned, loudly. This time I slipped my finger into #4's vagina and started to stroke in and out, with my fingertip pointing up. #4 started to respond by moving her hips around. After a while I turned my hand upside down. I pushed my finger down as I continued to stroke my finger in and out. #4 loved it and became increasingly hotter. Suddenly, she told me to put it right in, but darn, I didn't have my condom on yet.

When I laid back to get the condom from the nightstand, #4 grabbed my erection and started to pump it like there was no tomorrow. "Whoa!" I exclaimed. "Give me a chance to get this on." As quickly as I could, I put the condom on and returned to kissing her breasts and pumping my finger in and out of her, with my fingertip pointing down.

In just a minute #4 was on the edge again, so, I kneeled between her legs and very slowly entered her, slippery, smoothly shaved vagina (the missionary position) … Oh what a feeling. My erection slid right in, I bent over and started kissing #4 while continuously pumping in and out. #4 reached up and held my face, while she returned each of my inward stokes with an upward stroke of her own. After a while I tried stiffening my body and doing push-ups. It was neat, since all that was touching #4 was my erection, sliding in and out (I could tell that #4 loved it as well).

When I got back up on my knees, #4 shifted toward one side, so, I grabbed one of her legs and lifted it up until #4 was on her side and I was holding her leg against my chest. Then, I felt like each time I thrust inward, it seemed like I went even farther in. "Oh YAH!" #4 exclaimed.

I straddled #4's bottom leg and penetrated even deeper. It felt great to me, so I started to increase the pace of my thrusting. Suddenly, I became aware of my scrotum sliding back and forth on #4's soft, smooth, warm thigh. It felt fantastic and was increasing my pleasure to the point that I could not hold back any longer and I started to lunge back and forth, while #4 was grinding her pelvis with each of my strokes. Bang! Bang! Bang! Bang! Bang! I was shooting big, strong, hot loads into my condom as #4, fortunately, was having an orgasm with me.

I could feel her vagina tightening and loosening on my erection, over and over, as #4 was moaning, "I love it! I love it! I love it! … Keep going! Keep going! Keep going!" As #4 pumped her pelvis back and forth … and I kept thrusting.

Finally, I collapsed on my side, looking straight into #4's eyes as she said, "Sex … is … GREAT!"

"It sure is!" Was my reply. With that statement, I leaned my head in for a kiss. Then, we laid there for the longest time … just holding each other and kissing. It was fantastic!

Eventually, we got up, got dressed, and I left for home.

******

On my way home, I realized that I had just used my last condom and it was, unfortunately, time for me to purchase some more.

When I reached my house, I told my mom that I had to go to a friend's house to get a homework assignment. She just said, "Don't be late for supper."

I jumped on my bike and raced over to the next town, to my 'favorite' pharmacy to make my purchase.

On arrival, I walked through the back door and went into one of the aisles, to do my 'pre-purchase reconnaissance'.

The store had many customers, but only one old lady at the pharmaceutical counter. Once she left, I walked swiftly to the counter, to be greeted by the young, blond, female pharmacist who smiled and said, "Good to see you again … how can I help you?"

What did she mean by, again … I haven't been there for a while … oh well. "I need six condoms," I said confidently. I figured at the rate I am going with #4 a purchase of three would be futile.

She smiled, opened the drawer and with even a bigger smile she asked, "The regular?"

"Yes, lubricated," I replied. Gee, I am becoming a pro at purchasing condoms. I was hardly sweating this time and I was much more confident.

After she received my payment, she placed my order in a small white bag, folded the top, looked me straight in the eye as she handed me the bag and said, "Have a good time!"

That made me more nervous but I took the bag and said, "Thank you very much," and I ran out of the store.

Storage of that many condoms was an issue, since I didn't want my folks to find them. Fortunately, they don't take up a lot of room, so I stashed them in the bottom of my backpack.

******

For the next week, #4 and I kept up the same routine.

Walk home making small talk … we didn't have much in common. Jump in bed at her house, I would give her two orgasms, we would clean up, get dressed and I would leave. It was starting to become monotonous, but the sex was terrific!

Finally, one day #4 saw me in the cafeteria at school and yelled, "Tony!"

Gee, she got everyone's attention. All she had to do was wave to me, but she rushed over to me to tell me she would not be walking home with me that afternoon. She had met a senior boy and he is going to give her a ride home … yah, I bet she is going to get more than a ride home. (It sucks, I keep losing girls to guys with cars, jobs and money … three things that are difficult for a 15-year-old to compete with. I can't wait to become 16 so I can get a job, get a license and buy a car.)

Oh well, with a smile, I said, "Have a great time."

"I will," #4 replied, as she sauntered away.

Chapter 3
The Summer of Content

The next few dates that I had were duds. I went to a few dances but I didn't strike up any new relationships and the next thing you know we were coming to the end of the school year … wow!

Fortunately, #2 and I were invited to an end of school party at a rich girl's house in the 'ritzy' area of town. In a great, big, beautiful house, on a cliff, overlooking the valley. The entire lower level was a gigantic rec room, with sliding glass doors all across the back wall. Looking out onto their in-ground pool, with a majestic view … magnificent!

My dad gave #2 and I a ride to the party at 7:00pm and #2's dad agreed to pick us up at 11:00pm, when the party was scheduled to be over.

#2 and I made our way down to the rec room, where most of the 40 or so guests where already partying.

Our host was wearing just her black bikini, which matched her jet-black hair. She was just about five foot tall, petite, but had a super body. Her shoulders were a little wider than you would expect. Which made room for a pair of large breasts, which stood out in her tiny bathing suit top. "Glad you could come," she greeted us with a big smile. She had a great tan already and her pink lipstick lips, looked hot. "There are all types of soda at the bar, munchies on the tables, you can dance or even jump into the pool … have a great time!" Then, she strolled over to greet some more newcomers.

I knew everyone at the party since they were all classmates. Several of my good buddies were already there. So, I walked over and started to talk with B and J.

After everyone arrived, our host turned down the lights, turned up the music (which was great), came over to me and asked me to dance. We danced several slow dances is a row, which enticed more and more couples onto the dance floor.

My host looked up into my eyes and said, "You are a very smooth dancer."

I looked down at her, I was thinking how hot she was and how good she smelled. I answered, "That is because I have you in my arms," with that said, she just melted into my body and we danced very closely.

After a few more dances the tempo of the music quickened and we started to dance fast. Great! That was my forte, I was a really good fast dancer … and so was she. We were all dancing fast for quite a while … building up a sweat. "Let's jump into the pool and cool off." Our host announced to the crowd.

That moved most of the party out next to the pool, which was lighted. There were speakers out there, so we could still hear the music and the party was jumping.

Our host and I spent most of the night together, which was great. She had a great personality, plus she was HOT!

Later in the evening, we were snuggling in a chaise lounge, in a darker spot on the patio, when she just leaned over and started kissing me. Softly we kissed, but I didn't get carried away, because I felt a bit embarrassed since there were so many guests around.

At the end of the evening, I asked, "Can I help you clean up?"

She answered, "That would be nice … I'd like that! We are going to do it tomorrow morning … come over about nine."

******

The next morning, I rode my bicycle over to the mansion on the cliff and was greeted by my host from the night before and her best friend. "Tony! What a surprise!" She said.

"I thought I would come over and give you a hand cleaning up." I replied.

"Great, I am glad you came over."

My host was wearing a pink bikini top, and white shorts. She was always dressed perfectly (later I found out that all of her clothes were designed and made especially for her). The best friend had a white pullover blouse and black shorts on.

There really wasn't a lot to clean up and we were done in about an hour. We filled several black trash bags, which I carried up and put in the garage.

When I returned, my host said, "Oh Tony, I am so glad you came … you have such big muscles," as she caressed my biceps.

It felt great but it embarrassed me, "Anything to please you, my dear," was my humble reply.

When we were done, we retreated to the pool area where the girls would hang out each day. They were both extremely good swimmers and instantly made our high school swim team one of the best in the state when they joined the team. My host won a number of state titles the previous year.

My host's mother was a professional swimming coach and she was the one who made the workout for the girls each day. The mother was not home during the day, in the summer because she ran a huge swimming camp for kids. My host at 15 was not old enough to work there.

So, she made them a workout routine to follow each day. Twice each day they had to swim laps for thirty minutes, changing styles every five laps. Then, after thirty minutes of rest they would follow a list of exercises, which lasted about thirty minutes. Rest thirty minutes, then they would run for two miles. After thirty minutes, they would start all over again.

I couldn't last five laps, but I easily kept up to them with the rest of the routine … they got a laugh out of me working out with them.

The workout routine took up most of the day and didn't leave much time for romance. Most of the time between exercises we would hang out by the pool. Beside it was almost impossible to get away from her best friend, who was always by her side.

I had to come up with a plan to keep the best friend busy. I figured that we needed to get the best friend hooked up. Therefore, I spoke to my buddy S to see if he could come over and get something started with the best friend. It didn't take much to induce him to join us … at a mansion, by a pool, in the summer with two hot chicks. Done deal in no time.

The next morning, I told the girls that I had invited my buddy S to come over, because he had a crush on the best friend. The girls got all excited about what I had said and went off somewhere in the house to discuss it. When they returned, they couldn't wait for S to arrive.

This idea had the desired effect. S and the best friend got along famously and it left time for us to get some alone time.

The second day that S was there, my host and I left S and her best friend at the pool and we went into the family room. We started to make out on the sofa. She was sort of laying on top of me, kissing, delicately caressing my face and running her fingers through my hair (which I loved), while I was rubbing her back with my hands. I let one hand slide down to her butt and softly squeezed her cheek … what a body she had, it was trim and muscular everywhere and her skin was so soft and smooth … WOW!

Of course, I started to get hard and as I did, I could feel her start to gyrate her hips and rub her crotch around on mine, so, of course … I got harder. I think she liked it. She continued to grind away and she knew the effect that it had on me.

Finally, I said, "Let's go to your bedroom." She stood right up and led me to her extravagant bedroom. I led her to her bed and let her lay down first. I laid on my side next to her, kissing while caressing her side. When she turned on her side facing me, I slipped my hand behind and unhooked her top, slid my hand back around and cupped her breast. They were much more solid, compared to the soft ones I had felt in the past … I liked it. I caressed and fondled her breast and ran my fingertip very softly around and around her nipple as we continued to kiss more and more passionately. Her nipple hardened and I moved my mouth down to suck on it … it became rock hard! I moved my hand down between her legs and softly moved my fingertip around and around on the material covering her love lips. She seemed to be melting into the bed … she was soooo hot … and so was I.

When I slipped my finger in under the leg band of her bikini bottom, my host suddenly became startled, she pulled her mouth away from mine and said, "I can't do that!"

"What?" I said.

"Go all the way … it hurts too much."

"It does hurt the first time, but after that it should feel great," I pressed.

"Well, the second time it hurt as well! Just let me take care of you," she said as she pulled the waistband of my bathing suit down with one hand and she grabbed my swollen love rod with the other.

She repositioned herself so that her head was on my chest, watching as she stroked my penis up and down … softly and slowly at first … gosh it felt soooooo goooood!

She sat up and grabbed several tissues from the nightstand and handed them to me. Then, she went back to pumping my erection … WOW! It didn't take long for her to get the desired result … as I had a fantastic orgasm, shooting wads and wads of ejaculate into the tissues … over and over I spasmed, while she continued pumping … finally, when it was over, I tapped her on the shoulder and said, "That was GREAT!"

She looked me in the eye and said, "Good … I am glad."

As we started to get up and get ready to return to the pool, I said, "You seemed to know what you were doing."

"I had to do that with my last boyfriend, so he wouldn't become too frustrated," she nonchalantly answered.

That was all the romance for the day as we went back to the pool and had a great time with the foursome … playing in the pool and working out.

On the way home, on our bikes, S told me that he wanted to get intimate with the girlfriend and thought she did too (boy, that was quick). He asked what he should do.

I recommended that he bring her into the family room, lay on the leather sofa, kiss her softly, gently caress her breasts, then her vagina, put a condom on, a lubricated condom and then enter her slowly at first, then, slowly increase the pace. The key is to make sure that she is well lubricated before you enter her, use spit on your finger if needed.

He asked me where I get the condoms from and I told him that I go to the next town. I asked, "I need to buy some more, tonight … would you like me to buy you some as well?"

"Yeah," he said. "I don't think I have the guts to buy them myself!"

"It isn't easy for me either!"

******

That evening, I took a ride to my favorite drugstore to make my, our, purchase.

In the store, I had to wait in the aisle until the counter area cleared … then I made my approach. The beautiful pharmacist was there, just as in the past. When she saw me, she made a big smile, with those full red lips and she asked, "How can I help you today?"

Are you kidding me? She knew that I only came there for one thing … to buy condoms! Why would she ask me that?

While she was waiting for my reply, she moved over to the drawer that contained the condoms and as she opened it, I said, "Three, three packs … please."

Her head snapped back to look at me and she said, "That's nine!"

"Is there a limit?"

She burst out laughing (it was very embarrassing) and said, "You must be planning on really enjoying your summer!"

I am sure that I was bright red from blushing as I sarcastically replied, "Just trying to make it to the Fourth of July," which was only a couple of days away.

Then, she really cracked up … laughing hard, long and very loudly. It brought the attention of all that were in the store. Adding to my embarrassment … but it was funny.

I paid, she put my purchase in a small paper bag, folded the top down and as she handed me the bag she said with a smile, "Have a great time!"

"Thank you … I will," I replied. Then, as I was exiting the store … I could hear her laughing … it could not have been any more embarrassing!

******

The next day, I told S to wait for our hostess and me to go upstairs before he made his move.

When our hostess went in to go to the bathroom, I waited a few minutes, then I followed her inside and met her in the family room. Just like the day before, we kissed, went to her bedroom, laid on her bed making out, getting hot and bothered, then, she finished it off by giving me a 'happy ending'.

The next day was similar, but I felt guilty. So, I said to her, "Let me return the favor."

"What do you mean?" She replied.

"Let me give you an orgasm with my finger," I whispered in her ear … "You'll love it!"

"I have never done that."

I whispered, "Never had an orgasm?"

"No," she said with a smile.

"You're going to love it!" I assured her as I untied her bikini bottom, slid it away, put a large wade of saliva on my finger and pushed it down through the outer lips of her clean-shaven vulva.

I moved my mouth back to her nipples, gently running my tongue around and around, while I mimicked the motion with my fingertip, gently rotating around and around her clitoris … she was moaning. A little more saliva, then,

I pushed my finger down to her love canal. In and out, in and out went my finger and around and around went her hips … I could tell by her rapid breathing and her body that she was getting hotter and hotter. With my finger stoking in and out and my thumb rubbing her clit, I could feel her body start to stiffen. Faster and faster went my finger as I sucked her nipple into my mouth, sucking harder and harder.

Finally, she arched her body, pushed her thighs tightly together and pulled her knees up toward her chest. She made it difficult for me but I continued to gently stroke in and out with my finger. I noticed that she was holding her breath, grasping the sheets with both hands, while waves of spasms washed over her body, over and over. Soon she let out a deep sigh, started to breathe again, her body relaxed and she pulled my hand from her crotch.

She took my head in her hands, gave me as hard a kiss as possible and said, "That … was … FANTASTIC!"

My humble reply was, "I hope you enjoyed it."

The next day we both gave each other a 'happy ending' again. But the following day as I was stroking her vagina, I stopped sucking her nipple, looked her straight in the eye and said, "Let's put it in … it won't hurt."

"Are you sure?"

"I'll put it in a little at a time, if it hurts, we'll stop immediately," I assured her.

"Ok."

Quickly, I put a condom on and knelt between her legs. I put a bunch more saliva on my fingers and rubbed it around the opening that I was about to enter.

"Just the head," I said. Then I rubbed the head of my erection up and down between her love lips … I could tell she liked that. I held my love rod in position, then, I pushed gently in about an inch. She gasped, then held her breath. "Ok?" I asked, #5 nodded her head. I pushed in another inch, then stopped.

Next, I pulled out a bit, then pushed in a bit, several times, very shallow. "A little bit more?" I asked. She nodded her approval. So, I pushed in another inch or so as I continued to pump.

"This is great!" #5 said as she started to push herself further and further onto my rock-hard shaft. I could feel her vagina starting to self-lubricate.

As I had done with #2, I lifted #5's knees up to improve the angle of penetration.

"Right there," #5 moaned, as I pumped in and out faster and faster.

Just as she did for my finger, #5's body arched and spasmed as she orgasmed, and her pleasure made me orgasm as well. It was fantastic!

"You are magnificent!" #5 exclaimed. "I loved that … it felt great!"

"No hurt … right?"

"No … you knew what you were doing. You must be an expert," #5 complimented me.

"Not really," I replied.

******

My buddy S, even though he was inexperienced, had been having sex with the best friend each of the past three days. She evidently was not as reluctant as #5, to 'get it on'.

So, I had to sell S my other three-pack of condoms and the four of us continued to have a great time each day.

Of course, I had to return to the drugstore for more supplies.

The pharmacist could not believe I was back so quickly. "I suppose you want another nine?" She sarcastically asked.

"Can I get twelve?" I replied.

"You want a twelve pack?"

"No, four packs of three," I said. My thinking was that it is much easier to store a small package.

"You have been a busy guy," the pharmacist said with a wide smile.

A little less embarrassed than in the past, I replied, "I get lucky on occasion."

She laughed, I finished my purchase and left.

******

Our town celebrated the Fourth of July in a big way. We had a parade in the morning, a 5K run at noon, a big block party at night and a huge fireworks display.

For the block party, they would cordon off a short street in the center of the town, put up a stage for the band and string multicolored lights around the perimeter.

45

The band had just started when #5 showed up with her folks. When she saw me, she brought her mom and dad over and introduced me as her boyfriend. WOW! I have dated some girls but I have never been a boyfriend before … I liked it … to me it was a compliment.

#5 looked stunning. She wore a black blouse, white shorts with gold jewelry. Her long black hair framed her pretty face. Her lips were covered with pink lipstick … perfect!

I was wearing a black T-shirt and blue jeans, as usual.

When the band started playing a fast tune, we took the floor. Everyone started to watch as we put on a show. We could really dance well and very fast. We made a great couple!

******

The next couple of weeks were great. Our little foursome had a wonderful time each day.

Then, #5 went on vacation with her folks for two weeks. When they returned #5 was ecstatic that she had been accepted to train with some great swimming coach, hopefully for the Olympics. #5 spent the next several days packing so that she could move out west and live and train with the coach. She said she would write, but I never got a letter … out of sight, out of mind!

Chapter 4
Sophomore Year

The summer really flew by quickly. Here we were, #2 and I, walking to school for the first day of our sophomore year.

#2 had spent the entire summer sitting for her two brothers … boring! I spent the first six weeks laying by the pool at #5's mansion and the last month playing ball each day with my buddies.

I always liked the first day of school, seeing all of my friends and all of the other students, again. There was one Italian girl, a cousin of J that I had known and gone to school with since grammar school. As youngsters the three of us played together a lot. Last year she sat behind me in every class that we were both in, but I never realized it. She had never been very attractive. She had always been a bit chunky and short for her build and because I knew her for so long, I sort of pictured her as she looked in grammar school.

Well, over the summer this little Italian girl grew several inches taller, lost the baby fat and blossomed into a beautiful gal. When I sat down in my English class she asked, "So how was your summer?"

When I turned to answer her, I noticed the pretty details in her face, framed by her jet-black hair. Her bright white teeth glistened as she smiled at me.

"I had a great summer … how was yours?" I replied.

"Boring, I babysat for a two-year-old all summer," she answered. "Are you still going out with—"

Before she could finish, I interrupted her with, "NO! Not anymore … she went out west to train for the Olympics with some great swim coach." Then, with the saddest face that I could make, I said, "Now I am all alone and lonely."

"Oh, you poor thing," she said sympathetically. "Would you like to go with me to the back-to-school dance on Friday night?"

"I would love to escort you to the dance … it would be my privilege," I replied as she blushed brightly. Then the teacher came in and I turned around.

Later, we walked together to the next class, talking all the way. After that I didn't see her for the rest of the day.

The next day, after English class, she asked me if I would like to stop at her house after school so we could practice our dancing. I agreed since #2 had informed me that she was going to practice marching again with the band after school.

At the end of the school day, we met outside the school and walked the several blocks to her house. No one was home; her mom and dad both worked late and didn't get home until after 6:00pm. Most nights she cooked the meal so that it would be ready when they arrived home. She was a very nice daughter and had always been a considerate person.

We went down to the family room in the basement. It was large and wide open so it was conducive to dancing. She put on several fast songs and we danced well together. Then, she slowed the music and as we danced slowly, I looked down into her dark sultry eyes … I could tell that she wanted to kiss, so I lowered my head to kiss her lips … softly, gently we kissed … no tongue at first.

She moved her hands up onto the back of my head and while she stroked the back of my neck, she pulled my head down closer to hers. She leaned her body tightly against mine, so that I could tell that she wanted more. Slowly, I introduced more and more tongue. Her lips were very soft and inviting.

We made it over to the sofa and laid down on our sides, still in a lip-lock. I slipped my free hand under her blouse and caressed her lower back. Her skin was very smooth and very soft. Gradually my hand headed south … caressing the sleek curves of her butt. Then, down further to her leg. My hand pushed her skirt up as it made its way up her thigh.

When my hand made it to her panty, it jumped up to stroke her naval area before it made its plunge toward her love lips. I could feel her start to tense up as my finger slipped under the top of her panty … she pushed away and said in a whisper (not very convincingly), "I don't think we should go any farther."

I was thinking, 'give me a break … you brought me to your empty house … we made out on the sofa … you seem to be loving it … I am getting mixed signals here … but in my mind, when a girl says no, it's no! So, I asked, "How about just a little further?"

She nodded and sort of gave me the OK.

We went back to kissing and my fingers slowly worked their way down, sort of softly caressing and stroking. When my fingers made it to her pubic area, I could feel that her panties were like stuck between the lips of her vagina and the panty was like industrial-strength thick. My hand was undaunted and my fingers pushed the material out of the way and continued downward. I noticed that her vagina was unusually warm and very moist already. FINALLY, it dawned on me, she was having her period and it was her pad that I had pushed aside. Oh no, I better stop! So, I pulled my hand out, sort of abruptly, my fingertip was discolored up to the first knuckle with her menstrual blood. I said, "I'm sorry … I didn't realize that it was your time of the month."

She frowned and replied, "No, I'm sorry … I didn't think we would get that far today. I will be fine on Friday night."

I was not sure what that meant, but I replied, "Great!"

In the meantime, I wiped my finger off with my hanky and we went back to kissing for about fifteen minutes. It was nice. Then I left.

******

During the day on Friday, my friend K asked if I needed a ride to the dance. He had just gotten a car the week before. "Sure," I said, glad to have a ride.

When K picked me up, he told me his plan was to drive out to 'Lovers Lookout', so we could make out with the girls before we brought them home. He asked if I would take my date for a walk when we got there and not return until he put the parking lights on. I understood and agreed.

We picked the girls up and had a great time at the dance. When the dance was over, we told the girls that we had a surprise for them. K drove to Lovers Lookout. Lovers Lookout was a large cliff in the woods, overlooking the valley. It was a nice clear night, the lights from the streets and homes glistened below. It was very romantic.

After K parked the car, I said, "We're going to take a walk." There was a small blanket in the back seat, so I took it and wrapped it around my date when we got out of the car, to keep her warm.

With my arm around her shoulder and her arm around my waist, we walked into the woods and found a nice secluded spot to hug and kiss. Instead of caressing my head, as she did the other day, my date's hands went straight to my butt and she pulled my crotch tightly against hers. As we kissed more and more aggressively, she started to gyrate her hips and grind her pelvis into mine. I had the sense that she wanted to continue from where we left off the other day.

I took the blanket from her shoulders, opened it up and spread it on the ground. I sat on the blanket and reached my hand up for my date's. She smiled and sat down on the blanket to join me. "I hadn't planned for this," I said honestly.

"It's perfect," she replied.

We continued to kiss and this time I slid my hand up to her breasts. She had large firm breasts, which I softly caressed and squeezed. After a while she moved her free hand down between my legs and started to rub around. I was a little startled, I stopped kissing for a second and she said, "I am so sorry for the other day … I want to make it up to you."

"You are," was my reply. She smiled.

Now reassured, I became much more aggressive and task-oriented. I pushed up her blouse and unhooked her bra so that I could get full access to her breasts. Her bare skin felt great under my hands. I noticed her nipples were very dark brown as I took one into my mouth. Then, as I slipped my hand down toward her panties, she reached down and pushed off her skirt and panties in one movement … WOW! I was really surprised because she had always been so prim and proper. I could tell that she really wanted it.

I slowly caressed the outside of her hairy lips with my fingertip. Sliding down one lip, all the way to the bottom, then sliding up the adjacent lip. Both of us were getting hotter and hotter. When I went straight down between her lips, she held her breath. I pushed into the dry folds beneath and stroked up and down a few times. So, I wet my finger with a load of saliva and I deposited it between her lips. Then, as my finger started to slip effortlessly up and down, I felt her relax.

She spread her legs more and I continued to explore with my finger between her legs and my mouth on her nipple. I slid my finger into her vagina, with my fingertip up, she started to moan. She lifted up my head so that our lips met and she started to really kiss me hard (I liked that). With my fingertip stroking in and out, I used my thumb to rub her clitoris. She moaned, "Yes!" So, I continued for a while, until she said, "Let's put it in."

Quickly, I removed my pants and boxers, rolled on a condom and kneeled between her legs. I was cautious as I entered her dark hairy nest, because of what happened with #2 the first time. Fortunately, this wasn't #6's first time. I slid in with no obstacles (the missionary position). #6 closed her eyes as I slid in and when I was in all the way, she opened her eyes and said, "Oh boy … that is sooo good!"

I didn't reply … I have a hard time saying anything or making any noises when I'm making love. I just started pumping slowly, then a little faster. It wasn't long before #6 started to increase the tempo, as she moaned, "Yes … Yes … Yes!" As the yeses came faster and faster, I pumped faster and faster. Finally, I could feel #6's body start to spasm in waves as she had her orgasm. It caused me to orgasm as well, shooting large, strong loads into the tip of my condom.

Afterward, we kissed and hugged for a short time before we got up, straightened out clothes and walked back to K's car with our arms around each other.

When we got back to the car, K's parking lights were on so we got in and headed for home.

When we dropped #6 off, I walked her to her front door, she said, "Thanks, I had a great time tonight!"

I smiled, "So did I." Then, I gave her a little kiss on the lips and left.

Over the weekend, I thought a lot about that night. I realized that the spark that is usually there between me and a girl was missing with #6. Probably because when I kiss her or even when we made love, I pictured my chubby little nine-year-old friend and not a lover. I didn't think that we could ever be more than good friends.

On Monday, at school, as #6 walked to the next class after English, I explained how I felt and that I did not want to hurt her feelings. Remarkably, #6 had come to the same conclusion. We both agreed to continue to be close friends and we have continued to maintain that friendship.

＊＊＊＊＊＊

About a week later, K asked if I would like to double date with him and take out two hot sisters that he had met working in the next town. His plan was to take them to a drive-in movie and have sex, sounded good to me!

On Friday night, as we drove up to their house, K informed me that we had to act as though we knew these girls since their parents were very protective and would not let them go on a blind date. K knew the older sister, so it was just the two girls and me that had to pretend to know each other.

We all did a good job of talking, laughing, meeting the parents and leaving.

K's date was about 5'6" tall, a couple of years older than me, shoulder-length brown hair, pretty, nice figure and dressed neatly.

My date was my age, only 5'2", short curly brown hair, with a more athletic body, and cute.

It was a warm night but what amazed me was that the girls brought their long winter coats with them … well, girls always seem to feel cold.

When we arrived at the drive-in, K parked way in the back, where there were no cars on either side of us. The coming attractions were plying as we mounted the speaker in the window.

We watched the remainder of the coming attractions and some of the first movie. My date and I talked some and kissed a few times. We didn't have much in common … except for the kissing. K and his date kissed a lot more than we did and his date was really pressed up against him.

In the middle of the movie, the girls asked K to drive them down to the restroom. I was thinking, what a couple of prima donnas they must be, to have to be driven to the restrooms. Although it was a short walk, K drove them down to the restrooms. I also thought that it was odd that they took their coats with them into the restrooms. K and I waited in the car outside.

When the girls came out of the restrooms, they really looked odd, since they were wearing their long winter coats, plus it was a warm evening. Also, when they came out, they were both giggly and they didn't stop when they got into the car … I wondered what had gotten into them?

K drove back to the last row and fortunately, we got our secluded parking spot back. K mounted the speaker in the window and the girls were still giggling.

Well, it took a few minutes, but I finally found out what made our dates giggle. K's date whispered something in his ear, then she started to take her coat off. Which was a signal for my date to take her coat off as well. To my astonishment, the girls had taken all of their clothes off while they were in the restroom and had put on very sheer baby doll pajamas … I didn't know about K's date, but mine didn't have any panties on! WOW! I could see her pert, brown, stiff nipples through the fabric. My date was sitting on the edge of the seat facing me, with a cute smile on her face … a look that was asking, "What do you think?" In the meantime, I was salivating, thinking about how hot she looked, how wild she must be, and what move to make first.

Finally, I uttered, "Welcome to my slumber party … you look marvelous!" She smiled broodily as I slid across the seat to put my arm around her. She cuddled into my body. I lifted her chin and we gently started to kiss. When my hand left her chin, it went directly to her waist, under her top and directly up to her breast. Normally, I wouldn't be so forward but I felt this was appropriate for the way she was dressed … she didn't back away. Her breast was supple in my hand. As we kissed, I continued to caress her breast and tweak her nipple between my finger and thumb. Slowly, we slid down on the seat until we were flat (which is what K and his date had done some time before).

As we made out, my date pulled down my fly and put her tiny hand into my pants to fondle my package. I repositioned myself so that my date could lie flat on her back. We could hear K and his date breathing hard, in the front seat … good, they were busy, just like us.

I moved my hand down between her legs, which she spread immediately … boy, was she hot! After running my fingers around in her bush for a moment, I made the plunge with my middle finger through the soft, moist folds of her love nest. "UMMMM!" She moaned. As my finger would go in, she would push her pelvis out. so that my finger would plunge deeper and deeper. She was just as aggressive as I was and she seemed to be ready to put it in … but not before I had some more fun.

I moved my head under her nightie and started licking and sucking her nipples … they were rock hard. My date wasted no time in pulling my penis out of my pants and slowly began stroking it. I heated up pretty fast. At this point I was supercharged and my date was well lubricated. So, I broke suction on her nipple, rolled on a condom and pushed my pants down to my ankles … not much room in the back seat of a car.

I flipped over to get on top of her and my erection slipped right into her warm moist love canal (the missionary position). I tried to keep a low profile so that my butt would not go over the bottom of the windows. That made for shorter strokes than normal. #7 could not get enough of me. She reached behind me with both hands and grabbed the cheeks of my butt and she was pulling me in while she was pushing her pelvis up to reach each of my thrusts.

#7 was quietly panting and moaning, then she whispered in my ear, "You have a great love stick! Do me hard, Tony! YES! YES! YES!"

I could feel #7's vagina becoming warmer as she started to orgasm. I could feel each of her contractions as the waves of passion washed over her body and I kept on pumping faster and faster. I orgasmed with her, shooting what felt like amazing amounts of ejaculate into my condom. When #7 was done, she panted, "That was great!"

So, I dismounted, removed my condom into my hanky and pulled up my jeans quickly, not knowing when K or his date might look over the seat at us. I was very self-conscious with others in the same car. But they were still busy in the front seat.

#7 put on her coat and we snuggled in the corner of the backseat. We started to watch the movie for the first time. I could see that K was partially sitting up and his date had her head in his lap, bobbing up and down. Good for them!

After she was finished, K's date sat up in the front seat, put her coat on, then turned around and asked her sister if she needed to go to the restroom, which was answered in the affirmative. So, off to the restroom we drove and this time I went into the restroom as well (to wash myself off and to discard my used condom).

K and I waited in the car for their return … all dressed up and carrying their coats. Then, we drove them home.

K dated the older sister several more times. I wasn't interested in #7 since we had nothing in common … all she talked about were her friends and I didn't know any of them.

******

Of course, on our walks to and from school, #2 and I would discuss our dates, in vivid detail! Her dates were normally associated with a dance and didn't include sex because the guys were 15 and their folks usually drove them to and from the dance … so no luck.

#2 was always amazed at the amount of sex I seem to come across (my sense was that I was just lucky). She was impressed by the fact that whatever intimate question she asked, I had the answer. She felt that I had become an expert. So, #2 started to refer to me as … THE SEXPERT.

One day on the way to school, #2 told me about a girlfriend she had in the band. The girl, a junior, was dating a boy and when they had sex, it just didn't seem to work out well. #2 felt the girl needed some training, so she told her about the Sexpert. The girl knew who I was and was open to having me teach her the refinements of sexual intercourse. Therefore, #2 wanted to know if I was interested in helping her friend out. Her friend was a tall, slinky, attractive, brunette … who wouldn't be interested?

#2 said she would line up a rendezvous between the two of us. My interest was piqued.

During our walk home, #2 informed me that she had worked out the details. She would introduce the two of us after school tomorrow and the three of us would walk to her slinky friend's house together. #2 would continue home, while her friend and I would go inside the house.

The next afternoon, as I walked out of school and approached #2 and her friend, I noticed that the friend was looking goooood! She had on tight black slacks that made her legs and butt look fantastic. A tight red sweater accentuating her breasts, with bright red lipstick on her full red lips. WOW! Her face was very attractive and the rest of the package was great as well. What a lucky guy!

The three of us walked and talked freely until we reached the girl's house. Then #2 said, "I'll see you tomorrow," and she kept walking while her friend and I went into her house.

The girl's parents both worked and didn't get home until late, so we had plenty of time. We shared a soda, while the girl told me how pleased she was that I volunteered to help with her problem. I was very comfortable with this girl and I couldn't believe that she would have a problem with any guy. She was very nice, very attractive and HOT!

I explained that it was my pleasure to help, if I could (no kidding … MY pleasure) and I reassured her that I felt sex was great and she should feel the same.

She invited me into her bedroom, which was immaculate and very girly. I took her into my arms and gently started to kiss her. She had very soft, moist lips. She slowly parted her lips and introduced the tip of her tongue. Several times the tip of my tongue just touched the tip of hers, then it retreated back into my mouth, as an invitation to follow. Soon, her tongue was fully into my mouth. It was like our tongues were in a fencing match, darting and plunging about.

I pulled her closer into my body and slowly slid one hand down to her butt. When it reached its destination, I softly caressed and squeezed her butt cheek, gently. Things were warming up between the two of us and she nudged me over to the bed. We laid down on our side, still kissing.

I was letting her take the lead. She placed her hand, ever so softly, on the side of my face for a gentle caress (I loved it). She soon moved her hand down to my crotch where she started to rub a little harder.

Given her acts of aggression, I navigated my free hand under her sweater and up to her breasts, which were good-sized … she didn't flinch. After a while, I moved my hand down between her legs for some exploration. I just rubbed around on top of her slacks. All this time we continued to kiss, more and more aggressively. Soon she sat up and started to unzip my fly and unbuckle my jeans. I asked, "What are you doing?"

"Going to give you a blowjob," she replied matter-of-factly.

Although it sounded great to me, I didn't feel that it was warranted at this time, so I asked, "Why?"

"I always give my boyfriend a blowjob to get things going."

I smiled and explained, "I don't think it is wise to give a young guy a blowjob to get him going … a young guy is ready to go as soon as you touch him … It's the girl that has to get going first … I'll show you." With that said and my pants already undone, I slipped out of my jeans. She must have taken it as a hint, so she slipped out of her slacks and her sweater, as well.

As we started to kiss again, I put my hand between her legs and started to caress the entire area. I could feel her relax. After going around and around I started to move my fingers up and down over the center of her love nest, she spread her legs. I increased the pressure on my fingers … I could actually feel the heat from her body as she started to get hotter. Gently, I worked my finger under the leg band of her panties, pushed them to the side and I started to rub my middle finger up and down over her love lips. As my finger worked its' way between those lips the girl whispered in my ear, "Are you ready to put it in?"

"No … because you are not ready!" And with that said I put a big dollop of saliva on my finger, before it went back to her love lips. She started to moan as my finger slipped up beside her clitoris and then back down to her love canal. After a while I slid my finger to the middle, bringing it right up to the edge of her clit, then, with a little added pressure I would slide it down to her love canal. Lighten the pressure and start back up toward her clit. She started to squirm around and I could feel her vagina starting to self-lubricate … great!

She said, "I'm ready."

"Hold on," I replied. "Haven't you ever had an orgasm with a guy?"

"Never!"

"Well, let's see if we can fix that." Next, I pushed her bra up over her breasts and sucked one nipple into my mouth, while my other hand softly caressed the other. In a few minutes I put more saliva on my finger and returned it to her love lips. While I alternated sucking on one nipple, then the other, I slipped my finger up and down. Slowly at first, then I increased the speed, faster and faster. In moments she started to orgasm. Involuntarily arching her body, squeezing her thighs together and pulling her legs up, while she was moaning, "UGH! UGH! UGH! UGH! UGH!"

When she was done, I moved my mouth up to hers and started to kiss her again. She threw her leg over my body and said, "That was GREAT!"

"We have just begun," I replied. I was so hot for her, it was incredible. She pushed her face into mine and kissed me more intensely than I have ever been kissed. Slow, I pushed her back a bit and I started to rub between her legs again … she loved it and started to moan. I started to circle her nipple with my tongue as I gently circled her clit with my fingertip. Around and around, I went and she heated up like a burner on a stove … I felt she was just about ready when she pulled back my shorts, repositioned, with her head over my crotch, pulled out my fully aroused penis and went down on it. FANTASTIC! I had never had someone do that before, but after a few strokes up and down, I had to stop her before she made me orgasm. "Let's put it in," I sputtered.

I stood up next to the bed as I took off my boxers and rolled on a condom. She took off her bra and panties. Then she asked, "What are you doing?"

"Slipping into a condom," I said matter-of-factly.

"WOW … my boyfriend never used a condom," she replied.

"Weren't you afraid of getting pregnant?"

"Yeah … but he would pull it out before he orgasmed," she blushed bright red as she told me.

"Well, you won't have to worry this time," I said as I turned toward the bed with a stiff one in my hand. She spread her legs and pulled her knees up toward her head, but she was a little too far from the edge of the bed for me to reach her, so, I grabbed her by the hips and slid her over to the edge. Then, I entered her … just the head at first … very slowly and very softly. It was the first time that I had tried this position (the edge of the bed) and it was easy to control just how much I entered her. I leaned in a little more and I could see #8 smile.

When I pushed it in all the way and stopped, #8 gasped, "OH! You're sooo deep … my boyfriend never went in that far; he never went in more than halfway … afraid he would come inside of me."

I didn't say anything, I just wondered what the heck was on the other guy's mind.

I pulled out, all but the head, then slowly pushed it in again, a number of times, slowly increasing the speed. I could tell that she was really enjoying it because her face was wincing in pleasure and she was gyrating her hips. Then, I pulled out about halfway and started pumping fast, then really fast. #8 pulled her knees back to her chest as far as they would go and I pumped like there was no tomorrow. It was great! Just as I started to orgasm, I could see and feel that she was coming with me. WOW! Did that feel good … as my erection spurted, her vagina squeezed, in unison … and we both kept coming. All this pumping had pushed #8 further onto the bed, so I kneeled on the bed, between her legs, bent over and kissed her.

#8 grabbed my face with both hands and gave me a passionate, wet, lovely kiss and said, "Now, that was FANTASTIC! I was beginning to think sex was overrated … but you have proven just how wonderful sex can be … you really are the Sexpert."

I know where she got that name from. Then, confidently, I responded, "I really am glad … glad that you enjoyed it … so did I." I got up, grabbed my clothes and went into the bathroom to clean up and get dressed. When I came out #8, dressed in her slacks and black bra, again came to me, gave me another kiss and thanked me again.

I then said that she and her boyfriend need to follow 'The Three Rules for Having Sex', which I made up on the spot:

1.   The guy needs to heat up the girl first; she needs to be well lubricated.
2.   Then the girl can heat up the guy … just a little … if necessary.
3.   The guy has to use a condom, preferably lubricated.

#8 laughed as I enunciated the rules, I gave her a kiss on the cheek and a big hug, then left for home.

******

The next day on the walk to school, #2 wanted to know all the details.

First, I reminded her that a gentleman never tells. Then, I told her that her friend was a very nice girl. That was it.

On our walk home after school, I could tell that #8 must have shared many of the intimate details with her … #2 complimented me, saying, "Evidently, you really did a good job having sex with my friend yesterday … she said you gave her two fantastic orgasms and she had never had one before … she's telling all of the girls that you really are THE SEXPERT!"

"I wish she wouldn't do that," I said, but I guess it wouldn't hurt to advertise.

******

Somehow, I was voted onto the student council by my homeroom mates. I tried to stay under the radar at the meeting, but one day I volunteered to help decorate for a dance we were putting on in the gymnasium. The dance was to be a sock hop.

The prettiest girl in our class was in charge of decorating, so one Friday afternoon, right after school, I was only too happy to help her and a handful of other helpers decorate the gym.

I really didn't know the prettiest girl, but this gave us a chance to get to know each other better. She was sort of classy and she hung out with a group of kids that I didn't seem to fit in with.

At the dance she really looked hot! She was dressed for the occasion in bobby socks, a puffy red, short skirt (with a felt cutout of a white poodle on it), a white almost see-through blouse and a big red bow, pulling her shoulder-length brown hair back into a ponytail. She had a nice figure, with broad shoulders and medium-sized breasts … she looked great!

I danced with her several times. Normally, she would have come to the dance with her boyfriend, but she had just broken up with him. She had dated him for a year. Typically, she dated older guys, seniors. So, it was unusual to see her at a dance unattended.

I danced with a number of other girls, but I didn't seem to hook up with anyone. During a slow dance, the prettiest girl asked me if I would like to help take down the decorations the next day. Of course, I couldn't refuse, I was happy to say yes.

Saturday morning, ten of us (5 guys and 5 gals) met at the gym to clean up and take down the decorations. When our work was complete, the prettiest girl in our class invited everyone to go back to her house for a party … sounded good, why not?

We all walked the several blocks to her house. The girls walked in a group in front of the guys. As we were walking, I could her the prettiest girl ask the others, "Did you dance with Tony last night?" The others said no. She then said, "He's like the best dancer!" It was a great complement, but I was soooo embarrassed.

At her house, we were in the rec room, which was very nice, quite large. We had soda and chips and she was playing the same music as we danced to the night before. Everyone was laughing, dancing and having a great time.

I, of course, was dancing exclusively with our host. After a couple of hours, our host informed us that her parents had to go somewhere and the party was over. She pulled me aside and said, "After my folks leave, can you come back?"

"Sure, I would be delighted."

"When you see the garage door open and the car gone, come to the door," she explained.

I walked back to the school, got my bike and rode back to her house. Fortunately, when I got there the car was gone and I was met by the prettiest girl in my class. She had changed into a pair of red flannel pajama pants, with a gray T-shirt, tucked into the waistband of the PJ bottoms. It was evident that she had no bra on, due to the way that her nipples protruded through the fabric. I loved the look!

As I came in the door, she said, "I am so glad you came back … I'm wicked horny!"

We went to the rec room where the lights had been turned down and slow music was playing … we started to dance, closely. I looked down at her face and I could tell by the look that she wanted to kiss me as badly as I wanted to kiss her. As I tilted my head down toward hers, she rose up on her toes to meet me … I really liked that.

While we kissed, her body was at a slight angle to mine and she started to gyrate her hips, which rubbed up against my genitals, I had the feeling she knew what she was doing. I worked one hand under her T-shirt and then up to her breast. When my hand reached its destination, I cupped her breast softly in my hand and rubbed my thumb across her nipple. I could feel her body stiffen and she stopped breathing. I said, "Ummmm, very nice!" I don't normally say anything or make any noise when I am making love, but this seemed to fit the occasion and she relaxed.

After a while, as we stood there kissing, I slid my hand down the front of her T-shirt, past the waistband of her bottoms and gently to her furry nest. NO PANTIES! That blows my mind … how sexy can you get! I slipped my middle finger between her moist lips and pushed downward. She stopped breathing again. After a while she said, "You have such large, beautiful muscles," and she started to caress my bicep. By doing that it allowed me better access to her vagina. As we continued to kiss, her hand sort of massaged my arm and made its' way up to my shoulder and then to my neck, then into my hair. Oh boy! Did that feel good? The kissing became more and more aggressive, wetter and sloppier … in other words, it was great!

Then she moved her hand to the erection in my pants, which was bulging. "UMMMMM," she murmured.

I think she was pleased with what she had in her hand. I know I was. As she stroked my manhood through the fabric, I moved the two of us over to the sofa. When she sat down on the sofa, she said, "Let's lose the pants," as she pushed her bottoms off completely.

I unbuckled and pushed my jeans and boxers off, as well, but I was somewhat self-conscious since I had three-quarters of an erection sticking out. Then, as I sat down beside her, she pushed her T-shirt up over her head and off. Exposing her two good size lobes with extremely dark brown nipples sticking straight out. I surveyed the situation and it couldn't have been better; great face, great breasts, great legs with a dark brown nest between them and a great big smile on her face. FANTASTIC!

I turned on my side and took one stiff nipple into my mouth. As I circled the nipple with my tongue, I circled her clitoris with my fingertip. Around and around, I went. She reached over and was gently caressing my erection. I could feel her clit becoming aroused, as it grew and stiffened under my finger. After a while, I slid my fingertip to the side of her clitoris and started to pump up and down fast. That really turned her on.

"Are you ready?" she asked.

I moved my mouth directly off her nipple and went directly to her mouth, gave her a big, wet, French kiss. "Yes!"

I sat up, rolled my condom on and knelt on the floor in front of her. She pulled her legs back and spread them, to give me good access (it appeared that she knew what she was doing … it was definitely not her first time). With my rock-hard erection in my hand, I moved up against the sofa and directed my staff into her opening. As I entered her, I bent over and began to kiss her. She let go of her legs and put one hand on each side of my face, very softly, as I started to pump all the way in and most of the way out (the side of the bed position). "That is what I needed." Then #9 wrapped her feet behind my butt and urged me to push in hard and deeper. It felt great!

I started to increase the speed and she started to moan, "Give it to me … give it to me," over and over. I could feel her climax, shouting, "YES! YES! YES!" And as I watched the smile on her face, I started to shoot my load into my condom, BANG! BANG! BANG! I just kept coming and #9 seemed to be enjoying the moment as much as me.

When I was done, I said, "That was great!"

#9 agreed and complimented me, "You are very, very good!"

Again, in the deepest voice I could master, I replied, "All the better to please you, my dear."

We both laughed, got up, dressed, and #9 walked me to the door. "Thanks for coming back … I needed that," she told me as she gave me a small, but nice soft kiss.

******

Monday morning, I was met by #9 at the front door to the school. She informed me that she had gone back to her boyfriend. He had come over to her house on Sunday and they had a long talk. They decided that they loved each other and wanted to be together for the rest of their lives. So, she wanted to tell me right away.

Oh well! I lose another great gal to a guy with a job, a car and some money. Soon, I will be 16 and able to get a job and a car … then we'll see.

******

Not everything was wasted from my short fling with #9. It seems that ever since that weekend, one of #9's best friends, a gal that looks just like a model, had a gleam in her eye for me. She put on a big smile whenever she saw me.

Every day she would wait by the front entrance to the gym for her mother to pick her up and bring her home. Since it was spring and #2 had band practice after school, I was free to stroll by the gym after school and have a chat with the model while she was waiting. We seemed to hit it off fairly well, so I met her there the next several days.

Even though she hung out with a different group of kids than I did, I decided to ask her out, but there weren't any events happening soon. So, I asked her if she would like to meet me at the local ice cream shop that night. It appeared that she would like to meet me but her folks didn't let her go out after dinner. I suggested that she say that she needed to go to the library for a couple of hours. She liked the idea and so did her parents. So, that night she met me at the library.

We walked and talked and I took her to the ice cream shop for a soda (she didn't eat much … that was how she stayed so thin). My buddies were amazed that I was with such an attractive gal. They didn't understand that you always have to treat the girl nice, with respect, and remember what my mom always tells me, "Give every woman you come across whatever they want and you will be successful in life." It sounds corny but that is what I endeavor to do.

There was no place to kiss or hug, we were in a very public place, but we had a nice time.

I continued to meet with her after school, to chat until her mother picked her up. One day she even introduced me to her mom. Her mom seemed nice, she said, "Nice to meet you," and they were off.

The next day, the model told me that her mother liked me. She thought I looked like a model as well. I was very proud.

A few days went by and B asked me if I would like to double date with him and some girl on Saturday. A kid that used to live next to him had moved away into the country, invited B to a square dance that his new town was having, to commemorate the new firehouse. I knew the kid well and he was a nice guy. Also, I had been looking for someplace that I could take the model and the dance seemed to fit the bill. I told B that I would love to go and take the model, he was impressed.

The model liked the idea and her parents went along with it.

On Saturday, when B picked me up, he informed me that we were in luck! His folks went away for the weekend and his sister (#1) was staying at her boyfriend's house … we had B's house all to ourselves. So, we decided in advance to return from the dance early.

When we picked up the model, she looked outstanding. She was wearing a light, knit, tan-colored top with a brown, pleated knee-length skirt, with brown penny loafers. It was the opposite of what B had asked the girls to wear. He told us that the kid said for the girls to wear slacks and sneakers … nothing too fancy, because the girls get swung around a lot during the dancing. Oh well … she couldn't look nicer; she was happy and so was I.

When she got into the car, she sat close to me, not next to me, she didn't want to wrinkle her clothes. As we drove, I tried to put my arm around her and kiss her … again no way, she didn't want to mess up her make-up or her clothes. But we had a good time talking in the car anyway.

At the dance, we really looked like the novices that we were. You need four couples to square dance. The eight of us danced over by the corner, with our friend, his date and another couple he knew. They showed us what to do and we all did our best to try and follow. Although, we sometimes didn't know what we were doing, we had a blast, spinning and twirling and doing the rest of the moves. My date was at a disadvantage wearing her leather-soled, leather-heeled shoes. During one dance when she was getting spun around fast, she couldn't keep up and her shoes slipped on the floor and she got flung, feet first, into a row of empty chairs in the corner. It was really funny. Her head and back were on the floor and her perfect legs were up over the top of the chairs … her skirt was over her head … you could see her yellow and white lace panties. She was a good sport, she laughed it off and returned to the dance floor, but a few minutes later, all the chairs in that corner were filled with young guys hoping for a repeat performance … we all got a laugh about that.

Soon, we left so we could head to B's house. When I told the model, she seemed as interested as I was. GREAT!

When we arrived at B's, we went into the kitchen and got a beer. After a few sips B and his girlfriend excused themselves and went upstairs to his bedroom. After a few more sips, I got up the courage to ask the model if she would like to go upstairs to a bedroom. To my amazement, she smiled broadly and said, "I'd love to … I am horny!"

I love it when a girl tells me that she is horny. Sort of a signal to me that she wants to have sex.

I didn't waste any time in leading the model up to the room I had slept in that eventful New Year's Eve. It was tidy. Once the door was shut, I turned and gave the model a hug and a kiss. She did not push me away, good.

I continued to kiss her but it seemed awfully antiseptic. When I slid my hands down to her butt, the model said, "Wait … I don't want to mess up my clothes."

She walked over to the closet, removed her sweater and her skirt and hung them up on hangers.

She was very thin and tall (about 5'10"), with long, very nice legs and a wicked long torso. She was slinky sexy. When she returned in just her tiny yellow and white lace bra and panties … she became an ANIMAL! She just about stuck her tongue down my throat and she was all over me. What a difference!

With the model stuck to me like glue, I relocated the two of us to the bed, where I gently laid her down on her back, while I laid next to her on my side. I put my hand on her breast. Through the bra I could tell that there wasn't much in there. She reached back and unhooked the bra for me. What a difference when her clothes are off.

Her nipples were very small, medium brown, with a dark brown line around the outside of the areola. They looked like a target … and they were a target … for my hand. I softly caressed her breasts, and I ran my fingertip around and around the outside of her nipples, while we continued kissing wildly.

Then, I slid my hand down her long, long torso to her belly button, where I ran my fingertip around several times, before my hand headed south toward her tiny panties. I slid my fingers under the waist band and continued the trip down toward her love lips which was as smooth as her belly, absolutely no pubic hair!

Quickly, she slipped off her panties and my finger slopped into the folds between her legs, she said, "I love that!"

Just the kind of attitude I like. I moved my mouth to her tiny nipples and started to lick, suck and circle her nipples with my tongue, as I circled her clitoris with the tip of my finger. Then, I put my fingertip just below her clit and pushed softly down toward her love canal, just entering her with the tip of my finger before I would slide it back. By the way she was gyrating her hips I could tell that she wanted more. I continued to tease her that way for another five minutes before I slipped my finger into the entrance of her love canal … I paused … then softly, but relentlessly, I pushed my finger in as far as it would go. She loved it! I slowly slid my finger out and back up the slippery slope to her clit. Then, right back down and all the way in. She moaned in pleasure, ran her fingers through my hair and pressed my head down hard against her nipples.

After a few minutes, I pulled my head free and said, "I think it's time to put it in."

"Hurry, I can't wait," was her reply.

In a moment, I slipped out of my jeans and boxers, slipped on a condom and kneeled between her legs … ready to impale her with my swollen member. She just lay there with her legs barely spread, I grabbed and lifted her legs as I leaned in with my erection. With one hand holding it, I used the head to spread her love lips and I started to press into her (the missionary position). #10 was well lubricated but very tight. I slowly pumped in and out, while I lifted her legs. I tried to be gentle so that I would not hurt her. I continued to pump, increasing the pace from time to time. I could tell that #10 was about to climax.

Then, I became aware that my feet were cold … I shouldn't be aware of anything else at a time like that except for what I am doing. I realized that there was little emotion involved with what we were doing … we were just going through the motions. #10 climaxed, quietly, and sort of emotionless. I was nowhere near an orgasm. So, I started to pump even faster, closed my eyes and began to think of when I was inside #1 and it wasn't long before I was shooting long, hot wads of sperm into my condom.

Once we were done, #10 quickly got up, put on her clothes and went into the bathroom to fix her make-up and priss herself up.

We went back down to the kitchen and drank soda while we waited for B and his date…

#10 and I didn't speak much after we did it and as a matter of fact, #10 was pretty cold toward me on the way home … again with the not wanting to wrinkle her outfit. I walked #10 to her door and said goodbye.

I really wasn't interested in dating #10 anymore because all she cared about was her looks. I like a girl that can go out and have a good time without constantly worrying about her hair and her outfit. So, we continued to be friendly but I didn't ask her out again.

Chapter 5
The Sexpert Turns 16

"Tony … Tony … Tony," yelled my mom.

"I'm up," I replied.

"Happy birthday! … come for your breakfast … it's on the table." Mom always makes me waffles and syrup for my birthday breakfast and I can smell them as I am lying in bed … ummmmm … what a great way to start the day!

As I lay in bed, I was thinking, finally, after all this time, I am turning 16. What a huge milestone. I will be able to get a real job, earn some real spending money and get a car. Independence … that is what you get when you turn 16.

I want to remember this day the rest of my life, so I want to enjoy it to the fullest.

Breakfast was great. Mom reminded me, "Don't forget, we have a big birthday party for you tonight at supper time."

"I can't wait," was my reply.

Then, I had to shower, shave and dress for school. I put on a black T-shirt … my trademark. I have decided over the past several years, to always wear a black shirt, or a black sweater, blue jeans and black sneakers. Even when I get all dressed up, I wear a black shirt, black slacks and black shoes. I think it goes great with my black hair and olive complexion.

School went well. I looked for my latest girlfriend but I didn't see her around. She wasn't in any of my classes this year. She was a cute Italian girl, about 5'3" tall, sort of petite, with short, very curly black hair (kind of like an afro).

Last year, she sat next to me in math and we got to know each other then. Recently, I ran into her in the hallway and said I missed seeing her. She invited me to her house after school, so I met her there the last two Wednesdays. Wednesdays are the only days that she is free after school because she has piano lessons and she also, tutors some younger students on the other days.

She was a phenomenal pianist and her parents were pushing her to become a concert pianist when she grows up.

She lived in a nice house, only a block from the school. When I have gone to her house, we have had a good time; she plays the piano for me, we dance and talk in her basement recreation room. Unfortunately, her mom never leaves us alone.

Fortunately, her mom, in her mid-30s, is the most beautiful woman, from head to toe, that I have ever seen. She is always dressed very nicely; her fingernails are very attractively manicured and when she is at home, she does not wear shoes and her toenails are manicured to match her fingernails. She has beautiful, silky, waist length, black hair. Her face is gorgeous and her body is spectacular. At 5'5" tall, she had large breasts, a small waist, a great butt and even greater legs. Her posture was perfect and she had the nicest color skin. It has sort of a red blush to it … I have never seen another Italian with this skin color … and I have seen a lot of Italians. In other words, the mother is spectacular. We always said, "Take a good look at the mother, because that is what your date is going to look like in 20 to 25 years."

In any event, it was Wednesday, so I headed over to my new girlfriend's house.

It was a warm day, the front door was open and when I rang the doorbell, I heard the mother yell, "Come in."

I opened the screen door and went into the living room. Then, I called out for my girlfriend. I could hear water running. The mother yelled out, "Tony, is that you?"

As I replied, "Yes," I started to head toward her voice. In the hallway, I met the mother coming out of the bathroom. Obviously, she had just come out of the shower. She had her hair wrapped up in a towel and she was just finishing wrapping another towel around her body and tucking it in under her armpit. We stopped about two feet apart … how embarrassing … but look at her; even in a towel, with no make-up on, she was still radiant … I enjoyed checking her out, from head to toe.

"My daughter has had the break of a lifetime," she informed me with a great big exuberant smile. "She has been accepted to study with the top pianist in the country. He just relocated to a city just 25 miles away and her father has taken the afternoon off, to bring her there. The classes will be 3 hours long, every Wednesday, from now on. They won't be home till late."

I was thinking, oh well, there goes another potential girlfriend; in the meantime, I was studying how gorgeous the mother was.

"Do you like what you see?" She asked me.

"You are the most beautiful woman I have ever seen," was my humble reply.

She smiled, then she detached the top of the towel and held it wide open, behind her. OH MY … the most beautiful woman in the world was standing completely nude, in front of me … just for ME! In the back of my mind, I wanted to start singing, "Happy Birthday to you … Happy Birthday to you!" It was the nicest present … and she didn't even know it is my birthday. In the moment, I was thinking what a spectacular body she had. Broad shoulders, large breasts (big around and big protruding), dark brown nipples, the size of my finger (and dark brown areolas around her nipples … about 3" in diameter … I have never seen anything so big), a tiny waist, a jet-black triangle patch of pubic hair between her legs, and perfectly toned legs (that looked longer than they were) and finally her feet with the pedicured toenails … exquisite!

As I stood there, enjoying the view, completely stunned and in awe, she swiftly walked right up to me, dropping the towel. She stopped so close that I could feel here nipples were sticking through the fabric of my T-shirt. She looked up at me and pulled my head down as she rose up onto her toes. Her full, wet, lips softly brushed over my lips … I didn't move. She started to kiss me and her tongue parted my lips … I didn't know what to do, but I instinctively started to kiss … the best I knew how. After thirty seconds or so, as we kissed, she breathed in through her mouth and sucked the air from my lungs into hers … it was the first time experiencing this technique and it was HOT!

I put my hands on her butt and squeezed gently. She stepped back, took my hand, and said, "Come with me." She looked as good from the back as she did from the front. I followed her a short distance to her bedroom. She led me to her bed, which was already turned down. She started to hurriedly unbuckle my belt and she said, "Take off your shirt."

I immediately took off my shirt, kicked off my sneakers, then reached down and pushed off my jeans and boxers. Leaving on just my socks and a huge grin on my face.

She turned me so that my back was toward the bed, sat me down on the edge and pushed me onto my back, with my feet still on the floor. "Lay here … like this," she instructed … I didn't move.

She positioned herself between my legs, bent over and took my semi-erect manhood into her hand. She pulled the skin downward until it was taut, it swelled to full protuberance almost immediately … she bent over further and slithered the tip of her wet, hot tongue into the opening in my penis head, then ever so slowly around the rim of the head … OH HOW FANTASTIC! … then, she opened her mouth and put her hot, wet lips around the head and sucked my penis deeply into her mouth, while continually keeping my foreskin pulled down taunt. Her head bobbed up and down, as she sucked. I could not take much before I'd explode … I informed her, "You need to stop doing that right now or I am going to come in your mouth."

I could tell she was enjoying herself and her head continued to bob and suck. With her mouth full, she murmured something like, "Okay." Well, the vibration from her speaking went directly from her lips down the shaft of my erection and it felt soooooo gooooood that I started to orgasm harder than ever. She was a real expert and somehow, she timed the rise of her head with the contraction of my erection, giving me the feeling that she was just sucking the sperm right out of me … and she was! She was undaunted by my thick white juice and kept it up until she had sucked every last drop from me. It was the most fantastic thing that anyone had ever done to me … GREAT!

Then, she stood up and started to walk toward the bathroom, and with a mouthful of my sperm she murmured, "Stay right there," so I didn't move a muscle.

She must have spat my sperm into the toilet because I heard it flush. Then, I could hear the water running in the sink as she washed out her mouth. Next, I heard her brush her teeth and gargle. It only took a few minutes and she was back walking toward the bed with a big grin on her face. "Silly, you can make yourself comfortable," she said as she lifted my ankles and I swung my feet onto the bed.

She reached into the drawer of the nightstand and took out a condom. OH BOY! I know what that means. She snuggled up next to me in her bed, she smelled great (she must have put on some perfume when she was in the bathroom). She started to kiss me and to fondle my penis, it felt great. It only took a minute and I was fully erect, "That's what I like about a young guy …

you can get hard again almost immediately," she said with a smile. Then she sat up and opened the condom package, held my erection straight up, and unrolled a red condom with bumps on it onto my erection. It made me even harder.

Next, she straddled my hips, with two fingers, she reached down and spread her love lips apart, lowered herself down onto my throbbing shaft and started to slide forward and back (the cowgirl position). I didn't move a muscle, unsure what to do. #11 looked even more beautiful, sitting straight up on top of me; enjoying herself, sliding slowly forward and back until the head of my penis would get caught in the top of her love lips, where they come together. #11 would stop there a moment … it felt great to me and I could see she was loving it as well … then she would slide forward again. I reached up for her magnificent breasts. I lifted them slightly and caressed them, before I started to run the tips of my thumbs around her giant nipples. She moaned and pressed down more with her hips. Soon she bent forward, picked up an adjacent pillow and propped it under my head … so that my head would be in the ideal position for me to suck on her beautiful nipples … how thoughtful of her. She lowered her breast right into my mouth, which was only too pleased to suck one of those beauties in. I continued to caress the other breast and I would occasionally roll her nipple between my finger and thumb … she seemed to like that.

With #11 leaning forward, I could feel her rock-hard clit, sliding up and down on my shaft … oh boy, was she horny!

My right hand was free, so I moved it to the bottom of #11's back, and then slid it up to the base of her neck. With just the tip of my finger, I slid it back down to her butt, while I caressed and squeezed her fantastic butt cheek. Then, with just my fingertip, I went back up the middle of her back to her neck. Then, I got the crazy idea to slid down and feel her vagina. So, I started my descent, down her back, very slowly, down between her butt cheeks … I hadn't thought about it, but before I would get to her love hole, I had to cross over #11's butt hole. As my fingertip stopped on her butt hole, I could feel #11 stopped breathing. I circled my fingertip, having the feeling that she was enjoying this attention … and she did. She sort of pushed her tush back and pressed her breast further into my mouth. Teasingly, I continued my fingertip's trip to #11's love canal … I could hardly reach the destination, but I pushed my finger in, up to the first knuckle … into her very moist love canal. Then, ever so slowly, I dragged my fingertip back to her butt hole. I circled her butt hole again, with some of her own juices on it and then pressed in softly. To my surprise, with her lubricant on it, my finger slipped right into #11's butt hole! She moaned exuberantly, "You know what I like!"

I didn't have a clue what she liked but I was more than happy to try and find out. #11 was circling her hips, so that only her clitoris was rubbing on the head of my erection, while my fingertip was rapidly going in and out of her butt hole and my mouth was sucking on her nipple. She was about as hot as a gal could get. She instructed me to, "Nibble on my nipple!"

Not sure what to do, I put my tongue beneath #11's nipple and gently lowered my teeth onto the top of her nipple. "Yes … Yes," she moaned. As I nibbled, she orgasmed, over and over. The longest female orgasm that I have ever seen.

Next, she pushed herself up onto her feet and squatted over me. Lifting herself up on her legs, #11 grabbed my throbbing erection, pointed it straight up and lowered her dripping wet love canal down onto it. It was the most pleasure that I had ever felt, as she slid downward and my erection drove upward into her (the cowgirl position)! Up and down, up and down #11 went. I loved every stroke, especially when she would go all the way down and 'bottom out' … FANTASTIC! I reached up and started to caress and squeeze her breasts. It didn't take long before #11 orgasmed again. When she stopped moving mid-orgasm I started to pump up and down as fast as I could. Of course, it didn't take long before I orgasmed too, for the second time … this time inside the most beautiful woman, the most exquisite woman, the most sensuous lady that I have ever seen.

She was exhausted when she said, "That was great … I loved every minute of it … you were magnificent!" I was proud … #11 was an experienced woman that I had pleased … WOW!

Still sitting on top of me, #11 leaned back and put her hands on the bed and continued to slid herself back and forth on my semi-erection. It felt good.

Before I got too soft, #11 snuggled up next to me and gave me the most wonderful kiss of my life. She stuck her tongue deeply into my mouth and sucked the air from my lungs into hers, again … this time I was prepared, so I sucked the air back into my lungs … it was incredibly sexy!

When we stopped kissing, #11 told me how she really enjoyed what we had done and that she would like me to come back next Wednesday.

Of course, I told her that I would only be too happy to return; she said, "Don't tell anyone about what we did."

I replied, "Don't worry … a gentleman would never tell."

As I walked home, all I could think of was that I had just received the most magnificent birthday present of all time! WOW, was I lucky!

******

As I approached my house, I could see that there were several cars in our driveway and several more parked in the street. All of my aunts and uncles had been invited to my party … something special!

Inside, mom had decorated the whole house with all types of streamers, balloons and signs … it was incredibly festive. The party was extra special … feeling all of the warmth from all of my relatives and especially my folks. Somehow, they all seemed to know just how special this birthday was for me.

I received great presents from all of my relatives and my sister, but my most special present was from my parents; they paid for auto school, so I could get my license … FANTASTIC!

Even though it was a school night, we partied till late and when I went to bed, I just lay there and reflected on what a really special day my 16th birthday had turned out to be … it doesn't get any better!

******

The next day my mom instructed me to go to the big grocery store in the center of the town to get a job. It wasn't far from our house, so I could walk to work.

The grocery stores were owned by three Italian brothers and their sister. The store in my town was the first and largest of a chain of three stores. The oldest brother managed it, while each of his other brothers managed one of the other stores, in adjacent towns. The sister was not involved but her husband worked as a butcher in the main store.

My mom instructed me to go to the manager, tell him I was her son and he would give me a job.

That afternoon, after school, I went to the grocery store, I looked up the manager and asked him for a job. He was very nice and said, "Let's go to the office and put your name on the list."

On the way, I mentioned that my mom had sent me to see him and I told him her name. Immediately, he stopped and said, "Well then, you can start tomorrow, after school."

He scheduled me to work; Monday, Tuesday, Thursday and Friday afternoon and Saturday, the full day. I would have Wednesdays and Sundays off.

When I got home, I asked my mother why the manager just gave me the job when I told him her name. She laughed and said both of their families came from Italy about the same time and they lived right next to each to her. So, the boys that own the grocery stores were her next-door neighbors when she grew up. Their sister was her best friend.

******

Work went wonderfully. I enjoyed what I was doing and I fit in well. The staff was made up from kids from our town … I knew them all and the adults treated me well since they knew my mom well.

Mostly, I packed groceries and when it was slow, I put stock on the shelves … it was all good!

******

My folks bought me six driving lessons. Once the instructor saw me drive, he told me that he felt that would be all of the lessons I would need. My father had been teaching me for years and even let me drive on the roads with him if the traffic was light.

So, I just needed to study the book, preparing for the test of my life!

******

The week flew by and before I knew it, it was Wednesday afternoon again. Time to visit #11 after school. I couldn't wait … the excitement was almost too much as I approached her house.

I rang the doorbell, #11 yelled, "Come in." She met me in the kitchen, barefoot, wearing a thick, white, terry cloth bathrobe. Her long black hair was combed beautifully and it cascaded over her shoulders, her face was all made up like she was going to a ball … she looked outstanding!

"I could hardly wait for this day to come," she informed me with a big smile.

Not wanting to sound too eager, I replied, "Yeah, me too."

#11 took me by the hand and led me to the bedroom. I could smell her perfume as we walked. She smelled great!

She had me sit on the edge of the bed, as she stepped back and opened her robe … just so that I could look at her body … it was magnificent … like looking at some other great work of art. I studied her from head to toe. She just stood there … for me. Then, as she dropped the robe, she asked, "Do you like what you see?"

"You are the most beautiful woman in the world!" I said in complete honesty. "Magnificent!"

#11 smiled and seemed to like my reply. Next, she helped me get out of all of my clothes. Then, she had me lay flat, on the far side of the bed, on my back, with a semi-hard erection. She climbed onto the bed on all fours and went straight for my manhood. #11 delicately ran her hand over my semi-erect penis and then down to my scrotum. She gently took my erection in her hand and started to stroke it … it grew bigger, actually a lot bigger. #11 was looking at it much like I was looking at her body moments earlier … sort of in awe. "You have got a big erection," she said as she tightened her grip on my pounding rod. She licked her lips to moisten them before she lowered her head down to my waiting member, which she started to lick on the underside of the head … her hand had pulled the skin down taunt … it felt soooo good … I was like frozen in time as I watched as #11's mouth engulfed the entire head in her full, soft, warm lips and sucked it all in as her head went right down on it … WOW! FANTASTIC!

As #11 continued, I had to tell her, "If you continue, you are going to make me climax."

#11 took her mouth off for an instant and said, "Great!"

So, I laid back and enjoyed it as she brought me up to the brink … then she kept me waiting there as she licked up and down on the shaft … prolonging my ecstasy … then, #11 started to suck and stroke with even more vigor that before, as I filled her mouth with my sperm … she timed her upward suction on the shaft of my penis to coincide with its contraction to shoot out its' juices … it just couldn't feel any better … BANG! BANG! BANG! BANG! It was the most intense climax of my life … #11 was fantastic … and she seemed to love what she was doing.

When she stood up to run to the bathroom, I broke my silence, "That was fantastic! The most intense climax of my life!" I couldn't believe that I had said that. "You are magnificent!"

From the bathroom, she replied, "Great!"

She returned shortly with a small white towel, which she used to wipe off any remnants of sperm from my penis. Then, she just laid on the bed next to me. I laid on my side, softly rubbing my hand all over her naked body. As I cupped one of her breasts, I said, "Your skin is soooo soft … you are soooo beautiful … you are the most beautiful Italian woman in the world!"

As soon as I said that, #11 started to laugh so hard that her body was bouncing up and down on the bed. Eventually, she looked me in the eye and informed me, "Everyone thinks I am Italian just because my husband is Italian … but I am 100% American Indian … my husband met me when I was on the reservation."

That explained the color of her skin … how lucky can I be … I am making love to a beautiful Indian maiden! Then, I turned over a little further and started to kiss her.

#11 took my head in her hands and gently started to push it toward her waist … I kissed my way down to her belly button. #11 asked, "Aren't you going to reciprocate?"

"I don't know what you mean?"

She laughed, "Don't you know how to pleasure a woman with your mouth?"

"No."

"Let me show you," she replied. #11 had me kneel on the edge of the bed, while she turned and positioned herself so that her crotch was directly in front of my face. Then, #11 pulled her knees up toward her chest and spread them apart. With two fingers, she reached down and spread open the lips of her love canal. With the index finger on her other hand, she pointed to her clitoris, a small pink bump near the top, surrounded by layers of skin (labia) and covered with one thin layer of skin, she called the hood. #11 instructed me not to touch her clitoris directly because it is so sensitive. Instead, rub, lick, etc. around it. She had me start by just licking around the clitoris and up and down the lips … I could tell that she really enjoyed it by the way she was moaning. Next, she just had me suck her clit into my mouth like a clam … I would let it slide out then I would suck it back in … a few times I sucked it into my mouth and pulled my head away, stretching the skin until it popped out of my mouth … that gave her incredible pleasure. Sometimes I would run the tip of my tongue under the hood and that seemed to excite #11 even more.

After a while, I started to explore with my tongue … traveling all the way down to her love canal and sticking my tongue in as far as it would go. Then, sliding straight up the middle and stopping before her clit. As #11 became more and more excited I could feel her clitoris becoming larger and her vagina was becoming wetter and wetter from her own lubrication … It made everything very slippery for my face, lips and tongue to slide around on …#11 loved it and was moaning very loudly!

Next, #11 said, "Now take your middle finger and slowly push it up my love canal, with the pad on your fingertip pointing up." I did. "Feel for a small bump … that's my G-spot … Oh yes, that's the spot. Now rub that gently as you continue to lick."

I continued as requested and #11's breathing became more and more rapid almost immediately. #11 started to moan louder, gyrate her hips and in a minute or so she was having an incredibly strong orgasm … legs clenched together, uncontrollable spasms going through her body … her hands were grasping the sheets as though she was in pain … but she wasn't in pain … she was in pleasure.

I continued licking and stroking her G-spot until #11's orgasm was complete and she relaxed … she said, "Oh boy … that was very good! You are a quick learner!"

"Just trying to please," was my reply. I didn't know that I would enjoy doing that as much as I did and I probably wouldn't have enjoyed it if it didn't give her such pleasure. "Rubbing that G-spot really made you orgasm quickly."

"Yes … that is the most sexually sensitive area of a woman … and you stroked it just right."

All of this activity made me aroused as well, so I decided to get #11 hot again, so I could put it in. Therefore, I pushed her legs back toward her head and I started to lick around her clit again and run my finger up and down the middle, in and out of her moist canal … she responded by moaning. After a while, I got the idea to run my wet, slimy finger down to her butt hole … remembering how much she enjoyed me titillating it. #11 flinched and said, "Rule #1 … anything that goes into the butt hole does not go back into the other hole … it can cause an infection."

"Ok."

Fortunately, I had used my index finger, so I decided—middle finger, love hole … index finger, butt hole.

With that decided, I resumed my sucking and rubbing. The next time that I slid my finger down to her butt hole, #11 reached down and spread apart her cheeks, apparently to allow me better access. I put a big dollop of saliva on my index finger then slid my finger up and down her perineum and around her butt hole … when I pushed in … my finger slipped in up to the first knuckle. #11 squealed with pleasure … I pushed in and out a few more times and I could tell it made her hot … it excited me a lot having my finger there. I decided we were both ready.

I took the condom that #11 had put on the nightstand, and while I continued to lick, I slipped on the condom. Then, I spread #11's legs apart even more and guided my shaft to her love canal (the missionary position). As I slowly pushed in, I could see the pleasure that I was giving her. I could I could feel her G-spot as the crown on the head of my erection brushed over it … she moaned, "Oh yes!" I pulled out just enough to brush her G-spot again, then pushed in a bit. I could see that it was driving #11 crazy. So, I continued to do it and in a very short time #11 began to orgasm … moaning, groaning and coming with great force. I love giving pleasure … it gives me pleasure as well!

"Oh, you are good," #11 moaned. "Do you want to do it doggy style?"

"Aw … sure!" Although, I have never done it doggy style … give it a try.

#11 turned over and kneeled on the mattress with her arms supporting her shoulders. I kneeled behind her and slid my erection right in … WOW … did that feel good. #11 started to rock back and forth, pushing her hips back toward me. I pushed in when she came back and I pulled out as she rocked forward … it made for deep penetration. We both really enjoyed it. After a while I pulled out until the head of my erection was rubbing on her G-spot and then I went rapidly in and out while #11 braced for another powerful orgasm.

As #11 was coming, I noticed that her butt hole was looking up at me. To prolong her enjoyment, I thought I would rub it with my finger. So, I put a big glob of saliva on the tip of my thumb and without missing a stroke, I started to rub her butt hole which was somewhat open due to the position we were in. "You know I love that!" She yelled. "Do you want to put it in my butt?" She said, panting.

"I hadn't thought about that," was my reply … but it sounded intriguing.

"You'll love it … I do!"

#11 crawled to the nightstand and removed a tube and another condom. She squirted a big glob of the lube on several of her fingers, then she reached behind herself and applied it to her butt hole. "Remember Rule #1 … nothing that goes into hole two can go back into hole one."

"Yep!"

"Okay, Rule #2 … you need lots of lubrication … Rule #3 … you need to get the hole ready by relaxing my rectal muscles," she said with a smile, as she turned her butt to face me again.

"Got it!" So, I applied a glob of the lube onto my middle and index fingers. Then, I started to rub it up and down around #11's butt hole, she moaned. I kept adding lube and tried to stuff it in the hole with my middle finger … it started to slide in and out effortlessly. With my other hand I reached around to the front and started to rub her love lips and clit as well.

#11 was enjoying every minute of my manipulations, then she said, "Try to work two fingers in at a time."

It didn't take long before two fingers went in easily. "Put on the other condom, load it with lube and let's try to put it in," said #11, panting.

Quickly, I removed the red, bumpy condom and slipped into a very thin, clear condom, applied the lube and got into position (the lube is extra slippery).

#11 said, "Let's try to get three fingers in first."

I applied more lube to my fingers, slipped two fingers in and out a few times then I added the third. "I can only get them in about a knuckle and a half," I told her.

"Great … I'm ready. Put the head of your erection against my butt hole … good … now when I push back you push in, just a little … now when I push out like I am trying to poop, you should slide right in."

I pushed in, as instructed and all of a sudden #11's butt hole opened up and I slid in about one-third … WOW … it was very tight and very warm … HOT!

#11 froze in that position for a minute, and so did I, evidently, she was getting used to it being inside of her, breathing deeply #11 said, "I'll push out again, like I am taking a poop, and you push in."

WHAM-O, I slid all the way in. It was turning me on like never before but I held back. Then, slowly, I pulled out two-thirds, then back in. Each time it became easier. #11 was yelling, "I LOVE IT, TONY! … I LOVE IT!" While she rubbed her clitoris ferociously with her own fingers.

Ultimately, I was pumping fast and I couldn't hold back … I had the strongest and longest orgasm of my life, pumping #11 in the butt and enjoying ever stroke. Fortunately, #11 climaxed at the same time as me. When we were both done, I slowed my pumping and when I pulled out, I said, "That … was INCREDIBLE!"

#11 turned toward me, still on all fours, took my chin softly with her hand, looked me in the eye, smiled widely and said, "That was the best anal sex that I have ever had!" Then she started to kiss me wildly.

I responded by reaching down, cupping both of her beautiful breasts, while I was working my tongue savagely into her mouth and before she had the chance, I breathed in and sucked the air from her lungs into mine … #11 responded by sucking the air back … then I returned the favor … it was the perfect ending to a magnificent session of sex.

I was still glowing from #11's compliment when she said, "I am going to jump into the shower, then you can jump in and get cleaned up."

By the time I got up, removed the condom, and wiped myself off, #11 was out of the shower. The hot water felt great!

We dressed, had a nice hug and kiss. Then, I darted off for home, arriving just in time for dinner.

******

The next day, #11 showed up at the grocery store but didn't acknowledge that she knew me. When she came through the checkout line she said to me, "Boy, could you put my groceries in a box and carry it to my car, please?"

"Yes, mam."

At her car #11 informed me that we would not be able to get together again, since her daughter had a significant problem with her piano instructor the day before. Evidently, the piano teacher stood behind her daughter while she was playing, reached around, and started to fondle her breasts. She yelled and the father, who was waiting in the next room, came running in to catch the guy in the act. They left immediately and arrived just moments after I left. WOW!

Both of the parents were appalled. They went to the authorities to file a complaint.

So, our little fling had to end, at least for now.

******

It is funny how things happen.

The next day as I was leaving school, the junior class had set up a table near the exit, to sell tickets to the junior prom the next Saturday. As I walked by, the girl at the table asked, "Hey Tony, have you purchased your tickets for the prom next Saturday?"

"No, I haven't," was my reply.

"Why not?" She asked.

"You know that I am a sophomore and I haven't got a date."

"I would be happy to go with you," she replied.

I knew this girl a little. She had a great personality but she wasn't the type of girl that I was usually drawn to. She was average looking, with long brown hair and a bit overweight (with small boobs). She needed a date and based on what my mother has always taught me … I should attempt to please her. So, I said, "Well, that makes two of us … I would be delighted to be your date." Then, I sat at the table with the girl, purchased the tickets and we formulated a plan for prom night.

I informed her that I wouldn't have my license for several more weeks, so, she agreed to drive. I would get a tuxedo and flowers. She wanted the type of flower bouquet for her wrist, something to go with a blue dress. We would meet several of her friends for dinner, then go to the prom. After the prom, most of the kids go to a resort or some big hotel and party for the rest of the night, but she suggested that we go to her parents' cottage by a lake. It sounded good to me.

******

The following Saturday, I got out of work early, picked up her flowers and my tux, went home, and got ready for the prom.

My folks were really excited for me. Mom came along when dad drove me to the girl's house, so they could take pictures of us both, all dressed up.

The girl looked very nice in her light blue gown; which had a frilly skirt and sort of a halter top. Both parents were impressed with the yellow rose nosegay that I had gotten for my date. Of course, I wore a black tuxedo; with a black silk shirt and black bow tie with black, shinny, dress shoes. Everyone said I looked great. My matching yellow rose boutonniere stood out against the black material of the tux.

After copious pictures were taken by both sets of parents, we were finally off to meet her friends for dinner.

We met three other couples, none of which I had ever spoken to before. The dinner was nice, everyone was sociable and seemed to be having a good time. Then, we went to the prom.

The hall was decorated very nicely. We sat at a table for eight, with the same kids that we had dinner with. There was a live band and they played the type of music that we liked … great!

My father told me that I should initiate a conversation with each of the other guys at the table. Also, I should ask each of the other girls to dance at least once during the course of the evening. So, during our first slow dance, I informed my date that I felt that the right thing to do would be to ask each of the other girls at our table to dance with me once that night. She agreed and said she was impressed with my 'thoughtfulness'.

We danced a lot, but the others mostly sat at the table talking. As we went to sit down, after several dances, I asked one of the other girls at our table if she would like to do a slow dance with me. She popped up quickly and looked pleased that I had asked.

This gal was really pretty, nice figure, tan, blond hair in a fancy do on top of her head, with little curly strands of hair cascading down the side of her face … very nice. On the floor she pressed tightly up against my body as we danced. She asked, "Why did you invite her to the dance instead of me?"

"I didn't know that you needed a date," I replied.

She kept looking in my eyes and said, "I am available … you know. Why don't you ask me out for next Saturday?"

"I don't think it is appropriate to ask a girl out when you are on a date with another girl … let's talk next week in school."

She tightened her grip on me, pushed her hips in tightly against mine, smiled widely and said, "I'd love that!"

During the evening, I danced with the other two girls at our table … they were both very thankful for the dance … and neither one asked for a date … fortunately.

I did come across #2, who was there with her new boyfriend and as we shared a slow dance, she told me she planned to have sex with her date, later at a resort that they were going to, with a big group of other kids.

Later in the evening I ran into #8. We danced and she thanked me again for the lessons that I taught her. She said, "My boyfriend and I have great sex now!" I blushed … she laughed.

When the prom was over, my date drove us to a cottage next to a lake, about thirty minutes away. It was a cute cottage with a small living room, a kitchen and several bedrooms. My date asked me to 'get comfortable' in the living room while she got out of her gown in the bedroom.

I took off my jacket, tie, shirt, and dress shoes and sat on the sofa watching the television. When my date came into the living room, she had on a white terry cloth bathrobe and she was carrying a bottle of champagne, with two flute glasses.

She put the bottle and glasses on the fireplace hearth and turned on the gas fireplace. Next, she took a cushion from a chair that was adjacent to the fireplace and wedged it up and down in front of the chair, where there was a thick white rug.

"Come, lay on the rug and we can drink champagne and watch TV." She instructed me.

As I sat on the rug and leaned back against the cushion, my date went over to the lamp and shut it off. Then, only having the light from the TV and the fireplace, she returned and opened her robe, as she stood next to me. All she had on was a skimpy red bra and tiny red panties.

"Looking good!" I said in amazement, as she closed the robe and sat on the rug next to me, pouring the champagne into the glasses. She handed me one glass and as she raised her glass, she said, "Thank you for taking me to the prom and for being so much fun!"

I tapped her glass with mine and said, "The night is not over."

I put my arm around her shoulder and we leaned back against the cushion, drinking the champagne, soaking up the heat from the fireplace, watching late night TV and talking about various things that had happened at the junior prom … it was very romantic. When we were finished with the first bottle, my date got another. Soon we were kissing … softly, slowly, gently at first … then more aggressively. As things started to heat up, I sucked the air from her lungs into mine … she loved it and moaned with delight. I put my hand on her cheek, then slowly moved it down her neck and into the top of her robe and down to her breast, which she pushed willingly into my hand. She moved her knee up and started rubbing it up and down on my crotch … evidently, she had had some experience … this was not the move of a virgin.

I slid my hand down her torso into her panty, through her pubic hair and started to run my finger over her love lips … she raised her hips and pushed her mouth tighter against mine … she was definitely horny. I slipped my finger down between the lips and into her love canal, she caught her breath (as if she was surprised), then she relaxed as my finger slid up to her clit, then, around and around her clit, very gently … she was somewhat moist. I moved my head down and began kissing around the top of her bra. She got the signal and reached up to unfasten the hook, which was between the cups. While I watched her unfasten, I brought my finger up to my mouth and deposited a large glob of saliva on the tip, which went directly back to the area between her clit and her love canal. With the added lubricant my finger slid effortless around and she started to squirm and squeal with delight.

My tongue very gently started to circle her small nipples, while my finger circled her clit at the same speed … very slowly and very gently. She said, "I love that!" So, I continued what I was doing. Then, I lowered my lips down to suck her nipple into my mouth and when I would lift my head to pull on her nipple, I would slip my finger up from her love hole to her clit … then I would lower my head and suck her nipple back into my mouth while my finger would slide back down into her love canal. That really made her hot. My finger became all slimy from her lubrication … which made it slip around even better. I started to suck and lick her other nipple ferociously as I pushed my finger deeper into her love canal … she arched her body and gyrated her hips, forward and back my finger slipped in and out. I positioned my fingertip on her G-spot and softly started to circle it, while I sucked her nipple into my mouth … in thirty seconds she was ready to come … she yelled, "Put it in quickly … put it in now!" She was panting.

"Don't worry, I will," I consoled her. Quickly, I slipped out of my pants and boxers, slipped on my condom but during this time she cooled off … so I whispered, "Where did I leave off…" and I went back to what I had been doing … sucking her nipple and rubbing her G-spot. Again, it only took minutes to get her back to the edge of an orgasm.

"Tony … put it in … pleeeeeeeease!"

I kneeled between her legs and slowly started to enter her (the missionary position), she reached up and pulled my head down to kiss me, I pumped in and out ever so slowly. #12's kiss became extremely passionate. I quickened the pace. Her hips matched my rhythm. I pulled out until the rim of the head of my shaft was on her G-spot and then with rapid short strokes I pumped in and out, so that my rim would continually stimulate #12's G-spot. She climaxed in ten to fifteen seconds. Then, I went back to long, deep strokes. Her body seemed to relax even more. Then, as I continued, we started to get hotter and hotter. Again, I pulled out until the rim of the head was against her G-spot again, I stroked in and out rapidly … #12 pulled her knees up as far as she could and started to orgasm again, only this time much longer and stronger … I couldn't hold back any longer and I climaxed with her. Slowly, I went back to long strokes and #12 said, "Tony … you are fantastic … that was GREAT!"

"It was!" I replied. "I have to go to the bathroom." I pulled out and grabbed my clothes and walked to the bathroom, to clean up. When I came out in just my boxers, #12 had a light on in the bedroom.

"We can sleep in here," she instructed me. I went into the bedroom and #12 handed me a glass of champagne and said, "We still have half a bottle to finish."

I sat on the bed while #12 went into the bathroom. When she returned #12 took off her robe, picked up her glass and sat on the edge of the bed next to me … she looked at me and had a peculiar look in her eye … "Would you take off your boxers and sit back down … please," she requested … I did … then, #12 took a big gulp of her champagne and quickly kneeled in front of me, on the floor … #12 spread my knees apart and as she moved forward, she picked up my limp penis in one hand. Of course, it started to spring to life … she was staring at it … when she started to pump it, it became fairly hard … #12 looked at me, smiled and said, "I have always wanted to do this," and she poured champagne on my erection … then, she licked it off … it really felt great! I think it turned her on even more than it turned me on. She kept pouring champagne on my erection and licking it off, which really turned me on.

"Come here," I asked. When she stood up, I stood up and gave her a kiss … her lips had a salty taste from licking my erection. I pushed her panties down and instructed her to kneel on the bed, on all fours. I quickly slipped into a condom; fortunately, I brought three condoms with me. Next, I slipped my finger into her love canal from the back, while I rubbed her G-spot.

"That really turns me on," #12 whispered.

Next, I grabbed #12 by the hips and pushed my erection deeply into her, she moaned. I was in ecstasy, as I pumped and pumped and as I was getting close to my climax, I positioned the rim of my erection against #12's G-spot and when I stroked rapidly, we both started to orgasm at the same time … it was GREAT!

When we were done, we each cleaned up, came back and laid in bed. #12 laid on her side in the dark, stroking my chest, as I fell asleep.

I woke up first in the morning, quietly got up, showered and made coffee. #12 came into the kitchen and told me what a great time she had the night before … I agreed.

We both got dressed, tidied up and #12 drove me home. When I got out of the car, #12 said, "Thanks again … for a great time."

I smiled and replied, "The pleasure was all mine."

******

Back at school, I looked for the blonde from the junior prom and Tuesday I caught her coming out of the cafeteria.

"Would you really like to go out with me Saturday night?"

"Yes, Tony, I would!"

"Hopefully, we can go to the drive-in. I plan on getting my license tomorrow and I think I can borrow my dad's car."

"GREAT!" She was exuberant.

She told me where she lived and I told her that I would pick her up at 7:00pm … it was all set.

******

Saturday night was nice and warm. I got out of work, went home, showered and shaved, borrowed my dad's car and I went to pick up the blonde.

When she came to the door, she looked lovely. She was wearing white slacks, a tight red silky bouse, matching red shoes and lipstick. It was the perfect outfit given her long blonde hair and fair skin.

She was all bubbly about us going out. When we got into the car, she slid right over next to me. That was very nice but I needed to concentrate on driving. This was the first time that I was out driving on my own, and it was my father's car.

When we arrived at the drive-in, I parked in the back row, away from the other cars. The blonde and I talked about the junior prom and the party she went to at a hotel, with a group of other kids … it sucked! They were all drinking, her date drank too much, got in a fight, barfed on her gown and passed out. Everyone else acted like idiots. She really had a bad experience.

Once it got dark, the movie began and the blonde suggested that we move the front seat forward and relocate to the back seat where there would be more room. Once we moved to the back seat, the blonde kicked off her shoes and curled up against me in the back corner. We kissed for a while … she was very good … nice soft lips. After a while she sat up and started to unbutton her blouse. She said, "Take off your slacks," as she draped her blouse over the back of the front seat. I was reluctant … but once she had her blouse off, she unzipped and slid out of her slacks as well … she looked even more beautiful in her tiny bra and panties. I wasted no time; kicking off my sneakers, taking off my shirt and slacks.

Next, I slid down on the seat to lay on my back while she slid right on top of me and started to kiss me feverously. I put my hands on her butt cheeks and started to softly caress them … she squealed in enjoyment as she ground her pelvis into mine. I slid one hand up to the base of her neck and them, slid just one finger firmly down the middle of her back, very slowly, over the bra strap, down the base of her back, under her panty and down between her butt cheeks. As my finger traveled down her back, our tongues were busy going in and out of each other's mouths. Our mutual saliva was dripping down my cheeks from the corners of my mouth … I love sloppy kissing. When my finger reached her butt hole, she started to stiffen, at that moment, I suddenly sucked all of the air out of her lungs, while my finger continued south to her love hole. My other hand continued to rub and squeeze her butt cheeks.

Without her lips leaving mine, the blonde slid onto her side, leaning against the back of the seat, so that she could rub her hand over my semi-hard penis. Through the silky fabric of my boxers, I responded to her rubbing and soon had a full raging erection. The blonde was impressed and said, "WOW … you're big!"

"I promise … it's just the right size to please you," I responded.

She reached up under the leg of my boxers to grasp my erection and she started to stroke it … she was driving me wild!

While the blonde's hand was down there, I used my free hand to cup and fondle her breasts … we were both getting hot. Then, I pushed her bra up over her breasts and slid my body down the seat so that my lips lined up with her nipples, which I started to suck. She squealed with joy.

Then, I slipped my finger back into her panties, from the front. It traveled between the folds of her love lips. She moaned. My finger slithered up and down between her very well lubricated lips. I could feel her clitoris growing as my finger slipped back and forth along its side, gently pulling on the skin surrounding it. Her breathing was rapid. She unhooked her bra and pulled off her panties. In the dim light from the movie, she laid there in front of me. The only thing she had on was her nail polish.

I sat up, rolled on a condom and kneeled between her legs. I pushed into her vagina, which was very, very tight, but it had a welcoming feel to it … which turned me on! She gasped, then piped up with, "OH BOY! That feels soooo goooood!" So, I pushed in all the way. When I pulled out #13 pushed her hips toward mine and started to shout, "Give me that bad boy … slam it to me! NOW!" I quickened the pace and she orgasmed immediately. Her enthusiasm got to me and I orgasmed with her. It was over pretty quickly.

Then, feeling self-conscious about being in a car with no clothes on, we both sat up and dressed. We cuddled in the corner and #13 started talking about her friends … she was nasty. Not the kind of personality that I was drawn to.

Her discussion finally came around to me. #13 said that she just had to find out for herself if I was as good as the girls at school said … and I was! She said, "You are the expert … your lips, your tongue, your fingers, your penis are all trained to give a girl maximum pleasure."

WOW! What a compliment. I didn't know that I was that good!

#13 continued to say that sex with her present boyfriend was just fair. "Hold on … I thought you said you were available … do you have a boyfriend right now?" I asked.

"Yes, the guy I went to the junior prom with."

"That's not right. I don't date girls that have a steady boyfriend. I don't think that's right," I said to her.

"I am not going to tell him."

"Right, don't tell him or any of the other girls either," I instructed #13. "I don't want people thinking that I am moving in on other guys' girlfriends."

We moved back to the front seat and, with a 'chill' between us, I drove her home. I wasn't happy that she had duped me.

That will be the last time I would take her out.

Chapter 6
A Wild Summer

OH BOY! I bought a car right at the end of the school year. One of the seniors got a new car for graduation … he was the stud of the school. He came to me and asked if I was interested in purchasing his used car. He told me that the car was older, but in pretty good shape. It was dependable. Best of all, he informed me, the backs of the front seats reclined and became flush with the bottoms of the back seats. He referred to it as 'The Love Wagon'!

I was only too interested in checking it out. It was an older, red and white, four-door sedan, with red upholstery. All in pretty good condition. To the next guy it may have been a jalopy but to me it was a beautiful automobile.

The kid said that he had heard good things about me, and he wanted to pass it down to someone who would enjoy it. So, he gave me a good deal on it, and of course, I bought it.

What a grand day!

I spent the next weekend washing, waxing, and cleaning my new ride. I even bought some red throw pillows and a real soft, red and white 'Indian blanket' (which I kept in the trunk).

******

My job at the grocery store was great … I really enjoyed it and the boss seemed very happy with me. I made a suggestion that he implemented, and it worked out well.

Our procedure for bagging groceries was to place the items into a paper bag or bags and put them into a carrier for the customer, except if the groceries fit into a small bag, which we would hand to the customer.

My suggestion was for the person bagging the groceries to actually bring the groceries out to the customer's car and put the groceries into the car, for those times that there was a full bag or more.

Our customers, mostly the ladies but some of the men, loved it. They would say, "What a great service … no other grocery store gives this type of service." So, the owner was very happy with the idea.

******

One day a tall, thin, sexy, attractive girl from my school and her mom came into the store to shop. When they came through the checkout, I bagged their groceries. The girl seemed interested in me and struck up a conversation while I was bagging their groceries. She continued the conversation as I pushed the carrier of groceries to her mom's car. When I finished putting the bags in the car, I asked the girl if she would like to go to the drive-in with me on Saturday night. She said, with a huge smile, "I would love to."

On the way back to the store, I got to thinking that I had bagged a box of sanitary napkins and a box of tampons (this was very embarrassing at first, but now I was used to it). It was only Tuesday, so I hoped that she would be done with her period by Saturday.

******

Saturday night was very warm and when I picked up my date, she was wearing tight white shorts and a black blouse, which complemented her tan and her long, straight black hair. I, of course, was wearing a nice black T-shirt, black jeans and black sneakers … my trademark outfit.

She had a very nice personality, and we had a pleasant conversation on the ride to the drive-in. When we got there, I asked where she liked to park, and she said that she always parked in the back row … so be it.

Once situated, my date slid over against me. I put my arm around her shoulder, and we continued to talk during the comics and coming attractions. When the movie started, I informed my date that we might be more comfortable if we reclined the seat backs down. I said, "This is a new car to me and I haven't tried it yet."

She gamely replied, "Let's give it a try."

Once the seats were flat, we slid back to the back seat, and I put the pillows behind us for support.

"This is fantastic!" my date said as she turned and gave me a small kiss on the lips.

It was fantastic, like being in a king-sized bed. I replied, "You know what is fantastic … that kiss you gave me … only it wasn't long enough." She turned toward me, I put my arms around her and we kissed. It was very nice; she smelled great, looked great and kissed great.

Suddenly, she asked, "What is the blanket for?"

"In case we get cold," I replied. It sounded kind of stupid since the temperature was in the mid-eighties. She giggled … I think she figured out what the blanket could be used for.

We continued kissing on and off … each time getting a little more passionate. We slid down on the seats until we were prone, with our heads on the pillows. I was caressing her back with my hand, so I worked my hand down to caress her butt cheeks, she moaned, "Ummmmm." Based on this encouragement, I worked my hand back up her side. She reached down and pulled her blouse out of her shorts. I took that as a sign to reach under her blouse, which I did, caressing her soft skin. Just the feel of her bare skin turned me on. My hand finally made it up to her breast, which was amazingly large for such a thin girl. She rolled over onto her back; I think she was giving me better access. While our tongues were darting in and out of each other's mouths, I decided to try sucking the air from her lungs … which I did … she moaned, "Ummmmm … Ummmmm … Ummmm!" in a deep voice. Then she broke off the kiss and whispered, "I love that … you are really turning me on!"

"Is that OK?" I asked.

"It's great!" She replied. "Could you cover us up with the blanket?"

"You bet!"

Once we were covered up with the blanket, she unbuttoned and removed her blouse and black bra. Then, she pulled my face to hers to continue kissing. Only then it was extremely passionate. I fondled her breasts and tweaked her nipples, which made her hotter. I ducked my head under the blanket and sucked a nipple into my mouth. My free hand slid down her torso to the top of her shorts … but they were too tight to get my hand into, so I started caressing her love lips through the fabric of her shorts. Her breasts were supple; the nipples were very dark brown and stuck out like two small bullets. I alternated sucking on one and then the other.

She reached down and unzipped her shorts. I helped her push them down her silky, smooth legs. To my surprise and delight, she was not wearing any panties. … very sexy! I lost no time in getting my hand between her legs. I slipped my middle finger in between her moist love lips … she held her breath. I slid my finger up toward her clitoris, then, I sucked the air from her lungs, then, I exhaled it back into her lungs, then, I sucked it in again. She sort of growled, spread her legs wider and pushed her hips up toward my finger. Up and down, I stroked the side of her clit with my finger. I could feel her clitoris growing from my manipulations. She said, in a panting voice, "You … have got me all worked up … now I need to do the same for you." Then, she climbed on all fours, turned and went headfirst under the blanket. We both feverously, unbuckled and pushed off my jeans and boxers.

She grabbed my semi-erection and started to pump and suck on it … like she was in a hurry … and she was! Since her butt was facing me, I moistened my middle finger and slowly pushed it into love canal, she squirmed. I felt for her G-spot and softly started stroking it. In just a minute, she turned to me and said, "You are going to make me come."

I replied, "Fine." I smiled and continued to stroke her special spot.

She went back to working on my erection, but in thirty seconds or so, she stopped and sort of froze in position. Then, she pressed her thighs very tightly together, while the waves of pleasure coursed through her body as she orgasmed.

After her body relaxed, she continued to work on my shaft, which was as stiff as could be. Her technique was only fair but her enthusiasm was great. She began to sweat. I put two fingers into her love canal and started to swirl, then pump in and out. Stroking her G-spot and rubbing her clitoris with my thumb. She looked at me and said, "I can't stand it … we have to put it in! NOW!"

"OK!"

Quickly, I reached for my jeans, got a condom out and put it on. She had laid back down, flat on her back. I rolled over onto her, keeping the blanket covering us. I rubbed the head of my erection up and down between her love lips, she moaned, spread her legs and pushed her hips toward mine. I slipped right in (the missionary position) and slowly started to pump in and out. Each in, she moaned, "OH!" Each out, she moaned, "UWWWWW!"

As I pumped faster and harder, we both climaxed at about the same time. When we were both done, I lowered my head and gave her a soft kiss on the lips as I withdrew. #14 whispered, "That … was … phenomenal!" Then, with a great big smile she reached up, pulled my face to hers and gave me a very nice soft kiss. "Thank you!"

"Great … I enjoyed it too!"

We dressed under the blanket and sat up against the back seat. Just in time for the second movie; which was funny and entertaining. When the movie was over, I drove #14 home. We both seemed to have a good time, so, I asked #14 if she would like to go to the drive-in the following Saturday and she said, "I would love to!"

So, we went to the drive-in the next several Saturday nights and had a great time each night.

******

My father always took one week of vacation in the middle of the summer. My folks decided to rent a cottage on the beach. It was pretty big; four bedrooms, big kitchen, a living room and a big, screened porch with six comfy rocking chairs.

My boss gladly gave me the week off, saying, "You only live once, kid … enjoy!"

So, we moved in on a Saturday afternoon. Once we were all situated and I had unpacked, I slipped into a silky black T-shirt, black shorts and black sandals. After dinner, I went out to check out the area.

We were on the corner, two blocks from the ocean and one block over from the main street, where all the activity was … good location. There was an enormous arcade, and a variety of outdoor amusements, along with many different types of stores and restaurants.

There were tons of teens and adults out everywhere … the place was hopping! I spent a lot of time at the arcade. That is where I ran into a very pretty gal, which I felt stuck out of the crowd. She had a good tan, nicely shaped body, wearing a bright orange bikini top and white short pants. Her long blonde hair framed her face and her bright white teeth seemed to form a beacon of light when she smiled. I was drawn to her like metal to a magnet.

"This place is really hopping," I said to her.

She smiled at me and said, "We have got perfect weather for the beach."

"Are you staying here?" I asked.

"Yes, this is our third year in a row. We were supposed to head home today but the landlord allowed us to stay another day since the people that rented the cottage for next week aren't coming until late tomorrow afternoon." She asked, "How about you?"

"It's my first time coming to the beach, we just came in today, for the week."

She put her arms around my arm, cuddled up against my body, looked up into my eyes and asked, "Would you like me to show you around?"

"I'd love it!"

She led me up and down the streets, explaining where the best stores and restaurants were. Where the kids our age hung out and what we could do for entertainment. She was very nice and a lot of fun. Ultimately, she brought me for a walk on the moonlit beach. It was very romantic. She was a sexy gal, rubbing her boobs against me often during our tour … I didn't complain.

When we got to an area where there was nobody around us, I stopped, turned her toward me and kissed her. She just seemed to melt into my arms and responded by pulling me closer to her and kissing me back. The kissing progressed until it was quite passionate. She sort of broke off the kiss and panting said, "Follow me."

She took my hand and led me a short distance to a place on the beach that rented small boats, which they tipped upside down on the beach after hours. She led me to a boat in the middle where we could sit down on it and continue kissing. I wondered why my guide had led me there but I was enjoying myself and could care less. The kissing became incredibly passionate; she put her hand in my lap and stroked it over my manhood. Then, she asked, "Do you want to do it?"

"Of course," I replied. "But where?"

She smiled and showed me that there was a big beach towel on the sand between the boat we were sitting on and the next one (how convenient). So, we laid between the boats, out of view, on the towel and continued to kiss. I unhooked her top and fondled her breasts … they were very, very nice. She said, "Let's do it quickly … before anyone comes along."

So, we both disrobed as quickly and discretely as we could. Then, she laid flat on her back. In the moonlight her body looked perfect and very inviting. We began to kiss again. When my hand slipped down between her legs, her hand grabbed my shaft and she started to fondle and stroke it. Meanwhile, I pushed my middle finger down over her pubic hair free, very smooth, love lips. Then, into her love canal … she spread her legs and moaned … but it was dry down there and difficult to move my finger. So, I stopped kissing her, brought my finger to my mouth and deposited a huge glob of saliva on it, then, put it back between her love lips, as my mouth moved onto her nipples. Immediately we both could feel the difference when my finger re-entered her. Then, it slid freely up and down between her love lips and she whispered, "UWW … I like that!"

It didn't take long for her to be fully lubricated and she had me pumped up as well. I put a condom on, positioned myself between her legs (the missionary position) and she couldn't wait … she reached behind me with her hands, grabbed my butt and pulled me into her. I lowered my head and kissed her, while my hips pumped in and out. It could not have been more enjoyable … on the beach … with the sound of the waves … the warm breeze caressing my butt … in the moonlight. It doesn't get any better! After a while, before I got carried away, too far, I positioned the head of my erection to rub on her special spot, then, I started to pump rapidly. "OH YES!" She whispered, "Yes … yes … yes … yes … yes!" Again #15 reached out and grabbed my butt with her hands to pull me into her as she started to orgasm. She pulled her knees up and used her feet to pull me further into her. I could feel her vagina constricting and relaxing as she enjoyed a powerful orgasm. Her grabbing of my buttocks, the extra lubrication from her climax and her enthusiasm all combined to push me over the edge and I orgasmed as strongly as #15 had … and she seemed to welcome it as much as I did.

When we were done, we dressed and walked back to the main street holding hands. It was getting late, so I walked #15 to her cottage, gave her a kiss and a hug, and said goodbye.

******

The next morning, I met dad on the front porch, about 6:00am, as he was drinking a coffee. My dad and I were both early risers. I told him I found a little grocery store on the next block that probably sold newspapers. Also, I found a donut shop a block away. So, I ran out, the stores were just opening, got a newspaper and freshly made donuts and coffee. Dad and I really enjoyed the coffee and donuts as we read the paper in the cool morning breeze on the porch.

At 8:00am, I headed to the beach with my blanket and beach towel, to get a good spot. When I got to the beach, it was pretty deserted, so I easily found a good spot, put my blanket down, then I went to the stand that rented sand chairs and umbrellas. Dad had told me that the people that rented us the cottage also rents the umbrellas and they said the umbrellas and chairs would be free.

The stand was operated by their daughter, about 19 years old, with long brown hair piled on the top of her head. She was pretty, tall (5'10"), lanky, large-breasted, with an outstanding tan, wearing a small two-piece bathing suit … I'm interested.

"Hi, I'm Tony Tennaro … my folks rented one of your cottages just up the street," I informed the gal.

In a flirtatious way, she replied, "Really? So, what do you want from me?"

"I'd like to know when you are available?"

In a very sexy tone, she said, "I am always available, but I work until 5:00pm on Sunday. During the week, I work only until 1:00pm and then I am free the rest of the days."

"I like free … maybe we can get together tomorrow."

"I'd like that," she replied. "Would you like a beach umbrella?"

"Sure … but only if you show me how to stick it in."

She smiled widely and replied, "I would love to!" Then, she stood up, got an umbrella and a sand chair out for me.

"What do I owe you?" I asked.

"Nothing today … I will collect tomorrow." She was about as sexy as a girl could be.

"I can't wait," I said. "Hey, is there somewhere here that I can store my blanket and towel at night … so I don't have to lug them home and back each day?"

"Sure, you can put them in this box that I am sitting on … it doesn't lock but they should be safe here," she said as she stood up and lifted the seat on the wooden crate.

"Thanks … you're the best," I told her as I carried my umbrella and chair over to my spot.

Once I was set up, I laid on my blanket and watched the beach fill up with people … it was going to be another great beach day.

After a while I got hot from the sun beating down on me, so I went down to the water for a dip. The water was cool and refreshing. The waves were not too large … but they were large enough that I could body surf (which I love to do). I made several runs, then I sauntered up the beach to my blanket. On my way, I made eye contact with two hot gals sitting on a blanket near mine … I smiled … they smiled. I toweled off and laid on my back on my blanket with the towel rolled up, under my head like a pillow. I closed my eyes to contemplate how wonderful it felt to lay in the sun, on the sand, after getting out of the salt water … I love it!

When I opened my eyes, I was surprised to see one of the girls that I had made eye contact with, the taller one (about 5'6"), standing right next to my legs looking down at me. "Hi," I said.

"You know, you are going to get badly sunburned if you do not put some sunscreen on," she informed me.

Making the saddest face that I could, I replied, "But I don't have any."

"You're in luck, because I have a full tube right here." She kneeled down on the blanket and said, "I could put it on you."

"I'd love that!" I replied.

She smiled broadly and started to squirt the cream on my chest and smear it around. She told me that her folks had rented a cottage there, about eight blocks from the beach, for the week and she had brought her best girlfriend with her. I told her that my folks had rented a cottage as well. When she was done applying the cream to my chest, shoulders and arms, she had me turn over, to do my back. Suddenly, I sat up and asked, "Would you be my designated Sunscreen Applier this week?"

"Sure, I'd love to," she replied.

Then, I invited her friend to join us. She was about 5' tall but she had a smoking hot body and she always had a big bright smile. I told her I didn't want her to be lonely over there all by herself. She was only too glad to join us.

When I told her that I had made her friend my designated Sunscreen Applier for the week, she frowned. Feeling that she was hurt, I asked if she would like to be my 'left side applier' and her friend could be my 'right side applier'. She agreed and they both giggled about it.

For the next several hours, we talked, swam and joked around together. When her friend went back to her blanket to get something, the tall one asked me if I would like to go with her to see her cottage and, of course, I agreed.

Evidently, her mother had just come down to the beach and since it was a long walk, her mother wouldn't go back to the cottage until the end of the day … great!

We told the girlfriend that we were going for a walk, and we took off straight for the cottage. On the way we held hands and talked about our towns.

As soon as we got inside the cottage door, the girl turned, put her arms around my neck and pulled my face to hers for a sensuous kiss. It was like she hadn't been kissed in months. I put my hands at the base of her back. Her naked skin was soft and smooth. As we kissed, I moved one hand upward and the other hand downward … I swirled my hands and caressed her skin. When my hand reached her butt, I cupped the luscious cheek and softly squeezed. I worked the other hand down and squeezed her other cheek as well. When I pulled her hips toward mine, she gyrated her hips in a circle as she pressed against my loins … we were both getting turned on.

She separated from me and led me to her bedroom, which was very tidy. We sat on the bed, and she started to kiss me again. Then, she suddenly reached up under the leg of my swimsuit and cradled my penis in her hand. Instantly, it started to grow, while we kissed, she would occasionally close her hand around it and squeeze softly, then release her grip … it really turned me on. I untied her top and slid my hand under to caress her breast. Her nipple was as stiff as could be. I laid down and pulled her with me. When I slid my hand down toward her crotch, she pulled her hand out of my bathing suit reached down and removed her bottoms. I put my finger in my mouth and wet it, then, it slipped between her love lips which were already somewhat moist … good. I didn't have much chance to stroke her clitoris before she asked me to stand up. When I did, she grabbed the top of my bathing suit and I helped her push it down.

She sat on the edge of the bed as she pulled my erection toward her and lowered her mouth down onto it. She sucked and stroked, and it felt fantastic! As much as I hated to, I had to push her away, so, I could reach down and put on a condom, from my bathing suit pocket.

As I slipped it on, she positioned herself on the edge of the bed and pulled her knees to her chest … she couldn't wait.

As I approached to enter her, I put a big glob of saliva on my fingertips and applied it between her love lips. I could feel through the condom that she was not fully lubricated. So, I pushed in, in short thrusts. Then, I pulled out (the side of the bed position). That achieved the desired effect and she started to self-lubricate nicely. That made it more pleasurable for both of us. I put both hands on the bed and with straight arms I supported myself while I pumped my mid-section in and out. Only our genitals were touching, and it felt great! Next, I grabbed #16 by her ankles and spread her legs apart … it felt like I was penetrating much deeper. I let go of her legs and I bent forward to kiss her, while continuing to pump in and out. #16 sucked my tongue deeply into her mouth and kissed me wildly. Then, as I plunged in deeply in, I sucked the air from #16's lungs into mine … I completely stopped … as I withdrew, I exhaled the air back into her lungs … another pause … then I trust forward and sucked the air in again … then out, then in, then out, then in … what a fantastic sexual feeling … it was like we were completely 'into' each other, with the air going back and forth. I quickened the pumping, but continued breathing at the slower pace, I could feel #16 starting to orgasm. I took my mouth off hers and she started to scream uncontrollably, "Harder … Harder … Harder!" … I started to pump harder, I pumped as hard as I could into her spasm filled love canal. Then, I started to orgasm as well, while #16's body contorted in pleasure.

When we were done, we were both panting and covered in perspiration … we deserved it. I laid on the bed and #16 laid on top of me. While we kissed, #16 slid her body around on top of me, in the perspiration … I love to do that.

I had to stop at the drugstore on the way back to the beach, so I could buy a package of condoms, since I used my last one on #16. It was a simple transaction … I walked right up to the counter, told the older man that I wanted a three-pack of condoms, and I walked out with my purchase … no embarrassment. I must be getting used to it after so many previous purchases. When I reached the arcade, I went into the restroom, took the condoms out of the box and put them in my bathing suit pocket. Be prepared ... you never know what you're going to come across.

******

By the time we got back to the beach, there were two guys sitting on my blanket chatting with #16's girlfriend. All three stood up as we approached, I was a lot bigger than either of the two fellas. I said, "Relax, have a seat." Everyone sat down and we talked ... we got along well. In a short time, the guys retrieved their blanket and put it right next to mine and the girls moved their blanket next to the other side of my blanket ... we were like a big party getting started. I said, "The only thing that you guys need to know is that these two girls are MY sunscreen appliers, you'll have to find your own." They laughed and agreed.

We joked around, went in the water and we hung out in the sun until mid-afternoon, when I decided to go for a walk (alone). About a half-mile down the beach, I came across a group of gals, standing in waist-deep water, hitting a beach ball to each other. As I approached, one girl missed hitting the ball and it fell in the water and the waves washed it ashore. As I approached the ball, they yelled, "How about a little help?" I picked up the ball, took a few steps toward them and hit the ball back to the gals. They yelled, "Do you want to play?"

They were all somewhat attractive and they appeared to be having a great time, so I replied, "I would be delighted." They all laughed and giggled. I strolled out through the water and got between two girls that I noticed later were twins. They were cute and they were petite (less than 5' tall but they had nicely proportioned bodies). I had a great time playing 'keep the ball up' with the girls. When we were done, I dove into the water to get cooled off, while the girls all headed back to the beach. I was right behind them as I made my way back to the beach and the view was terrific. I followed the girls back to their blanket, to find out where they were from. They were with a group of sorority girls that rented a big cottage for the week (some of the other girls were off doing something else).

One of the twins seemed more interested in me than the others. She came over with her towel and dried me off. I think she was just looking for a cheap feel.

She did not seem to like it when the others took my attention away from her, so she asked me to take a walk with her. She led me to their cottage and as soon as we got inside, she led me to a step stool that she stood on so that she could put her arms around my neck and kiss me. It seemed like Deja vu, since I had just gone through this with #16. So, I went directly for her goodies. I cupped the cheeks of her butt and started to caress and squeeze … she loved it … she had a cute little squeal that showed her enjoyment … I found that sexy.

After a while, I asked her to show me her room. When we went inside, I closed and locked the door. We sat on the edge of the bed kissing … she wasn't as aggressive as #16, so I took the lead. I fondled her breasts through the fabric of her bathing suit … she moaned in acceptance, so I moaned as well and took off her top. She had lovely round, not large, but very nice breasts. I had her lay on her back, while I played with her breasts and told her how lovely they were … she liked that. Then, I started to lick and suck one nipple while I caressed the other. She completely stopped breathing as I slid my hand down between her legs. I moved my fingers up and down over her love lips. She started to relax and I moved my thumb up and hooked it on the top of her bathing suit bottom. Then, I made a sound like, "Hum … Hum."

She got the hint and she slipped off her bikini bottom. She laid back down and started to kiss me again. I put my hand on her black hairy triangle, which was cut very short like a three-day growth of beard … she lifted one knee and put that foot on the bed. When she turned her knee out, her love box opened right up for me … how thoughtful. She was obviously worked up because when my fingers got to their destination, she was very wet. Very slowly, I slid my finger up to her clitoris, then down to her love canal. After my finger made several return trips her hips began to grind slowly. I could tell that she wanted me to put my finger into her love canal … so, I did … I slid it in slowly, little by little until it was all the way in … then, slowly out until I found her G-spot. There I stopped … then stroked … then swirled … then I just put my fingertip gently on it … she did the work by gyrating her hips so that my fingertip would stroke her special spot. I kept my fingertip there until she said, "You have just got to put it in me … NOW!"

"Don't rush … you're enjoying what I am doing … go with it," was my response … so, she laid back and in seconds she began to orgasm … her body curled up, she squeezed her thighs together, almost crushing my hand but I kept rubbing that spot and she seemed to really enjoy it.

When she was done, she looked at me with a very serious face and panting said, "That … was powerful … no boy has ever done that to me … thank you!"

I just smiled back at her, then, I slid off the bed onto my knees. I took off my bathing suit and removed a condom, but I wasn't ready yet. So, I spread her legs and positioned my head between them to get her worked up with my tongue (cunnilingus). I separated her love lips with my thumbs and stuck my tongue between them. She was very wet, from her previous orgasm. I had to keep my tongue in the middle since her short pubic hair was prickly on my tongue. I just manipulated my tongue up and around her clitoris then back down to her love canal. I sucked her clit into my mouth, and she squealed with delight. So, I continued to suck it in and then swirl my tongue around it. Simultaneously, I slipped my finger in and stimulated her G-spot. In a very short time, I brought her to the edge of her next orgasm, and she begged me, "PLEASE … PLEASE … PLEASE PUT IT IN!"

Now I had an enormous erection, so I put on a condom (good thing that I stopped at the store earlier), stood up and held her legs apart as I gently entered her (the edge of bed position). Fortunately, she was very well lubricated because she was very tight, so I went in slowly at first. #17's short pubic hairs were stabbing my shaft … it was like sex in a prickly patch, but somehow it also felt good … it turned me on. As I continued to pump, I looked down at her body and her nipples were calling for my mouth. I slid #17 further onto the bed, so I had room to kneel (the missionary position), then I bent over to suck one of her beautiful nipples into my mouth. It made #17 orgasm. As I pushed in and out, #17 clenched the sheets tightly with her hands, arched her body, wrapped her legs around my waist and squealed, over and over, as she orgasmed. #17 didn't have to wait long before the tightness of her vagina and the enthusiasm of her orgasm pushed me over the edge. I orgasmed in long, strong wads … Fantastic!

We didn't lay there long before #17 said we better get back to the beach. On the way back, I told her I'd see her later and I headed back to my blanket.

******

When I got back to the beach our gang had grown by two. A fairly muscular guy and a thin blond … both seemed to be nice people.

We spent the remainder of the afternoon joking around on the beach and in the water. At 5:00pm everyone started to leave the beach. So, we decided to pack it up as well. I took the umbrella and the sand chair back to the stand. The girl there said, "Looks like you have made some friends?"

I looked into her eyes and replied, "None as good as you … or as nice as you."

She smiled at me and asked, "Will I see you tomorrow?"

"You bet!" I snapped back. "I will see you at 8:00am … to get my umbrella … and I am really looking forward to seeing you tomorrow afternoon … remember our date?"

She put her hand on my cheek, winked, and replied, "I can't wait!"

As she stowed my umbrella and chair, I opened the box she sat on and as I stuffed my blanket and towel into the box I asked, "OK if I put these in here?"

"No problem."

Then, I headed back to my cottage to shower, shave and get ready to go out for the night.

It is amazing just how good a shower feels after a day in the sun and the salt water … WOW!

******

After dinner I went back to the beach and took my big beach towel out of the umbrella girl's box and I laid it between two of the boats that were tipped over, in the middle of the formation. Just in case.

Then, I hung out at the arcade. One of the sorority sisters came in, found me in the crowd and came directly to me. She looked great, long, clean, red hair, just a little overweight but still she had a very nice figure. She wore a navy-blue halter top with a matching short, tight skirt and most importantly, a great big smile. She looked great!

When she got close, I said, "You look beautiful!" She blushed bright red and that wasn't easy since her extremely light skin was already a bit sun burned from exposure to the sun all day.

"Thank you." She replied, "I wanted to look good for you."

"I'm impressed." She put her arms around my waist, I bent over and gave her a kiss on the forehead … she giggled.

We hung out for a while; I introduced her to several of the friends I had made on the beach. She held my hand the entire time.

I asked, "Would you like to go for a walk outside?"

"I'd love to," she replied.

So, we walked down the street toward the beach holding hands. When we got to the beach, I put my arm around her shoulders … she leaned into me. We walked down the deserted beach to the waters' edge. I turned and kissed her. Then, she kissed me … it was very good and extremely romantic. The moon shinned brightly on the water and the sound of the water crashing on the beach was all you could hear.

We walked along the beach, just above where the water reached. We stopped often to kiss again. My little red head seemed to want to go even farther. So, we made our way over to where the small boats were tipped over and I told her, "This is one of my favorite spots on the beach."

I walked her over to the boat in the middle, we sat on the boat, and I started to kiss her more aggressively … she responded in kind. While our tongues were darting from mouth to mouth, I put my hand on her breast, she went, "NNT … NNT!" And pushed my hand away.

I asked, "What's the problem?"

She replied, "I would like more privacy."

I instructed her to follow me, as I walked to the other side of the boat, and I laid down on the beach towel that I had put down for such an occasion. "Please join me," I requested.

With a big smile, she kneeled, then lay back on the towel next to me. "How did you know about this spot?" She asked.

"This is my spot. I put this towel here earlier," I said proudly.

"How convenient," she said as she went back to kissing me.

Then, when I put my hand on her breast, she did not resist. I fondled her delightful breasts for a while but when I tried to take her halter off, she went, "NNT … NNT … I don't want to take anything off while I am on the beach."

"Would you like me to stop?" I asked.

"No, I'd like to go all the way … but I am not going to take off my clothes, on the beach," she informed me. Then, she pushed her halter up over her breasts and pulled my head down to her chest. I sucked her soft nipple into my mouth, while I caressed the other nipple with my fingers. She pulled the bottom of her skirt up to her waist, and she pulled the crotch of her panties to one side, exposing her bare love lips with a very small patch of red pubic hair above. I put my middle finger in my mouth to wet it, then I started to slide my fingertip between her love lips. Almost immediately she started to moan, "Yes … Oh Yes!" Soon I could feel her self-lubricating … she was getting very hot very quickly. She said, "I better get you ready," and she turned around so that her head was between my legs, then, she tried to unbuckle my short pants … I just reached down and pushed them off. She then reached over and pulled my erection into her mouth. For a shy girl she seemed to have good technique. She pulled the skin back and circled the head, teasingly with her tongue. Then she started to suck on it, while pumping her head up and down … it drove me crazy!

Of course, I was positioned perfectly between her legs, which were spread in front of me, so I continued to stroke her clit, as she got me hotter and hotter, I pushed my finger into her and softly stroked her special spot. She stopped sucking and panting said, "You have got to put it in … now!"

As I turned around, I put on a condom; she laid on her back, spread her legs and pulled her panties out of the way. As I entered her, I could feel her body tense up, I slowly pushed in and said, "Are you ok?"

She was wincing and, in a murmur, she said, "I'm coming!"

I have never seen anyone orgasm that quickly but #18 just did … and she enjoyed every last second of it … great!

I continued to pump in and out and when her climax was over, I bent forward to kiss her. She grabbed my face and kissed me wildly. I pulled out until the head of my erection was at her special spot and then I started to rapidly pump short strokes to stimulate her. It worked, in a minute #18 was in the midst of her second orgasm. Then, I made long, deep strokes and just as my orgasm started to well up, #18 orgasmed again … it felt great! We stopped kissing and #18 was out of breath as she said, "WOW! That was as good as it gets … Thank you!"

As she tidied up her clothes and I put my short pants back on, I said, "Yeah … it was really good."

I walked her hand in hand back to her cottage and kissed #18 good night. Then, I went back to the beach to retrieve my towel and put it back in the box for the next day.

While I walked back to my cottage, I got to thinking what a special day today had been. I had had sex with three terrific girls in one day … it must be a record … at least it was for me and it was only my first full day at the beach.

******

At 6:00am I was off to get the paper and coffee for dad and I. I really enjoyed sitting with my dad on the porch, with the soft breeze blowing through, rocking, reading the paper and drinking my coffee. It was a great start to any day.

At 8:00am I was at the beach to get my blanket, towel, umbrella and sand chair. The gal that rents the umbrella looked even hotter than she did yesterday. She was wearing a florescent green bikini with her long hair in braids and bows to match her swimsuit. "You are not going to forget about our date this afternoon?" She asked me.

"That's all I can think about," I snapped back.

She smiled, she liked to joke around. "Stop over at my cottage between 1:30 and 2:00 … cut through from the street behind our place, so my mother doesn't see you coming down the street."

"Sounds good," I replied, then I took everything and set up my place on the beach.

When I was done setting up, I sat in the sand chair and watched the activity on the beach. The vendors were opening up their shops; families were coming onto the beach and setting up for the day. It was very interesting.

Then, WOW! A girl with the hottest body I have ever seen was walking down the beach by the water. She had; very clean, brown hair, a great tan, about 5'6" tall, wearing a brown bikini, that matched her hair. Her body was exquisite; perfectly proportioned legs, flat tummy, small waist, great butt and gorgeous skin. Her most outstanding attribute … she had stunning breasts … which were accentuated by the way she walked; shoulders back and breasts pushed out in front of her. She oozed sex from every pore in her body.

I jumped up and walked down toward the water to intercept her. "Going for a long walk?" I asked her.

She stopped, looked me up and down, smiled then said, "I walk about three miles every morning."

"Would you like company?" I asked … hoping she would say yes.

"I would be delighted to have you join me," she replied. She was very flirtatious … I like that.

So, we walked for the next forty-five minutes. As we walked and talked, she confided that she lived in a town about an hour north of my town. She was a sophomore in high school, and of course, she was a cheerleader.

She told me that she came to the beach for two weeks, every summer, with her mom, little sister (7), little brother (6), and her aunt. Her dad brings them down, drops them off and picks them up, but never stays because he is allergic to the beach! Evidently, the mixture of salt water in the air and the sun makes her dad's lips break out in huge, oozing, painful sores. Something she saw first-hand several years ago when he tried to visit the beach for just one hour.

On the other hand, her mom and aunt love the beach, so dad stays home and works and they take another vacation, inland together, as a family, later in the summer.

Everywhere we walked people turned to watch and it wasn't to look at me … it was like walking with a goddess.

Her cottage was several blocks over from ours and ten blocks from the beach. She went on to say that she used that to her advantage. It was such a huge project for her mom and aunt to lug all their stuff, plus the little kids, to the beach that once they got there, they stayed on the beach, for the day. Leaving the cottage free for her to entertain her friends.

"When does your mom head down to the beach?" I asked, with an ulterior motive. The sooner the mom gets to the beach, the sooner I can get this beauty alone in her cottage.

"They'll be starting to come down shortly," she told me.

"Let's take a walk to your cottage … maybe I can help," I suggested. So, we started off to her cottage.

She had a very nice cottage with a great screened-in porch. It was set up like a living room (sofa, chairs and a daybed that they used as a sofa).

The mom seemed very nice; she was an older version of my goddess. Mid-thirties, tall, nice figure, big boobs, wearing a one-piece bathing suit. The aunt was twenty-nine, divorced, one kid (6), short, petite and she had the body of a teenager. She looked like she really worked out to keep herself so fit. She wore a nice, two-piece bathing suit. She had short, curly hair and a bubbly, friendly personality. The three kids were cute, running all around, excited to be going to the beach.

I piled the blanket, towels, umbrella and sand chairs on top of the cooler, which I lugged to the beach. The mother and aunt followed; herding the kids and carrying canvas bags of personal items, sunscreen, etc.

When we reached the beach, I put down the blanket, set up the umbrella and sand chairs. I still had to go back to the cottage to retrieve two large canvas bags of beach toys and floats.

The mother and aunt were so thankful, since it was a major project for them each day to bring everything down to the beach. Just watching the kids was a job in itself. I couldn't believe how thankful they were. Saying that I was the only boy that the daughter brought home that ever helped them … they were very nice.

Once they were situated, the daughter and I said that we were going for a walk on the beach, but all we did was to walk down the beach to the next street, which we took back to her cottage. Once we reached her cottage, we sat on the daybed, because it was against the front wall of the porch and we could see down the street … to see if her mom or aunt were coming.

We kissed … my goddess had great lips and was a great kisser (she made her lips soft to kiss, her tongue was not aggressive, yet it invited me into her mouth and it was playful … much like her personality). We laid back at first, but then we laid down … the kissing became more intense. She would sit up every now and then, to look down the street … at first it broke the mood, but I got used to it.

With one hand she caressed my face, neck and chest … but her knee was masterful with its manipulation on my groin. I just rubbed the back of her neck with one hand while the other circled around on her back … but what she was doing to me was driving me crazy … additionally, she had the ability to moan and squeal very gently … it turned me on … she was very good.

I couldn't wait any longer to feel one of her magnificent breasts, so I worked my hand across her soft, soft skin, under her arm and up to her breast … immediately … she went, "NO! NO!" and she removed my hand. Then, she went right back to what she was doing to me. It was hard to believe because her lips, her hands, her body, her entire being was sending me the message that she wanted to go farther, but when I touched her breast, she stopped me … maybe she just wasn't ready yet.

As time progressed, she was getting really hot (and so was I). She was rubbing her body all over mine, I had a raging erection, we were both sweating and panting. So, I made my next attempt to fondle her breast … again a stern, "NNT! NO!" and she removed my hand.

I was confused, so I asked, "Why don't you like that?"

Her reply was amazing, she said, "I don't want my breasts to become floppy … and my mom says that the hormones in a man's hands and the manipulation help deteriorate the muscles that keep them firm … she hasn't let men fondle her breasts and look how nice her breasts still are."

I didn't believe it, but she sure did. We went back to the heavy petting again. As we kissed, I realized that when she removed my hand, she didn't just move it … she put it in her lap both times … maybe she would like me to go to second base. So, with that thought, I worked my hand down to her marvelous butt and fondled her cheeks … she seemed to like that and she didn't object … good. As my hand caressed its way over her hip toward her loins, she rocked back to provide room for me to access the area between her legs. My fingers started to caress her love lips (through the fabric of her bikini), she started to gyrate her hips. It was a very good sign … it gave me the feeling that she wanted more … I know I did.

As I pushed the fabric to one side, she said, "Let me help you," and she removed her bikini bottom, probably so it wouldn't get stretched out. My finger slid right into her perfectly shaved cave … as I slid my finger up to her clitoris she moaned loudly. She sat up, looked down the street, then she laid back down and reached for my erection, which she stroked like a pro through my bathing suit. As she stroked, she moaned, "UMMMMM." In a few minutes she informed me, "I can't wait any longer … put it in!"

I had been thinking the very same thing. I sat up; took my last condom from my bathing suit pocket, slipped out of the bathing suit, rolled on the condom and as she watched she told me, "You have a great body!"

Minga! I was thinking the same thing about her body. Next, she positioned herself; spread eagled, flat on her back with her tummy sucked in. As I looked down on her I thought again what a spectacular body she had (even though she still had her top on … and I couldn't touch her breasts). I slid right into the most inviting love canal ever (the missionary position) … it felt soooo good … #19 gyrated her hips and moved sensuously under me. I bent over and started to kiss her again … she was rubbing her hands on my chest and my butt … #19 was driving me crazy. I started pumping faster and faster … her hips matched me thrust for thrust. I decided to try sucking the air from her lungs into mine … OH WOW! Did that feel good … #19 moaned in enjoyment. I exhaled the air back into her lungs, then sucked it back into mine, a number of times … each time #19 moaned with enjoyment. We both orgasmed simultaneously, while I was manipulating the air between us … it was the most glorious orgasm of my life … it was FANTASTIC!

I lifted my lips off #19's and she immediately said, "That was fantastic … it felt as if we came as one … I loved it … you were fantastic!"

"No," I said, "you were fantastic!"

"NO, you!" She shot back.

"It was both of us … it takes two to tango."

#19 sat up, looked down the street and said, "We better get back down to the beach quickly … before they miss us."

We got up, dressed and #19 and I walked back down to the beach, hand in hand. When we got back to where her mom was on the beach, I realized it was 1:15pm already. I had to rush off to my date with the umbrella girl.

I had to come up with some sort of excuse, so I said, "Oh wow … look at the time … I have got to run … I promised my dad I would help him fix the chairs on the porch after lunch."

I told them that I would be back later in the afternoon and that I would bring all of their stuff from the beach back to their cottage … they liked that … then, I said, "Goodbye."

******

As I rushed down the beach, I thought it best to take a dip in the ocean, to wash off any perspiration, love juice or perfume from #19. I would never want the next girl to smell the last girls on me.

My body and suit dried quickly in the heat of the day during my short walk to the umbrella girl's house. On my way I had to stop and buy several more packs of condoms … I put two in my bathing suit pocket and stuffed the bag with the remainder under a bush in the umbrella girl's backyard.

I approached from the back, as she asked, but I surprised her when I walked up onto her back porch and caught her lying on a chaise lounge, soaking in the sun. She was wearing a white bikini, with loads of sunscreen (which I found out later was baby oil). She looked great and was pleased to see me.

"I thought you had forgotten about me," she teased.

"I could never forget about you."

"It's hot, would you like a beer?" she offered.

"Sure."

She pulled two bottles from a cooler next to her chair and gave me one. We drank from the bottles. The ice-cold beer really hit the spot; sitting in the hot sun and with the taste of the salt water still in my mouth. "You are the best hostess," I said as I leaned over and gave her a small kiss on the lips.

"That's no way to kiss a girl," she said teasingly.

"Really, then you better show me how," I challenged.

I was sitting sideways on the next chaise lounge. She stood up, came over, put one leg on each side of me and sat on my lap facing me. Then, she put both arms around my neck, pulled my face to hers and savagely kissed me. Open mouth, full tongue and all!

"That's a good kiss … for a beginner," I said with a smile. "Let me show you how a professional kisses." With that said, I slipped one hand up the middle of her back, up to her neck and into her hair. I pulled her lips to mine and started softly kissing her lips (while making my lips as soft as possible, by making them like fish lips), I increased the pressure by pulling her head toward me, with my other hand. I entered her mouth with my tongue and as I slid my tongue out, I inhaled the air from her lungs into mine and I held it for a moment. Then I stopped the kiss.

As she breathed deeply in for air, she whispered, "We better go into my room." Then, she got up and led me to her bedroom, which was very colorful and bright even though the shades were drawn.

I watched as she bent over to pull back the covers on the bed. She was tall, with a lanky body, but she had very nice breasts and a fine butt. She was a little older than most of the girls that I have been with, at 19, but that just gave her a little more maturity and probably more experience.

I approached her from the back and slid my arms around her, crossed them in front of her and brought my hands up to her breasts. She didn't flinch. She pushed her rump back into my groin and rotated her hips, then, she moaned, "Ummmmmmm!"

Gently, I alternated squeezing her breasts … she reached back, undid her top and removed it … without stopping the rotating of her hips. I continued to cup, lift and caress her breasts as I slipped her nipples between my fingers. Her nipples stiffened and a chill came over her body … she got goose bumps.

"Oh," I whispered in her ear, "you've got goose bumps … I'll have to fix them." As I said that, I slid one hand across her oily abdomen, circled her belly button several times and then my hand went right under the top of her bikini bottom. Then, directly between her love lips. Simultaneously, with my hand's descent, she held her breath.

As my finger stroked up and down, the umbrella girl mumbled, "You know what I like … I love it when a guy is gentle but direct."

"Just trying to please you … my dear."

"Oh … I'll bet you really know how to please a girl," she said; as she took off her bikini bottoms, turned around, laid on the edge of the bed, and pulled her knees up to her chest, while she spread her legs apart.

I took this as a gesture that she would like me to perform cunnilingus on her. I was pleased to have the opportunity. So, I kneeled down on the floor, spread her love lips apart with my thumbs and ran my wet tongue up from her love canal to her clitoris … she squealed … my tongue circled her clit several times then went back down and I tried to push it into her love hole as far as it would go … I licked around and around her love hole (because that is where there are tons of sexual receptors) … then, slowly back up and around her clit (which I found was much larger than during my last rotation). I sucked her clit into my mouth (forming my lips like those of a fish), and then I flicked my tongue over her clit. It drove her crazy, she started breathing faster and faster, she moaned, "You are good … very good!"

I brought my finger up and pushed it into her love canal and started to rub her G-spot. "I can't take much more of that … or I am going to explode!" She said while panting.

I pulled my head back for a second and said, "So, explode!"

I went back to what I was doing, with even more vigor and soon her legs started to come together, her breathing stopped, she pulled her knees tighter against the sides of my head, I sped up my tongue and my finger (I was licking like a hungry dog). Her body started to bounce on the bed as the waves of her orgasm washed through and over her body and the entire time, she squealed a soft, "Ooooooooooooooooooooooooooo!"

When she was done, she let her legs go, sat up on the edge of the bed, grabbed my head with both, hot, sweaty hands and still panting heavily, said, "You are not good … you are fantastic … sweetie." Then, she pulled my face to hers and savagely kissed me, sucking my tongue into her mouth she gave me a big, wet kiss … she was not concerned about the fact that my mouth, lips and face were covered with her love juice … it was a wonderful kiss.

"Stand up," she instructed me. She pulled my swimsuit down to the floor, and then she reached for my semi-erection and she started to pump and suck on it. I became rock hard in an instant. Once I was fully erect, she continued to suck and lick, while one hand softly caressed my scrotum and the other caressed my butt cheeks. Her hands turned me on … what she was doing was driving me crazy, it felt soooooo good!

I hated to stop her from what she was doing but I just had to say, "I'm ready … we better put it in."

As I rolled on my condom, she took a huge bottle of baby oil from the night stand and she squirted it all over her love lips and into her love canal, then she spread the oil around with her finger, she was covered in oil. She slid completely back onto the bed, still holding the baby oil bottle and as I approached, she said, "I have got some for you too."

I kneeled between her legs. She poured copious amounts of oil all over my shaft, my scrotum and stomach. Then, she put one leg between my legs and rolled onto her side. She lifted her leg and put her ankle on my shoulder. I entered her (the split leg position) … of course, with all of the lubricant I slid in with no problem … and it felt very good … very sexy. It felt like I penetrated #20 deeper in that position … it turned me on.

I started to pump. After I would complete my stroke in, #20 would rock her hips forward, sliding her vagina further onto my shaft … wow that felt … great! I started to pump harder and faster, #20 responded in kind. I put my arms around the leg she had on my shoulder and as I pulled tighter, I pumped even faster. I could feel that #20 was going to orgasm soon and so was I. As I thrust forward and back, I realized the sensation of my scrotum and testicles sliding back and forth on her cleanly shaven, silky-smooth inner thigh was driving me to heights that I have never reached before … it was a sensation that drove me wild … #20 rocked her hips forward and back violently as she started to orgasm and I matched every stroke with one of my own. I couldn't hold back. I started to orgasm halfway through #20's orgasm … mine was as strong as hers and lasted longer than ever. I was not sure if it was the oil or the girl or the position, but it was a magnificent orgasm.

When we were done, we were both covered in perspiration and oil … pretty messy … #20 put her leg down and I laid on top of her, kissing her as our bodies were sliding around without any friction due to the lubrication.

"Let's jump in the shower," #20 suggested.

#20 led me to the bathroom, turned on the water and we both got into the shower together … how interesting. I took her lead. She moved the shower head to wet down the front of my body, then, very sensuously she applied the soap … devoting plenty of time to my genital area … standing beneath the shower head she was getting all wet, so I grabbed the soap and started to lather up her back and neck, then, her large breasts … it really aroused me … #20 was delighted to see me getting hard again … as she continued to stroke my erection with a soapy hand, I applied more and more soap to #20's crotch … even applying some between her love lips … she was squealing again … #20 stepped forward and with one hand pulled my head down so she could kiss me and with her other hand she positioned my engorged erection between her legs and given its' soapiness, it slid right up and into her … wow … it never felt so good … then I realized … it was the first time I have been inside a girl without a condom on … and it felt soooo good … we both had our arms around each other, and we were pushing our respective pelvic areas forward and back, while non-stop kissing … the warm water was cascading over us … I didn't think that it could feel any better.

Fortunately, I had just climaxed earlier, so I wasn't going to orgasm again in a hurry. When, I thought it just couldn't get any better, it did. #20 pulled away, turned around, soaped up her butt and started to slide my erection up and down in her butt crack … OH WOW! Then, she reached between her legs and guided my enormous erection back into her love canal … #20 bent over halfway and pushed back, as I grabbed her hips and pumped as hard as I could, "I love it like this!" she shouted (the doggy position).

Without missing a stroke, I grabbed the soap, rubbed it in #20's butt crack and pushed my soapy finger into her butt hole (it went in without any resistance). "YES! YES! YES! YES! YES! YES!" She repeated while she came to another powerful orgasm, as both my finger and penis were sliding effortlessly in and out of her.

When #20's orgasm was complete, she turned with a worried look in her eye and asked, "You didn't come inside me … did you?"

"No, but I am close."

"Good," #20 murmured, as she knelt on the floor of the tub and slid her soft, moist lips over and around the swollen head of my erection. As she licked and sucked, she soaped up my scrotum and butt. Then, after softly stroking my scrotum and testicles, #20 slid one fingertip down the little seam from my scrotum to my butt hole. When #20 got there, she paused a moment … then she slipped the finger back … it created an intense feeling (stoking my perineum), which I hadn't experienced before … it was great! #20 kept applying more and more soap and after the third or fourth time that her finger caressed my butt hole … without hesitation she pushed her finger right up into my rectum … WAHOOOOOO!

I almost jumped six feet into the air … no one had ever touched me there and nothing had ever penetrated my anus before … but it felt great and while #20 sucked my erection into her mouth as far as it would go, she found and massaged my prostate with her soapy fingertip … it brought me to a climax immediately … my groin (and my butt hole) convulsed in one powerful spasm after another … and #20 sucked out every drop!

When #20 was done, she spit a mouthful of my love juice into the drain and stood, allowing the shower water to fill her mouth (which she spat out into the drain several times). Then, she turned back toward me and asked, "Well, what do you think?"

"That … was … MAGNIFICENT!"

#20 laughed and said, "I meant, are you still interested in kissing me, after what I just had in my mouth?"

"Hell yes!" I replied as I pulled her to me and gave her a long, aggressive, French kiss.

She shut off the shower; we toweled off, got dressed and went back out onto the back deck. We each drank an ice-cold beer, which really hit the spot … then, I was on my way back to the beach.

******

As I left, I retrieved the bag of condoms from the bush that I had stowed it under. Then, I headed back down to see my friends at the beach.

There wasn't anyone at the blanket when I got there. They were all together in the water. I put my condoms into my backpack, ran down and dove into the water (so that my friends would not notice that I had just showered).

"Hey Tony!" They screamed as I emerged from the cool water. "Where have you been all day?"

"Oh, I was busy helping a friend's mother to bring all her stuff down to the beach and then I had to help my dad with a project," was my reply, which satisfied their curiosity.

I went back to the blanket and laid in the sun for a while. Then, I explained that I had to run to help my friend's mom bring her stuff back to her cottage.

******

When I got back to #19's, her mom and aunt were just starting to gather all of their stuff for the return trip to the cottage.

I said, "I am glad that I got here in time to help you." I could see by the looks on their faces that they were very happy to see me.

After lugging everything back to her cottage, I asked #19 if she would like to go out with me later. She looked surprised that I invited her and said, "I would be delighted!"

I told her that I would pick her up after dinner. Then, I hurried home to change and eat.

******

After dinner, I had to perform my evening ritual of putting my towel on the sand between a couple of boats. Then, I headed for #19's cottage.

When I arrived at the cottage, I met #19 on the porch. She looked spectacular. She was wearing the shortest of shorts, that appeared to be lower than normal at the top, a white blouse which was tied in a knot just below her magnificent breasts, pink lipstick and her long beautiful hair flowing over her shoulders and down her back. HOT … HOT … HOT!

I asked, "Are you ready to go?"

"Yes."

Her mom and aunt said, "Goodbye … have a good time," and we were off.

I felt like the king of the world with #19 on my arm. Everywhere we went, all eyes were on #19. Not only because she had a great body and dressed very sexy, but the way she carried herself was extremely sensuous. On top of that, she always walked with her shoulders back and her perfect breasts sticking straight out. She sure grabbed your attention.

We hung out for a while at the arcade, where I introduced #19 to many of my friends … all of the guys were enamored … the girls were not so enthused.

I suggested a nice moonlit walk on the beach and #19 liked the idea.

So, we walked down and along the water's edge toward the small boats, of course. Kissing at various stops along the way. When we reached the boats, I led #19 to the boat in the middle, where we sat and started to kiss more sensuously. I slid my hand up and down her silky-smooth thigh; she ran her hand through my hair, around my neck and shoulders. It was perfect. Almost a full moon, with a warm breeze, the sound of the waves crashing in the beach, a very sexy gal kissing me and she was the best kisser. She just had great lips, great technique and great enthusiasm. It just couldn't get much better!

As we kissed, I was ready to take it to the next level, on the towel on the sand. So, I slid my hand between her legs and started to stroke up and down. #19 pushed my hand away and said, "You are going to get me too hot."

I replied, "We can lay on this towel on the sand and do it … you'll love it!"

"I'm not lying in the sand, crapping up my hair and my outfit … wait till tomorrow morning and we'll do it on my porch, again."

My water chilled … so I asked, "You want to swing by my cottage and pick me up in the morning?"

"Sure," she replied.

We kissed for a while longer on the beach and then we kissed on and off on the walk back to her cottage.

I left #19 off and headed home … what a fantastic day … I had sex with two of the hottest girls that I have ever met … I LOVE THE BEACH!

******

The next morning, as my dad and I were finishing our coffee and reading the paper, I noticed #19 coming around the corner and heading down the block toward our cottage. She looked spectacular; wearing a tiny tan bikini, sandals and her long brown hair flowing behind her.

At the same time that I noticed #19 coming, so did dad. He was looking over the top of his paper and watching her every step, walking down the street, turning at our front walk and walking straight up to our screen door. His eyes were enormous as she said, "Good morning, Tony," with a huge, happy smile.

"Come in," I said. I introduced her to my dad and in her always flirtatious way, she sat in dad's lap and put her arm around his shoulder. Of course, she had her boobs in his face and she bounced up and down as she talked … I think he liked that … he didn't complain.

We talked for a few minutes, she explained where her cottage was to my dad and then we decided to leave and head back to her cottage to help her mom relocate to the beach.

When we arrived at #19's cottage, her mom had almost everything piled up and ready to go.

"Oh Tony, you have come to help us again … thank you very much … you're such a dear," #19's mom told me.

"I am just happy to help out … my mom always tells me if I please every female I meet, I will be a very successful man," I replied.

We were like a parade marching to the beach … #19 and I, then the mom, the aunt and the three kids.

Soon after we got the family settled, #19 announced that we were going to take a long walk on the beach.

Of course, we made a beeline to #19's cottage. Inside the porch I started to head for the daybed but #19 asked me to sit in the big wicker chair … you could see very well down the street from there. #19 kneeled on the chair, straddling my legs, facing me and when she brought her head down to kiss me, her hair cascaded down across my shoulders … I found the feeling of her hair very sexy. #19 kissed me softly, slowly and sensuously … at first. Then, she stopped for a moment to say, "I am sorry about last night … leaving you all hot and bothered. I want to make up for that … right now."

Then, #19 kissed my chin, then all around my neck and shoulders. All the while her soft hands were caressing my body. The feel of her hair delicately flowing over my naked chest turned me on. #19 continued downward until she was kneeling on the floor and pulling at my bathing suit. I helped #19 remove my bathing suit and she started to masterfully suck, lick and stroke my throbbing erection. #19 would pull the skin back, circle the head slowly with her tongue, then lick at the tip … but what really drove me wild was when she made tiny circles with the tip of her tongue on the small piece of skin attached to the top of the head along the shaft, then, she started to flick the same area with the tip of her tongue … small flicks at first, only at the top … but then she started down along the bottom of my shaft … WOW, did that feel goooood!

After a while, I had to tell #19 that I couldn't take much more of what she was doing and we had to get ready to put it in. She must have taken her bikini bottom off while she was fellating me, because when she stood up, she had no bottom on … just a condom in her hand … while I put the condom on, she opened the drawer on the table and took out a small bottle of lube oil and squirted it in and around her love canal. She was ready.

#19 resumed her position, straddling my legs, facing me on the chair, with one hand #19 guided my erection directly into her love canal and we both moaned as it slid up into her (the cowgirl position) … #19 lowered her head and started to kiss me, as she moved her body up and down on my swollen manhood. We both loved it. After a while I could feel #19 position the rim on the head of my erection on her sweet spot and then she bounced up and down in quick short strokes while she brought herself to climax. Then, she relaxed into long slower strokes.

"This is what I have been waiting all night to do for you," she said, surprisingly. She stood up, turned around and backed up between my legs. #19 bent over, reached through her legs and pulled herself toward my erection, which she guided, back into her very wet love canal.

I felt the most intense feeling of my life as my erection slid back into #19's magnificent body. Then she started to rock her body back and forth … taking it all in and then letting it all out (the reverse cowgirl position) … the vision of my erection penetrating #19 and then coming out, glistening from her lubricant only added to the erotic pleasure she was giving me … fantastic!

I experienced my most powerful orgasm ever in this position. I just held onto the chair and let #19 do all of the work … and she was happy to be doing it.

"Magnificent!" I said with conviction. "That was the best climax I have ever had."

"I loved it too … I orgasmed twice … I was HOT from last night … you have a great erection. Now, let's get ready to go back to the beach."

On the way back to the beach, I talked #19 into joining me and my friends. First, we stopped by to check on her family, and then we went to my blanket.

My beach friends were happy to see me … the guys were ecstatic with #19 … the girls, not so pleased with her.

I had a great time lying in the sun, joking around and playing in the water with the group. In the meantime, #19 flirted with all of the guys and entertained them. Later in the afternoon, #19 and I helped her mom bring all of their stuff back to her cottage. #19 and I decided to meet after dinner at the arcade.

******

After dinner, I went over to the arcade and was hanging with the group. When #19 hadn't showed, I decided to go see what the delay was. As I was walking down a side street toward her cottage, I saw #19 headed down the next side street toward the arcade … she didn't see me. Just then a really hot red convertible sports car pulled up to her, as she was strutting her stuff down the street. She spoke to the driver for a while, then she got into the car and they drove away.

I went back to the arcade to wait for her. After an hour, I was irritated, so I started to mingle and look for a girl to be with. Then, along came #17 (the twin sorority sister from the beach) and she was looking HOT … great tan, contrasted by her yellow halter top and matching shorts.

As we started to talk, I realized this was not #17, it was her sister. She was alone since the other girls went off to a movie that she had previously seen with a boyfriend. "I understand that you are fantastic on the beach," she said.

Not being exactly sure of what she meant, I replied, "I am fantastic everywhere. Would you like to go for a walk on the beach?"

"Sure," she replied with a big smile. "Let's go!"

As we walked down the street with my arm around her shoulders, she asked, "Would you rather go over to my cottage? We'll have it all to ourselves."

"Great, let's go there."

We kissed several times on the way to her cottage … she had very soft, sensuous lips.

At her cottage she led me directly to her bedroom, then she turned and started to kiss me. The room looked familiar … I had sex with her sister in this very same room, just two days ago.

We sat on the edge of the bed and started to kiss. She had a very gentle soft moan and it really turned me on. Also, I noticed that her hands were very small and gentle as she caressed my body. I moved my hand from her back to cradle one of her breasts, in her halter. Without stopping the kiss, she moaned, "Ummmmm," reached back and untied and removed her halter. Her breasts were petite, like her sister's, with very small dark nipples … but they were beautiful. Shortly, I pushed her onto her back and while I continued to fondle one breast, I took the other into my mouth.

"I am very hot and horny," she said.

"So … what would you like me to do about that?"

"Let's get naked and under the covers," she replied. Then, as we were both disrobing, she said, "I have been hearing how good you are for the past several days … and I have to find out for myself."

I didn't know what to say, so I offered, "I just try to please."

She pulled back the covers and we both nestled in. She only pulled the top sheet up to cover us. I noticed that she was clean-shaven, unlike her sister's prickly patch … very good. Also, the outer lips of her vulva seemed to be puffier than I had seen before, they seemed to protrude further from her body, in a nice way … very interesting. I couldn't wait to put my hand down there, but I decided to take my time. She didn't. She turned on her side, right up against my body, and she reached for my manhood, which she started to fondle and stroke … it felt great … she was in a hurry. So, I didn't waste any time reaching down between her legs. I just softly caressed the area between her legs, from just above her love lips, then down almost to her butt hole and from one inner thigh to the other inner thigh. It drove her wild (and the softness turned me on, as well).

She lifted one leg so that her foot was on the bed and her knee was in the air. That parted her love lips and was my invitation to enter. Her sister had made a similar move … it must be in their genes.

So, I slipped my middle finger down into her moist cavern, slowly circled her clitoris, then very slowly, very softly I slid my fingertip straight down the middle to the entrance to her love canal. She was moaning, but when my finger reached its' destination, she held her breath. I circled the opening several times. Then, I slid my fingertip back up and around her clit. As my finger made its' next decent, she started to breathe again, but she stopped breathing as my finger continued from the entrance of her love canal to deep inside it. Slowly, I started to pull my finger out until it reached her magic spot. Once there I started to massage it with the pad of my fingertip. Simultaneously, I reached up with my thumb and stroked her clitoris. She let out a large sigh, squeezed her thighs together and said, "I'm coming!" She had a powerful climax and almost violently spasmed and shook, but when she was done, she grabbed my face and wildly kissed me, she crawled up on top of my body … it felt great … her body slithered on top of mine … her skin against my skin … it was wonderful. As my tongue went into her mouth, she closed her lips around it and sucked on it and moved her head up and down so that her lips would slide up and down my stiffened tongue … great technique.

I couldn't resist, I had to tell her, "You are excellent at that!"

She looked me in the eye and said, "Yes … and you're going to find out right now just how good I am." She slid off my body, kneeled on the bed, turned so that her head was over my crotch and her butt was toward my head and just took my manhood directly into her mouth and she started to do to my penis what she had done to my tongue … only it felt much better as she slid her wet lips up and down on my erection. I was stunned at first but as I got used to what she was doing, I decided to slip my finger back into her vagina. My finger would playfully enter her all the way, rub her hot spot on the way out, slid up and around her clit and then tease her inner lips.

One time while coming out of her tunnel, I turned my finger around and pushed up … sort of a different feel. When my finger exited the canal, I slid my index finger down her perineum to and over her butt hole. It must have surprised the heck out of her, because she jumped, her head coming completely off my shaft, she sputtered, "OH!" and she went right back to sucking on my massive erection. I wasn't sure if she liked what I did but when she went back to what she had been doing, she was much more vigorous. So, I did it again and again … each time she increased her intensity.

"I cannot wait any longer," she announced. She was sweating and panting.

As I put my condom on, she turned over onto her belly and spread her legs, I positioned myself between her legs, as she brought her knees up under her thighs and pushed up with her arms. Although she was small and tight, my manhood slid right in all the way on the first push (the doggy style position). Once I was all the way in, #21 started to rock forward and back, while grinding her hips … I could feel that she was having another orgasm, almost immediately after I penetrated her … good for her. Once her spasms subsided, she put a pillow under her belly and lay on it, I leaned forward as she went down, while I was still pumping away (the lying dog position).

I didn't seem to penetrate very deeply, so, I decided to try and straddle her hips. I put one foot on each side of her hips then squatted and re-entered her, she spread her legs even wider. OH WOW! This position (the squatting dog position) was FANTASTIC … she loved it as well. I could pump in and out easily, with just our genitals touching … it was really great. My thrusts became faster and faster, deeper and deeper … the feeling was intense. Finally, I exploded … it was the most magnificent orgasm of my life because #21 orgasmed again and at the same time as me … her spasms and my spasms were simultaneous … her vagina would contract on my erection at the very same time that I was thrusting forward and ejaculating … it was as though we came as one … it really was phenomenal!

As I pulled out of her, #21 turned on her side and even though she was panting said, "That … was the best … it doesn't get any better. You really have a talent. You made me orgasm three times … that's a record."

"Great. I like to set records," I answered.

"If you were in the Olympics, you'd have just won a gold medal."

I started to laugh, "Can you imagine telling someone, I won the gold medal for sex in the Olympics."

That got #21 laughing as well and she replied, "They would name the sport after you. It would be called the Tony Award."

"Isn't there a Tony Award already, for the best in Broadway Theater?"

#21 looked at me very seriously and said, "You haven't been doing it with everyone on Broadway, have you?"

After that statement, we both broke up laughing, got dressed and I headed home to my cottage.

On my walk home, "I contemplated … I could not believe what a great vacation I was having at the beach … it was only Tuesday night … it felt like I had been on vacation for 10 days … I had met lots of new friends … had had great sex with phenomenal girls … can it get any better than this?"

******

The following morning, while dad and I were finishing reading the newspaper on the porch, I saw #19 coming down the side street. As she turned down our street, my dad asked, "Are you screwing her?"

That shocked me, because dad and I had never talked about sex or anything sexual in nature. I didn't know what to say so I said, "No … I wouldn't do that."

Dad shot back with, "Well, if you wouldn't … you're no son of mine." Then, he followed with, "If you do … you want to make sure that you use a condom … you are too young to get a girl pregnant … you have too much living to do first."

It was touching … I didn't know what to say … so I said, "OK."

Just then, #19 was at out screen door looking spectacular, as always, in her tiny black with yellow polka dots bikini. She came in and went directly to dad's lap. Then I knew … he was jumping for joy inside.

We gabbed for a while, then I asked her if her mom was ready for me to carry all her stuff down to the beach. #19 said that her mom was piling it up when she left to come and get me. So, we left and went to her cottage. When we arrived, they were all ready for me to lug all of their stuff down to the beach. Off we went.

After I set them up on the beach, I asked #19 to go for a walk. I was concerned about what I had done the night before, and possibly what she had done.

I asked #19, "What happened to you last night?"

#19 was very honest. She told me she had met a guy on her way to the arcade and went for a ride with him in his sportscar. They had a blast. #19 went on to say that she did not want an exclusive relationship at this point in her life … she felt that we both should be free to see whomever, but she would still like to have sex with me because it was special.

How could I argue with her logic? I agreed with her explicitly.

******

#19 did not like to hang out on my blanket, because there were too many 'distractions'. So, when I headed for my blanket and friends, she headed in the other direction for a walk.

As the morning heated up, more and more of our 'gang' arrived. It was fun, flirting, joking … just fooling around.

My other official Sunscreen Applier started to devote more and more time to me. Finally, she told me, "You have been neglecting me lately."

Not really knowing what she meant, I asked, "Whatever do you mean?"

"You have been running off with the other girls and leaving me here."

"Well then," I replied, "would you like to run off with me now?"

"I'd love to," she answered as she grabbed my hand and led me off the beach and toward her cottage. She had a bubbly personality, was always fun to be with, but most of all … she was pretty hot!

When we reached her cottage, she led me into the bathroom, which was next to the back door. She locked the door and said, "We won't be disturbed in here." Then, she put her arms around my neck and pulled my head down, so that my lips met hers … very softly she started to kiss me. I didn't waste any time … I started to give her some tongue and I pulled her hips toward mine. In no time we were kissing so aggressively that our lips and chins were covered with saliva … and that is a good thing! As we kissed, I caressed the perfectly formed mounds of her butt … and she loved it!

After a while, I was getting uncomfortable, all scrunched up bending over kissing. So, I decided to move over to the toilet and sit down. But when I stood up, my erection stood straight out and the girl coyly asked, "What is that?"

"That is my Love Meter," I answered.

"And what is it reading?" She suggestively asked.

"On a scale from one to ten, it is presently at," I looked down convincingly and said, "seven."

"We'll just have to make it a ten … won't we?" She said as she reached into my bathing suit with one hand, grabbed my erection and held it out of the way, as she pulled my bathing suit down with her other hand. She bent over and as she slipped the head into her mouth she started to pump vigorously with her hand. Her technique was not great but her enthusiasm was terrific! Most females think that technique is key to giving a male great pleasure. Technique is important but the key ingredient to pleasuring a guy is enthusiasm, and this girl was very enthusiastic! WAHOOOOOOO!

Shortly, I had to stop her … but first I untied the top of her bikini, while she was bent over … when I sat down on the commode, she pulled her top aside and her magnificent breasts were right in front of my face. They were spherical, like two big juicy grapefruits the skin around her huge protruding nipples was very dark brown and about four inches in diameter. Her nipples were the size of my thumbs and stuck out over an inch and I could hear them calling to my mouth.

I reached out and pulled her to me and she reached out and hugged my head, which was pressed between her lovely globes. I reached down and untied her bikini bottom, then I pushed her away far enough to relocate my mouth to one of her fantastic nipples. My free hand came up and stated to caress and fondle her other breast and nipple. Her breasts were soft, but supple and her nipples were stiff … like me … from the excitement. I pushed her a bit farther away and as she stepped back her bikini bottom fell to the floor. I sat there for a moment just looking, like a judge, at her nude body. I couldn't contain myself, I had to say, "Magnificent!"

She smiled happily and moved closer to me. I slid one hand down between her legs, the other hand on one breast and I sucked the other nipple into my mouth. As my finger parted her labia, I could tell that she was almost ready, so I just rubbed my fingertip, softly, up and down on the side of her clitoris, and I could feel it growing … her nipples stiffened even more … I said, "Let's put it in."

"Where?" She replied as she looked around the bathroom.

"How about the tub?" I said as I grabbed a blanket from a shelf and draped it over the old fashion freestanding bathtub. While she settled down in the tub, I slipped on a condom and knelt between her legs (the missionary position). I guided my erection to her vagina with one hand and supported my upper body by holding onto the top of the tub behind her head. As my erection approached, she spread her legs and arched her body, which made it ideal for me to enter her hot, moist cavern. It took a few strokes in and out to achieve full penetration, as #22 sort of repositioned herself to accommodate my manhood. Then, we both started to push together and pull apart, simultaneously. It was great! I bent my head forward and as we started to kiss, I sucked #22's tongue deeply into my mouth. #22 put her feet up over the top of the tub and lifted her bottom up, which gave my erection better access to penetrate her even deeper. My deep, fast stroking brought #22 to climax fairly quickly in this position and I started to orgasm just moments later … FANTASTIC!

I kept stroking until both of our orgasms were complete and when #22 relaxed and lowered her bottom back down to the tub, I said, "That was great … you are beautiful!"

#22 pulled my head down and kissed me gently, she was still catching her breath. "Tony … that was great! You are great! I really enjoyed that!" Then, #22 kissed me again.

I was starting to lose my erection and I was afraid that my condom could fall off and make a mess, so I lifted myself out of the tub, removed my condom and wiped myself off with toilet paper. #22 hopped out of the tub, folded the blanket and returned it to the shelf. She put her top on then asked me, "Could you please step out of the bathroom for a minute?"

"Certainly," I replied as I pulled my bathing suit up and left the bathroom. I think #22 wanted to wipe herself off and go to the bathroom, since a few minutes later I could hear the toilet flush. When she came out, her bikini was all intact.

We were both sweating pretty good, so #22 suggested that we go for a nice, cool refreshing swim.

I agreed!

******

After lunch I swung over to check on #19's mom. They had just finished lunch as well and didn't need anything. #19 had gone for a walk.

So, I headed back to my blanket. When I got back to my blanket, everyone had gone to lunch. There was only a very hot girl sitting in the shade of my umbrella. I had seen her on the beach several times but hadn't spoken to her. With a big smile on my face, I plopped down beside her and asked, "Where is everyone?" Gosh, she was hot!

"I guess they all went off to lunch," she replied.

"I'm Tony … unfortunately, we haven't met … and let me say … you are beautiful!" I stuck my hand toward her and looked deeply into her deep blue eyes.

She reached out and gently held my hand with both of her hands, she smiled and said, "I'll bet you say that to all the girls." She blushed.

"You know, it probably would not be a bad opening line … but in your case, I mean it … I have noticed you on the beach a few times and thought how beautiful you are." She blushed darker red. We both were looking into each other's eyes. To break the tension in the air, I continued with, "What brings you to my little group today?"

"I have started to hang around with your two Sunscreen Appliers and they have told me all about you," she said confidently.

I laughed and asked, "ALL about me?"

She giggled, looked me in the eye and replied, "ALL about you … and it was all GOOOD!" She then asked me if I would like to join her for lunch … of course, I accepted the invitation (even though I had already had lunch, I could eat another). So, we got up and she led me off the beach and up the street to her cottage. On the way, she explained that her folks owned three cottages and she stayed in one, with her mom, all summer long. That day her mom had gone off to a fair with some ladies and she wouldn't be back until suppertime … how convenient!

Her cottage was very nice. We went straight into the kitchen and she made two sandwiches and poured us both a glass of iced tea. We talked as though we knew each other forever. She had a great personality.

I asked, "So, you know my two official Sunscreen Appliers?"

"Yes."

"One of my official Sunscreen Appliers does one side, while the other does the other side … where will you apply the lotion?"

She got up from her chair, with a very serious look on her face and came over and stood next to me. Then, she bent over and put her hand on my lap and said, "How about right here?" Then she gave my penis a gentle squeeze.

Her face was directly in front of mine and she was looking right into my eyes … it was a very sensuous moment. "Do you think I need some lotion right now?" I asked softly.

Her hand softly rubbed my manhood, which was starting to stiffen, she said, "You're going to need a lot!" she replied as our lips came together for a kiss. She led me into her bedroom and while she spread a big beach towel on the bed, she instructed me to remove my bathing suit … done! She had me lay on my back as she took out a bottle of baby oil and squirted a huge puddle in her hand, which she then spread all over my semi-erection and scrotum … it really felt great and it turned me on. She was very serious about what she was doing … and very good at it.

Before she got me too hot, I said, "Let me return the favor." She smiled widely. "Let's take this bathing suit off." I removed the top while she removed her bottom. Then, she laid next to me. I applied some oil on my finger and circled it around her nipples … they started to grow. I squirted some oil on my hands and started to massage her perky breasts … very nice! We started to kiss again, very passionately. I moved my hand down to her crotch, which was covered with hair … unusual at the beach … she spread her legs apart. Then, I applied a big load of oil on my fingers and worked it into her labia as she moaned. After a while, I started to rub her G-spot as I started to kiss my way from her mouth down to her vagina. I softly kissed my way down her neck … around and around her nipples … I noticed that she was grabbing the sheets with both hands, I continued to rub her G-spot as I moved down to her belly button … when I French-kissed it, she orgasmed … very strongly … I continued to rub and kiss … she moaned and moaned and continued to orgasm.

When her body relaxed, I kissed my way back up her oily body to her mouth. We kissed very passionately. Then, she held my head in both of her hands and said, "I have got something special for you! Can you put on a condom?"

"Of course," I said, as I sat up and slipped into a lubricated condom … little did I know that the lubrication would not be necessary.

When I laid on my back, she squirted oil on my chest, belly and privates. Then, she got on top of me and started to squirm and slide around to spread it out … it felt GREAT! Next, she applied even more, then she started to slide all the way up, so that her breasts reached my mouth, then, all the way down, so she could press her breasts around my massively engorged erection … then back up … FANTASTIC! She made round trip after round trip and we both got hotter. Then, she applied even more oil to our genitals and as she slid her body down, she spread her legs wide so that my erection would enter her (the cowgirl position) … it slipped right in with no resistance … #23 made a few quick strokes and then she slid up so I could suck her nipples into my mouth … she was panting … as #23 slid back down and I slipped back into her … she started to kiss me. I reached up and pressed her lips to mine, while she was making short, quick strokes with her pelvis … I sucked her air into my lungs … she moaned … I exhaled the air back into her lungs and inhaled it again, over and over. #23 rocked her body feverously back and forth as quickly as she could and we both climaxed simultaneously … our lips never parted … it was intense … it was MAGNIFICENT!

When our mouths parted, #23 gasped for air, pushed up, still impaled by my erection. "That was SPECTACULAR!" #23 told me. "The girls on the beach were right. You are … terrific!"

"What do you mean the girls on the beach?"

"Your Sunscreen Appliers … they talk incessantly about how good you are in bed."

I was embarrassed that the girls on the beach were talking about me. On the other hand, I took it as a compliment. I didn't know what to say, so I asked, "Is that why you brought me here?"

"Yea, I couldn't wait … you were even better than I expected … that was great!"

"I don't think that it is right to be telling anyone about what we did in private. I would never do that. Do me a favor, don't go telling anyone what we did," I asked.

"OK, I will try to contain myself. Now, why don't you jump in the shower across the hall, while I will shower in my folks' bathroom."

I got up, all covered in sweat and oil, and took a shower, it felt great. I was hoping that #23 would join me, as #20, the umbrella girl, had. But #23 took her shower in her parents' bathroom and she was just putting her bathing suit back on when I returned to her bedroom. We kissed and hugged and walked back to the beach.

When we got back to the beach, everyone was sitting on the blankets and when they saw us together, my official Sunscreen Appliers asked, simultaneously, "I thought you guys didn't know each other?"

I said, "We just met on the beach." Then #23 sat on the blanket while I headed for the water to take a dip. When I returned to dry off, the girls were all giggling (I bet I know what they had been talking about).

I let my official Sunscreen Appliers apply their lotion on me and then I laid down to soak up some sun. Later in the afternoon, I checked on #19's family and they were ready for the trek back to their cottage. So, I helped them pack up and, as usual, I carried the majority of the burden. The mom and the aunt could not be more thankful for my help. I hadn't seen #19 since the morning, when we brought the family down to the beach. I wondered where she was.

******

At dinner, my dad announced that we were going to the drive-in for a special showing of three 'spy' flicks … the movies were very good and we had a great time!

******

The next morning started like the last few; I set my stuff up on the beach, got the newspaper, donuts and coffee for dad and me … #19 came to my cottage, bounced around on dad's lap, we went to her cottage and helped her mom carry all their stuff down to the beach.

Then, I had to hurry back to meet up with my mom, dad and sister to go for a ride on some guy's yacht.

The day before, my dad had gone to the bar on the beach for a beer and he got talking to the guy that owned a big motor yacht, which was moored not far from shore. Evidently, dad hit it off well with the guy and he invited our family to go for a ride on his boat … it sounded special.

We met the guy, his son (who was my sister's age) and his daughter (who was my age) on the beach where they rented the little boats. It took two trips to bring us all out to the yacht in their dinghy.

The boat was gorgeous, 65 feet long, three bedrooms, three baths (called heads on a boat), a beautiful living room (salon), kitchen (galley) and a back deck.

Once we were all on the boat, we traveled about an hour to a restaurant that had docks that we could pull up and tie the boat to. On the ride over, the daughter showed me all around the boat. She was fairly hot but the fact that her dad owned the boat made her really hot!

The father bought all of us lunch and then we traveled back to our beach. The daughter asked me if I would like to return to the boat once everyone else left. I told her that I would be delighted.

Our dads decided to go play golf, mom was a little seasick so she went back to the cottage to rest and my sister and the boy from the boat took a ride over to where they lived, to see their home (which was a mansion).

Once they had all left, we jumped into the dinghy and returned to the yacht. Inside, the girl opened a bottle of wine. We sat on the back deck as the boat swayed on the waves, drank our wine and talked. It was delightful … I started to think, "What are the poor people doing?"

After the second glass of wine, the girl asked if I would like to get out of the sun and go inside. Of course, I agreed. Inside we began to kiss, she was very sensuous. She led me to a bedroom (stateroom on a boat). We continued to drink our wine, sit on the edge of the bed and kiss, while the boat rocked on the waves. It was very sexy.

The girl was an excellent kisser, she smelled great, and her skin was smooth as silk. As we kissed, I reclined the two of us to a prone position and put my hand on her abdomen. I wasn't sure if I should move it up or down. I didn't need to make the decision because as I pondered what to do next, she pushed my hand down between her legs. Then, I knew what to do!

Next, she reached up and pulled one of her breasts from her bathing suit and pushed my head down onto it. I sucked the nipple into my mouth and ran my tongue around in circles. I had slipped one of my fingers under the leg portion of her bathing suit bottom and tried to rub her clitoris, but it was a tight fit because of the bathing suit. I think she sensed the problem, so she lifted up her butt and slid her bottom off. That allowed me all the access that I needed to perform my titillations of her love lips. I put a big glob of saliva on my finger and moved it up and down between the lips. I could really feel the effects of the wine … giving me an inner glow. She turned on her side, slid a hand up under the leg hole of my bathing suit and sort of massaged my erection.

"I am ready for you, baby!" She murmured.

She took off the top of her bathing suit, as I disrobed and put a condom on. I positioned myself between her legs and entered her (the missionary position), in almost one move. Slowly, I started to pump. #24 reached up for my head and brought it down for a kiss. Then, #24 moved her hands down and grabbed the cheeks of my buttocks. Her massaging of my butt drove me crazy, and I started to pump faster and faster. Then, I supported my upper body by pushing my head into the pillow next to her head. I reached down underneath #24 and grabbed her butt cheeks with my hands. As soon as I started squeezing #24 started to orgasm and so did I … we both kept pumping and squeezing until we were completely finished.

"I'll bet the boat was bouncing on the waves," I said.

Then, we both turned onto our sides, connected by my shaft. We cuddled and kissed on and off. It was so peaceful with the boat rocking and the water slapping against the hull.

Finally, #24 said, "Let's finish the wine and get ready to go back to the beach."

So, we got up, cleaned up and finished the wine … I felt a little tipsy.

When we got back to the beach, I invited #24 to join our group on the beach. After introductions, I laid down and fell asleep (most likely an effect of the wine).

Dinner was late because we had to wait for dad to return from the golf course. At the dinner table, we all talked about what a great time we had on the yacht, except for mom, she was still a little sick from the boat ride.

After dinner, I headed over to the arcade to hang out with my friends. All of a sudden, I saw a girl come in the door. She was from my town, from my school. She had an identical twin sister, but I didn't see her come in. I have known these sisters and they were always unattractive and kind of chubby. But over the summer, this girl had blossomed into a beautiful, slender, hot chick!

"Where's your sister?"

Surprised to see me, she replied, "She met some guy and they have gone for a ride."

Standing there in a silky top that went over one shoulder and stopped just under her breasts, gathered in some sort of elastic, tan silky shorts, light brown hair and a bronze tan, she was the most beautiful girl in the arcade. WOW!

"How long are you here for?"

She answered, "We came down on Saturday and we are her until tomorrow afternoon, then we have to go home for my cousin's wedding on Saturday."

"You look lovely," I said. "Would you like to meet my friends."

"Sure," she said as she put my hand in hers.

We spent about thirty minutes hanging out with my friends. Then, I asked her if she would like to go for a walk on the beach. She accepted and as we walked and talked, she held onto my hand. When we got close to the rental boats, I decided to try and kiss her. She was more than willing. After a while I encouraged her to sit on a boat and our kissing became more passionate. I asked if she would like to lay on my towel, between boats, for more privacy … she was intrigued and impressed.

Then, we became more passionate. I slid my hand up under her loose pant leg toward her crotch. When my hand reached its destination, I was surprised to find that she was not wearing any underwear. WOW! I softly rubbed my fingertips over her love lips, and she started to grind her hips. I parted her love lips; it was very dry. So, I brought my finger to my mouth, put a big glob of saliva on the tip, returned to her labia and slipped my finger between her love lips. I circled her clitoris, then, I slid down to her love canal and back up. The saliva was the perfect lubricant and my finger moved without much friction. As my fingertip traveled downward, she made an, "Uuuuwe," sound, then,

"Ummmmmm," during the trip back up to her clit. Her hip gyrations also became a bit more vigorous.

I decided to touch her breasts … they were not big but they looked inviting. As I worked my fingers under her top, she stopped kissing me and she pulled the top over her head and off … she wasn't wearing a bra (how sexy). We went back to kissing while I manipulated her vulva with one hand and her breasts with the other. Soon, she moved her knee up and started to rub it on my crotch … she wasn't an expert at the technique but her knee got the desired effect, as I grew a massive erection.

I started to softly kiss her breasts and suck on her nipples. My other hand moved down to her very moist love button. I started to softly circle it with my fingertip and soon I could hear her stop breathing … she was ready.

I stopped and said, "Pull down your pants," as I took off mine, and quickly put on a condom. She pushed her shorts off one leg, she was panting, heavily. I knelt between her legs and guided my stiff shaft toward her waiting canal (the missionary position). It took several lunges before I was all the way in, because she was so tight.

#25 briefly stopped kissing and whispered in my ear, "You are sooo big … it fills me up."

Whispering in my ear while we are having sex really turns me on … how sexy! I asked, "Are you all, right? Does it hurt?" I wouldn't want to hurt her.

She whispered again in my ear … oh boy, I love the whispering, "No, I love it … go harder!"

I usually do not talk when I am having sex, but I thought, if #25 could turn me on with her whispering in my ear, maybe I could turn #25 on more if I whispered in her ear. So, each time I pushed in all the way, I would stop and whisper something in her ear, "You are beautiful … this feels so good … I'm soooo deep in you." As I whispered, #25 would contract her vagina as if saying, "Thank you." It was delightful.

With my head next to #25's ear; I supported myself with my forehead. So that I could slip my hands down and cup her butt cheeks, continually whispering in her ear. We were both on the edge of coming, as I gently squeezed and pulled #25's butt cheeks apart … it felt great for both of us … I seemed to be able to slide in and out even easier, and it must have turned #25 on even more because she started to moan, "Yes … Yes … Yes, Yes, Yes!" and VOILA! We both started to climax simultaneously … it doesn't happen every time, but when it does, it adds another dimension, a step up in the pleasure, when both people are thrashing about in orgasm simultaneously … and it was perfect!

I think we had both forgotten where we were. It was just perfect and surprisingly private. After the waves of pleasure subsided, we quickly dressed. Then, we just laid there kissing and hugging. It was very romantic.

Finally, we got up and walked back down the beach, kissing and hugging. I walked her to her cottage and said, "Too bad you are going home tomorrow."

"Don't worry … we can see each other when we get back home," she consoled me.

******

WOW! It was Friday morning … my last full day at the beach … we need to be out of our cottage by noon Saturday. I was thinking that I need to get up and get going to make the most of what's left of my beach vacation. I don't know how I could have had more fun, met more girls or have had more sex than I have been getting. So, I will go with the flow and follow my present routine.

When #19 showed up, she was wearing a very light tan bikini, which seemed to make her body look even better … if that was possible. Of course, dad was only too glad to see her, as she bounced around on his lap while rubbing her boobs all over his face.

When I finished helping #19's mom, carry all their gear down and set it up on the beach. I said, "I don't think that I will have time to help you guys tomorrow because we have to pack up and be out by noon."

The mother and aunt looked astonished. "I don't know how we'll ever get by without you," the mom said. "You just cannot go home!"

I laughed and asked #19 if I could join her for her walk down the beach.

As we strolled away, I asked #19 if she wanted to go back to her cottage. Since it would probably be our last chance to do so. She didn't hesitate to agree and we headed back to her cottage.

When we reach #19's cottage, she said, "Let's do it in the chair again … I like it that way since I can see down the street."

"Why not," I said. Actually, I loved it that way. #19 seemed to be far less inhibited in that position.

We kissed as we stood in front of the chair … gosh, was she a good kisser … soft lips, sensuous noises, the way she moves her delicate hands all over my body … I am going to miss it … my hands traveled down her back to cup her perfectly shaped butt cheeks. I was always impressed at what a perfect body #19 had to look at or to touch … firm, toned, soft and silky skin … she oozed sex from every pour in her body … I was REALLY going to miss her.

#19 had a way of turning her hips slightly, so that she could rub her hip against my manhood, similar to what she did with her knee, it really turned me on. Also, her position allowed me to rub my hand between her legs. We both knew what turned the other one on.

I remembered how good it felt the last time we did it in the chair, so I said, "Let's sit down."

#19 replied, "Take of your bathing suit first." She removed her bikini bottom as quickly as I discarded my bathing suit. I sat down but #19 did not straddle me, instead she bent over to kiss me and took my manhood into her expert hand and started to slowly pump. In a flash she kneeled between my legs and started to fellate me. #19 was extremely good, the way her tongue would flick and flirt with the head of my erection. Then, she slid her lips up and down my shaft. #19 knew what a guy liked and she knew how to give a guy incredible pleasure.

"Let me return the favor," I asked. "You sit in the chair."

We changed places. #19 spread her legs and I buried my head between them. I lifted her legs up over my head and spread them apart as far as possible. It opened up her love lips with my thumbs and my tongue slipped right in between them. I circled her clitoris several times, then, I sucked it into my mouth, while French kissing it, like a tongue. Then, I licked down the inside of one love lip to her love canal, then back up the inside of the other lip and around her clit again. #19 loved it and was squealing in delight. I lifted #19 a bit higher and positioned my mouth right in front of her vagina … and I stuck my tongue in as far as it would go and circled it around. Then, keeping my tongue as stiff as I could, I moved my head back and forth.

I could tell that #19 was extremely hot, by how wet her love canal was … #19 asked me to put it in. As I put on my condom, she got up and had me sit down. She turned around and backed up with my legs between hers. #19 reached between her legs and pulled my massive protuberance into her love canal (the reverse face to face position). #19 started to gyrate her hips and grind them up and down. "MINGA!" I said. "That is driving me wild!"

#19 said something through her groaning … but I couldn't understand her. I grabbed her hips and arched my body to stick my erection in even further. The reverse face to face position excited both of us and #19 started pumping up and down quicker and quicker. That was it, I started to orgasm and so did #19 … it was GREAT!

Before I could say anything, #19 turned and said, "I am going to really miss you!"

I cracked up laughing, and I said, "I was thinking the very same thing." I was!

As we walked back to the beach, we both discussed how much we were going to miss each other (and the great sex).

******

#19 headed down the beach for her walk and I returned to my blanket where the group had already congregated. We had a good time, talking, joking around and going into the water … building pyramids with the guys on the bottom and girls forming the top. Higher and higher we would go until we would collapse into the water. It was loads of fun.

After a little nap on the beach, I was off to say goodbye to the sorority sisters. The girls all gathered around me on the blanket … all saying how sorry they were that the week was coming to an end. So, I suggested that we make the most out of the time we have left. I grabbed their beach ball and ran down to the water with a trail of girls running behind me. We played 'keep the ball up' for quite a while, when all of a sudden, I felt a sharp pain in my foot. I yelled, "Ouch!" And headed out of the water. Either, I had stepped on a sharp shell or a sand crab had bitten my toe and it was bleeding.

The 'head' sorority sister wrapped a tissue around it and asked me to go with her to their cottage where she could put some medicine and a bandage on it. So, we left the other girls in the water and walked off to the cottage.

She brought me into the bathroom and although it was just a little nick in my toe, she made a big deal out of cleaning the wound, putting medicine and a band-aid on it … she was very gentle … very nice.

"Thank you very much, how can I ever repay you?"

She smiled and said to follow her upstairs to her bedroom. When we got there, she said that she had heard that I was a good kisser, and I could repay her with a kiss. She was a very pretty redhead, buxom, curvy with lots of freckles, brought out by the sun … full lips. So, I was happy to pull her to me and start to kiss her. At first, I gently slid my lips on hers. Then, I applied a little more pressure and when her lips parted I slipped just the tip of my tongue in. Her breathing quickened … her tongue started to flick at mine and the kissing became more passionate. I moved my hands slowly down her back to cup her butt cheeks … as I softly gave them a squeeze she seemed to melt into my arms. My right hand made a slow trip around her hip, to the front, she instinctively rotated that hip away from me, so that my hand would have room for its approach. With my other hand, I unhooked her bikini top … she reached up and threw it aside. She had beautiful white globes, with tiny pink nipples (tiny because of the cool, wet bathing suit). I bent over and took one of her tiny, cold, salty nipples into my mouth … I could feel it relax in the warmth of my lips.

I said, "Why don't you lay on the bed?" She laid down on the edge of the bed. Still standing, I bent over and started to kiss her as my right hand continued to massage between her legs … she was squirming around. Slowly, my lips moved down to suck her other nipple into my mouth. Flicking it over and over with my tongue … it grew in my mouth. Next, I started kissing my way to her navel … I French kissed her belly button … I untied the sides of her bikini bottom … at just the right time she lifted her butt so I could pull the bottom off without any resistance. She was motionless, as I kissed my way down to her cleanly shaven vulva. I pressed her legs apart and slipped my tongue between her love lips … she stopped breathing. I started to slide the tip of my tongue up and down her slit. She started to moan with pleasure, and she reached between my legs to fondle my genitals.

After she felt around for a while, she reached up and pulled my bathing suit down and took my semi-erection into her warm hand. It only took a few of her golden strokes to bring me to full protuberance. She said, "WOW! You have a big one!"

"I hope you like it," was my reply. She pulled me closer, so I lifted my leg and put my foot on the other side of her head, on the mattress. It opened up my entire crotch to her as she pulled my bulging manhood down into her mouth. I spread her love lips and sucked her clitoris into my mouth. The more she sucked on me, the faster and more ferocious I sucked on her. Finally, I couldn't wait any longer, I stood straight up and without a word I slipped on a condom. She turned to face me and pulled her knees back toward her head. Standing right next to the bed, I just had to lean toward her for my erection to enter her (the side of the bed position).

As I pushed inward, #26 sighed, "OH!" When I pulled out, she sighed, "Yes!"

I loved #26's response and I knew that she must be enjoying it as much as me. After six or seven strokes, I asked #26 to turn on her side … I straddled her lower leg, and I took her upper leg and lifted it straight up, as I re-entered her (the split leg position). MINGA! Did that feel good. I was going in soooo far, it felt fantastic! #26 started to grunt with each of my lunges. Then, she mumbled through a grunt, "Faster … harder … faster … harder!" I wrapped my arms around her thigh and tightened my grip and started to pump faster and harder. Finally, #26 looked at me and said, "You're making me come … come with me, baby." That was all it took, and we both orgasmed together. It was amazing … we both really enjoyed it … I just love this position and I am sure #26 did as well.

As our passion subsided, I put #26's leg down on the bed without pulling out of her. I bent over and kissed her. As she hugged me with her arms, I could feel her vagina contract around my member … it was a 'complete hug'. "You are the king of the beach!" #26 pronounced. Her reply surprised me. "You are the BEST looking guy on the beach … you have a KING-SIZE penis and you use it like an EXPERT … you are the KING!"

I just laughed (and I am sure that I blushed), but I was proud, even if #26 was the only one that thought that, it was a great compliment.

We had to hustle back down to the beach so that we didn't arouse any suspicions.

The other girls were in the water again when we got back to the beach, so #26 and I went right in to join them (and cool off). We all had a ball!

******

Friday evenings were special for teens. A really good dance band would come to the bar on the beach and their huge dance hall was open to teens only (Saturday night was the same deal for adults only).

Everybody was excited and having a terrific time dancing and singing to the tunes belted out by the band. I danced with a number of girls, but I had my eye on one beautiful blond, with a ponytail, dressed in a rawhide halter and matching short shorts. There were hundreds of strips of rawhide hanging from her outfit that bounced all over as she danced, and boy, could she dance. Just as I made my way over and asked her to dance the bandleader announced that they were going to have a dance contest. Perfect, we'll dance together. The bandleader selected three judges and then said, "If anyone wins two times during the summer, they will be the undisputed king or queen of the beach." Well, I just had to win, to keep the title that #26 bestowed on me just hours before.

We danced as fast and as good as we could … then I did a split … the girl seemed surprised, but she was smiling … when my partner danced down into a squat position … I jumped over her into another split. When we were done dancing, we were tired. The judges huddled together and after their deliberations, they came over and brought my partner and me up onto the stage where the bandleader announced us as the winners! The crowd gave us a good round of applause … it was embarrassing.

Then the bandleader said, "Let's show everyone how you won the contest!"

We went back to the middle of the dance floor and the band started to play my favorite fast tune. My partner and I started to dance as fast as we could … the audience was clapping and singing and while she was shaking her moneymaker, I dropped down into a split … the audience erupted into a wild mass of screaming and clapping … we both started to dance again and after a while my partner danced down into a squat position and I jumped over her again, into a split … that sent the already excited crowd into an uproar. When the dance was done, we walked off the floor to a standing ovation … WOW! Was that fun!

I was 'off the chart' hot and sweaty and so was my partner. So, I suggested that we go outside to get some cooler air.

We kicked off our footwear and holding hands we walked out onto the beach. I noticed that the tide was out. So, when we reached the water's edge, I picked up my partner and carried her out to the sandbar. The cool water felt great on my legs. When we reached the sand bar, I put my partner down in about a foot of water, I turned her toward me and we kissed … very passionately for two people that didn't really know each other very well. It could not have been more romantic: the light warm breeze, a full moon shining on the water and small cool waves slapping against our legs. We kissed over and over … it was really quite nice. We were both starting to get heated up.

Then, my partner asked, "Why don't we head over to my motel room?"

"Let's go."

She drove about a mile to a nice, clean motel. On the way she explained that she was 20 years old, came down for the weekend with her best friend and was just looking for a good time. Her room was small, with two beds and clothes everywhere … messy.

As my partner walked toward the bathroom, she said, "I just have to change my outfit … I have sweat right through this one." While she was talking, she pulled off her halter top and threw it into the corner. Of course, when she did that, her breasts came springing out and I reached around her and cupped them in my hands.

I said, "Let me help you with these." I lifted them slightly and caressed them.

My partner moaned, "UMMMM … that feels good!" In the next instant, she pushed off her shorts and was then standing completely naked in front of me.

"You have a perfect body," I said, while running my hands up and down her sleek, toned body.

She turned toward me and said, "Get naked." Then, she went into the bathroom and shut the door. I stripped down and sat on the bed. In a few minutes I heard the toilet flush and she came out, leaving the bathroom light on. She shut off the light in the room and walked over to me. She pushed me back on the bed and laid on top of me. Looking into my eyes she said, "I hope you are as good in bed as you are on the dance floor!" Then, she savagely started to kiss me … Oh boy, was she horny.

I turned so that we were both on our sides and started to run one hand up and the other hand down … our lips were stuck together. She was grinding her pelvis up against me and we were both getting hotter. I placed my hand between her legs and slipped a finger between her moistened love lips, while she gently caressed my growing erection. I was surprised at how softly she stroked me given how aggressive she had been … I think she didn't want to get me too hot, too soon … good idea!

All these manipulations had the desired effect and soon she asked me if I had a condom. Of course, I said I did, and I put it on. As soon as I turned toward her, she put one leg around me and pulled me toward her … one of her hands reached down and guided my shaft right into her waiting vagina. We rocked forward and back and ground our pelvic areas against each other. I had never done it in the side-by-side position before … it was nice. It didn't get me too hot too quickly and I could enjoy the pleasure of it … GREAT! After a while, I pulled out until the crown of the head of my erection was against #27's special spot. Then, I made quick, short, jerky motions, just to rub against the spot. I could feel her body tense as she approached her first orgasm. I reached over and grabbed the butt cheek of the leg #27 had around me and I started to pull her toward me, then back. It increased the pleasure for both of us and I could feel #27 start to come. As the waves of pleasure flowed over and through her body, I continued to slowly rock in and out. #27 was biting her lip, hugging me as hard as she could and grinding her pelvis like there was no tomorrow.

When her orgasm was complete, #27 lifted her leg straight up into the air and I could pump in deeper and deeper. #27 looked me in the eye and asked, "Did you come too?"

"Not yet," I replied.

"Good!" She answered.

I got up on my knees, holding #27's leg straight up (the split leg position) and I started to pump in and out … she really liked it, so did I.

Shortly, #27 brought her leg down to the bed and got on her knees. I entered her from the back (the doggy style position). This style was great too … then, she put a pillow under her belly, and she laid on it (the lying dog position), as I continued to pump in and out. In the lying dog position, I could only get shallow penetration. So, I put one foot on each side of her hips, squatted and re-entered #27 (the squatting dog position) … she let out a gasp and spread her legs … OH! WOW! The feeling was FANTASTIC … I went deeper and deeper into her cavern, as though there was no end. I started pumping ferociously and #27 started to rock forward and back … our rhythm was right on, just like when we were dancing. #27 started to climax just before me and when I started to climax, I changed my pumping into long, deep, slow strokes. #27 was great … she would contract her vagina for my forward stroke and loosen as I pulled out … it was as though she was milking me and OH BOY!

Did that feel good. It was the longest, strongest most intense climax of my life. What an end to a fantastic week!

We dressed and during the ride back to the dance #27 all of a sudden blurted out, "Better!"

"Better what?"

"You make love … even better than you dance," she said.

I started to laugh.

Back at the dance, we went our separate ways. Since we had won the dance competition, everyone wanted to dance with us, and we obliged them.

******

The next morning, as dad and I read the newspaper, we saw #19 and her mom walking down the street. They came right up to our screen door and came in. I introduced #19's mom and #19 sat on dad's lap as the mom pulled up a chair.

#19's mom told my dad that he couldn't possibly take me away from the beach. She explained how much help I had been all week transporting all of their stuff to and from the beach and how they could better watch their small children, since I was doing the heavy carrying. How difficult it was, without me, for her or her sister to watch the kids while the other took trip after trip from the beach to their cottage. She went on and on and on, even saying that they would drive me home at the end of the week.

Dad just sat there and smiled. I wasn't sure if it was because of all the nice things that she was saying about me, or the fact that he had the nicest breast in town rubbing on his cheek. Finally, he said, "Well, Tony … would you like to stay here another week and help out?"

I was jumping up and down like a maniac inside, just thinking about the proposition of staying another week. I had to calm my emotions to stoically say, "You know, this is all a surprise to me … I didn't know they were going to come over and ask for me to stay another week." I continued, "I would be happy to stay and help, but what about my job and what will mom say?"

Dad said, "Don't worry … I'll talk to both of them and explain how you have become indispensable to #19's family."

#19 and her mom went back to their cottage, while I went up to pack my stuff to bring to #19's cottage. Dad explained to my mom and sister that I was going to stay.

I kissed mom and sis goodbye, and dad gave me some money and told me, "Have a good time … and behave."

I knew exactly what he meant.

Chapter 7
The Beach Week 2

I was numb as I walked over to #19's cottage. I do not know how her mother ever talked my father into allowing me to stay at the beach, alone, for another week. It was blowing my mind.

When I got to #19's cottage, her mom said I could sleep on the daybed on the screened porch. So, I put my stuff out of the way in the corner. Meantime, they were gathering everything for the trip to the beach.

I brought everything down to the beach and set it up. Then, I went over to #20, the umbrella girl. To tell her I was staying another week. She was happy to hear my story and she was happy for me.

"Maybe I could come over and have you for lunch some afternoon," I told her.

#20 smiled and told me, as nicely as possible, that she had a serious boyfriend who was 20 years old, and he worked in a machine shop all day during the week. She told me that she had felt guilty ever since we had gotten together and although it was great with me … she would have to save herself for him. I concurred with her, but she never stopped flirting with me every time she would see me.

I set up my umbrella and blanket, then, laid down for a rest. As I reflected on how lucky I was, a shadow came over me. I opened my eyes to see a really hot girl, with an incredible tan and a sumptuous body, looking down on me. She asked, "Do you need some tanning lotion?"

Since my official Sunscreen Appliers had gone home, I would need some lotion … so I said, "Sure."

She kneeled on my blanket, and I looked at her selection, before I made my choice. A bottle of SPF 15, coconut smelling oil. She wore the smallest bikini on the beach and she had just the right body for it. Her jet-black hair framed her bright white smile. I guessed she was about 20 years old.

I asked, "Now, who is going to put this on me?"

"I take a break about two o'clock and I go back to my trailer for an hour. If you would like, I could fit you in then," was her reply.

"Great … I will meet you in front of the donut shop at two," I said.

She was right on time, and we walked several blocks to the field where her trailer was kept. It was small, clean and adequate, but it was warm, baking in the sun all day. As we entered, she turned on a fan … it really helped. I sat on a chair at the table, and she came over and sat in my lap. "We don't have much time," she informed me. Then, she started to kiss me. She seemed very experienced. Her lips were full and very soft. Her tongue, curious. As we kissed, she ran her fingers through my hair. It felt great! I had one hand on her back and the other on her tummy and I was moving both hands in circles. I reached for her breast which were a nice size and very muscular. Her nipples were rock hard. My other hand untied her bikini to so that I could slip my hand beneath the fabric. She took my head and put it on one of her nipples. Then, she moaned as my lips and tongue went to work, she said, "Let's get out of our suits and into the bed."

The bed was not made from the night before, but it was comfy. Knowing that I liked the smell of coconut, she picked up a bottle of coconut oil and poured it on my crotch with one hand, while she started to massage the oil on my genitals with the other. She was very, very good and in no time, I had a raging erection. Then, she laid on her back, motioning for me to get on top of her. "Missionary style," I said, "you're not ready yet."

She replied, "I have been horny for you all day!"

So, I got up, put on a condom and kneeled between her legs. With one hand I spread her hairless labia and with the other hand I applied copious amounts of the oil. Then, I slid the head of my erection around her clitoris … she moaned in approval. Then, I pushed my shaft up and down between her love lips … she was enjoying all of this. Next, I slid into her love canal for a few strokes (the missionary position). #28 was really moaning. I made a few slow strokes, then a few fast strokes. #28 started to meet my thrust with thrusts of her own … it felt great!

I bent forward and started to suck on her nipples. Alternating, one for a minute or so, then the other. Then, I supported myself with one hand and slid the other under her butt and started to squeeze her butt cheek while pumping very fast. I started to orgasm and midway through so did #28. I was done way before she was, but I continued to stroke until #28's climax was complete. When #28 was done, she said, "Okay … now let's get back to work … that was a great quickie," very matter-of-factly.

We got up, dressed and back to the beach so that #28 could sell her lotions. I went into the water and swam out to where it was deep, so that I could push down my bathing suit and wash off the coconut oil. Then, I swam back, went to my blanket and took a nap.

******

When I awoke, I headed over to help #19's mom to carry everything back to their cottage. "Boy, you smell good enough to eat," both mother and aunt told me.

I explained during our long walk to their cottage that I had purchased some coconut oil sunscreen, which was what they probably smelled.

#19's mom and aunt prepared an excellent dinner, and I complimented them a number of times. They really liked the fact that someone complimented the food, and they pointed it out to all the kids at the table.

While the mom and the aunt cleaned the dishes, #19 and I went out for the evening to do our thing. Following my past routine, I headed for the beach to put my towel between the little boats on the sand and #19 told me that she would meet me at the arcade.

When I got to the arcade, #19 was nowhere to be found … what's new. All of my friends from the previous week were gone and the arcade was populated with all new faces. I just needed to make some new acquaintances.

It wasn't long before I came across a really pretty, petite, brunette, wearing a short, denim skirt and light blue polka dot tube top … she was showing a lot of skin and she caught my eye. She had super nice legs and nice size breasts, and the rest of the package was very nice as well. Her eyes were a beautiful color of blue.

As I approached, I said, "You have the most beautiful eyes that I have ever seen."

She blushed and replied, "Give me a break … I bet you say that to all of the girls."

"You are right … I say that to all the girls I meet, even if they have brown or green eyes," was my retort. She had a bubbly personality and I liked that. I went on, "You know, honestly, I was here at the beach all last week and I never said that to anyone, I'll bet you get complimented by lots of people."

She looked at me seriously and said, "You're right ... many men and women have told me that."

"And your eyes are actually not your best feature," I followed up (now that was a line).

"Really!" she responded. "What do you think my best feature is?" She asked as she brought her hands up under her breasts.

"I would say ... your beautiful face ... or your bubbly personality."

She looked very pleased with my response, and I think she was at a loss for words. So, I continued, "Is this your first day at the beach?"

"Yea ... first night, we didn't get here until late afternoon."

I looked into her beautiful eyes and said, "I was just like you last week, but by the end of the week, I had hundreds of friends. You are my first this week."

"So, your parents booked a cottage for two weeks?"

I explained that last week I had spent with my family but this week I was staying with a family that I befriended. The family consisted of a mom, an aunt and four children. The father did not come to the beach and the family had a cottage way up the street. So, I carried all of their junk down to the beach and back to their cottage each day. They found it so helpful that they asked me to stay with them and continue to help them this week. She was impressed.

"Would you like to go down and see the beach?" I asked.

"Let's go."

It was just getting dark as we reached the beach. We left our shoes next to the boardwalk and strolled down to the water's edge. She started to hold my hand ... we walked very slowly along the beach. Talking about where we live and what we do at home. I asked if she was a cheerleader, she said she was and then I didn't need to say a thing. She did all of the talking.

We walked about a mile and then turned back. During this time, we transitioned from holding hands, to my arm around her shoulder and her arm around my waist. All of a sudden, I stopped walking, looked into her eyes and asked, "Would you mind if I kissed you?"

She smiled very widely and replied, "I'd love it!"

We faced each other, I bent over, and she stood on her tiptoes and we kissed ... surprisingly passionately for a first kiss. She was the aggressor with the tongue. She put her hand behind my head and ran her fingers through my hair

… how did she know that I loved that? My hands were on the silky skin of her shoulder blades. We alternated walking and kissing until we approached where the small rental boats were stored. It was very romantic on the beach, and we were in the mood.

I asked, "If you would like a little more privacy, I know of a place on these boats."

She nodded, so I led her to a boat, but the bottom was still sort of wet. So, I gave her a seat on the only dry spot. It was on the back corner of the boat, she sat with one leg next to the side and the other next to the transom. I sat on a damp spot next to her and we went back to kissing. We were both kind of worked up, sexually.

She started to caress my crotch, so I put my hand on her leg and as we kissed, I slowly slid it up her thigh and under her skirt. It was fortuitous that she was sitting on the back corner of the boat, for that caused her to spread her legs, in a position that I could easily reach second base … to my amazement she was not wearing any underpants. ZINGO! That always gets me excited. I gently stroked my fingers over her love lips. She was moaning and kissing me. When I started to part her love lips with my finger, she stopped kissing me and asked, "I thought you said you had somewhere that is private?"

"I do," I said and gestured toward the towel between the boats. I stood up and led her there.

We laid on our sides and resumed kissing. She was sexy, kissing my neck and ears. Then, she pulled my fly down and reached in for my manhood, as I slipped my finger between her love lips, and I started to stroke … It wasn't very slippery, so I put a glob of saliva on my fingertip and spread it around her love nest. When I pushed my finger into her love canal, she would rotate her hips toward me. As I slid my finger out, she would rotate her hips back. Eventually, as I pulled my finger out, I stopped at her special spot and circled it with my fingertip. She held her breath. I started to tap it gently with my fingertip and she started to moan, "OH YES! OH YES! OH YES! OH YES!"

In the meantime, she had managed to extradite my erection from my pants, and she was pumping it expertly. I went back to circling my fingertip on her special spot and she said, "Put it in!"

As I put my condom on, she laid on her back and pulled her skirt up over her waist. I entered her missionary style. Then, I bent over to push up #29's top so I could caress and fondle her breasts, but she stopped me … she said that she was uncomfortable taking off her top on the beach. So, I just bent over and started to kiss #29 as I pumped in and out. #29 picked up the cadence and started to raise her pelvis to meet each of my strokes. I found this very sensuous (when the girl participates … rather than just lay there). It turned me on more and more. #29 reached behind me and started to caress my butt cheeks and say, "Give it to me hard … faster … faster!" Rubbing my butt wicked turns, me on.

I looked down at #29's face and I could see that she was already having an orgasm and I started to climax just moments later. We were both panting. I continued pumping for a while, then I pulled it out and we quickly got dressed and I walked her back to her cottage.

After I kissed #29 goodnight, I asked her to join me on the beach the next day.

Then, I rushed back to #19's cottage, I didn't want to keep her mom up.

******

When I got to the cottage, #19 wasn't home yet. The mom asked where #19 was and I explained that we were in two different groups at the arcade and we got split up. Fortunately, we only had to wait fifteen minutes before #19 returned.

After #19's mom and aunt put their kids to bed, they would retreat to the porch and drink rye and ginger. That night, they were both a little tipsy. As it got later, I think they realized that I couldn't go to bed until they did, since I was using the daybed to sleep in. So, we all said goodnight and they went to their upstairs bedrooms. I made the daybed and laid on top of the covers to cool off (I sleep in my boxers).

It was pretty quiet, just the sound of tree crickets and the waves crashing on the shore in the distance, and it was very dark, just a bit of light from the streetlight several cottages away made it to the porch, filtered through the trees.

Once I cooled down, I covered myself with just a sheet. I laid there on my back, hands behind my head, staring at the ceiling, contemplating how lucky I was to have met so many terrific girls in the past eight days, and for the incredible sex. Just mind-blowing.

Over an hour passed. As I was just starting to doze off, I heard a squeaking noise from the threshold of the door to the cottage. I had wondered if #19 would come and 'visit' me in the middle of the night. As her shadow moved closer, I could tell that it wasn't #19. It was #19's mom, wearing a terry cloth bathrobe.

She bent down beside my bed and as she bent over to put her face close to mine, one of her hands slid under my top sheet and traveled ever so delicately up my thigh, into my boxers and around my penis. Then, as she gave my penis a tender squeeze, she whispered very softly, "I just wanted to make sure that everything was ok down here."

I was completely stunned … almost in shock … I couldn't move … except for my penis, which was growing into a rocket, from her touching it. Smugly, I replied, "I'm doing fine … now that you are here."

She lowered her lips to mine and started to kiss me, as she gently stroked my manhood several times. It gave me a raging erection. She stopped kissing and whispered, "I was just lying in my bed and all I could think of was you down here." Then, she pushed back the sheet and pulled down my boxers and while she was holding my erection straight up, in the dim light, I could see her lowering her head toward it. First, her moist tongue came out to circle the head and to tease the little piece of skin that attaches the foreskin to the head. I don't think that I have ever had a bigger erection than at that moment and I think she was impressed. She murmured, "UMMM!" Then, she pulled my foreskin down with one hand as her soft lips encircled the head of my erection, then she sucked it into her mouth as far as she could. I was wrong … it had just gotten bigger than ever before!

She just made two magical trips up and down, then pulled her head off it, stood up and took off her robe. Even though there was very little light, I could see that she was naked. Her long brown hair cascaded down her back, her very large breasts still stuck out very nicely, her tummy was fairly flat, with a full triangle of pubic hair between her longish curvy legs … very nice for a woman of her age (I was guessing 36-38).

I still had not moved a muscle, I hadn't taken a breath and I don't think my heart had made a beat since she knelt beside me and touched my penis. I laid there like a log, with my hands behind my head … mesmerized … not knowing what I should do.

She effortlessly lifted one foot and put it on the mattress next to my far side, then she knelt over my crotch, facing me. She had a bottle of lube oil in one hand … it must have come from the pocket of her robe. She squirted some oil along my engorged shaft and between her love lips. Then she lowered herself down on top of my shaft, with one love lip on each side of it, and she slid forward so far that my erection popped up like a spring behind her. She reached back and pushed it down and slid back until the head of my erection was caught by the top of her love lips … she paused there and moaned, "OHHHHHHHH!" Then, she started to slide back and forth. I could see the intense pleasure on her face as her motions stroked her clitoris along my swollen shaft.

I still had not moved a muscle … not knowing what to do or what she was going to do next … but at this point I started to get a pretty good idea. So, when she leaned forward to put more pressure on her clitoris, I reached up and took her beautiful breasts into my hands. I started to softly squeeze and caress them. She murmured, "UMMMMMMM!" Just the opposite of her daughter, she liked me to handle her breasts. I took one breast into mouth and started to suck on her extra-large nipple. WOW! Then, I started to slide my free hand up and down the silky-smooth skin on her back. She seemed to like what I was doing (I know that I was super enjoying it!). So, as I gently nibbled on her nipple, I slid my hand down to her butt and decided to slide my middle finger down her butt crack to her vagina, not stopping to think that I would come to her butt hole first. I stopped at her butt hole and circled it very slowly with my fingertip … she must have liked it … she stopped breathing and slid way forward, so I could reach behind her better. As I pressed my fingertip into her hole up to my first knuckle, she slid back to rub her clit on the tip of my erection and then she froze in that position … while her body started to shiver.

I wasn't sure what was happening … was she having some sort of fit or something? I just continued to do what I was doing. Once the shivers passed, she started to move again and she slid way back, bent down and took my head into her hot hands and kissed me … thankfully. Then, she reached over and opened the end table drawer and removed a condom. Incredibly quickly, she opened the package and slid the condom down over my erection, like a professional. It felt so good that she almost made me orgasm … I was just holding back as best as I could.

Next, a squirt or two of lube oil and then she squatted on her feet, she held my love rod straight up as she lowered herself down onto it until the head of my swollen member disappeared into her. Ever so slowly she slid down … down … down, until she bottomed out. There is no more intense feeling than that feeling … FANTASTIC! #30 evidently concurred since she grunted,

"OHHHHH YESSSSS!" Then, she raised herself up … then down again (the cowgirl position). I reached up and started to fondle her breasts … squeezing her nipples … #30 was smiling widely. I don't know how I kept from coming … I just held back to wait for her … then, she had another attack … #30 froze, with me half in her. So, I started to bounce up and down, pushing into her as deeply as I could, then pulling almost all the way out. Like a jackhammer, I bounced. Then, she started to shiver again … I felt so sorry for her … just when we were both really getting hot … she must have some sort of disease!

When her 'episode' was over, #30 bent over and asked me if I had climaxed. I said, "Not yet."

#30 shook her head, smiled widely and said, "Good!" Then, she turned around, with my erection still inside of her, so that her head was toward my feet and she started to pump her hips up and down on my erection, which was bent far more forward than I would ever believe it could be bent, in its hardened condition (the reverse cowgirl position). Boy oh boy! It felt super intense, and I loved it! I didn't want to lie there doing nothing, so I reached for her butt and started to squeeze #30's butt cheeks. Then, I noticed the bottle of lube oil on the bed. I picked it up and squirted some on my shaft … it seemed to slide in much easier.

Then, boldly, I squirted some in #30's butt crack, stuck my middle finger between her cheeks and it slid right into her butt hole (I think it must have been open in that position). #30 loved it! As she would slide down my shaft, my finger would slide into her and as she raised herself, my finger would slide out. I could feel #30 tightening and loosening her butt on my finger. #30 quickened the pace more and more. I just couldn't hold back any longer. As I started to climax, I pushed into #30, as she bottomed out. PUSH … PUSH … PUSH! Then, darn #30 had another 'episode' of the shivers … I just couldn't stop … I had to keep pumping as I succumbed to the looooongest, most inteeeeeeense orgasm ever … I felt it from the top of my head to the tip of my toes … UNBELEIVABLE!

As my body relaxed, so did #30's. She raised up off my softening erection and my finger, stood on the floor, bent over and gave me a very soft, gentle kiss. Then, #30 whispered in my ear, "Thank you, Tony … I needed that!"

I whispered back, "The pleasure was all mine," as I smiled.

#30 put the bottle of lube oil in the end table drawer, quietly slipped back into her robe and sauntered off to her bedroom upstairs.

I just laid there on my back contemplating what had just happened. Was I dreaming? No, I pinched myself. I was awake. Very awake! I just could not believe how everyone seems to be having sex at the beach … everyone!

My sense is that people get horny from the sun beating on them, the sight of others in their skimpy bathing suits, from the freedom that they feel that their sex partner is not from their town and nobody at home will find out. Whatever it is … it works for me … at 16 years old, I have never been more pleased.

******

The next morning, I was up early as usual. There were no shades on the porch, so I awoke to the bright shine of the sun.

While everyone else in the cottage asleep, I went down and set up my place on the beach, bought a newspaper, went back to the donut shop for a warm donut and got three coffees to go. One for me, one for the aunt and one for #30, #19 didn't drink coffee. … only healthy food entered her body, or should I say, 'The Temple'.

When I got back to the cottage, everyone was in the kitchen, except for #30. The aunt was making pancakes for everyone and said that her sister probably had too much to drink the night before and was sleeping it off.

The aunt was so pleased that I had brought her a 'real' coffee. She couldn't stop thanking me.

Just as we were all finished eating the pancakes, #30 arrived. She walked in looking only half awake. The aunt gave her the coffee that I had brought for her and #30 took the cover off the cup, holding the cup as if it were gold, took a drink and as it went down her throat, she moaned in delight. Looking at me with a twinkle in her eye, #30 said, "Tony … thank you … I needed that!"

I wasn't sure if she meant the coffee or what we had done in the middle of the night. I just smiled at her and replied, "I just try to please."

While everyone else got ready, I went back to the donut shop, to get away from the small children screaming.

As I drank my coffee, I saw a beautiful, thin, young lady exiting the grocery store carrying two full bags of groceries … well, we can't have that. So, I ran over and volunteered to carry her groceries home for her. Of course, she was very pleased and handed them right over to me.

She had a delightful personality and we talked as we walked. She told me that she had come with her sorority for the week. Surprisingly, she was staying in the same cottage that a different sorority had stayed in the previous week. She told me that the owner was tied in with the national association that her sorority belonged to and that the cottage was rented to a different sorority each week, during the summer … very good information for someone like me to know!

When we arrived at the cottage, I stayed only long enough to meet the rest of the girls. Then, I had to excuse myself to run back to #30's cottage and carry everything down to the beach.

When everything was set up, I went back to my blanket, laid in the shade and fell asleep. I must have slept for two or three hours and when I awoke, the entire beach was packed with people. There was hardly any room to walk between the blankets to get to the water. Sundays are the busiest time at the beach. You have all of the vacationers, plus all types of people have the day off from work. And … it was HOT! The heat really brings out a crowd to cool off in the water.

I went for a dip and a swim, then back to my blanket. I really enjoyed watching all the various activities on the beach … especially with a large crowd. By mid-afternoon, I was getting restless. I got up determined to take a walk. So, I walked over to the sorority cottage to see what was happening there. I half expected to not find anyone there because it was so hot, but fortunately the girl that I had carried the groceries for was there.

She was happy to see me. It was her job to cook dinner for the girls and she was just about to start the oven to bake a roast. I suggested that she use the grill outside to cook the roast since it was stifling hot and turning on the oven would just make the kitchen that much hotter.

So, as I filled the grill with charcoal and started the fire, she prepared the potatoes and veggies in aluminum foil packages. We put the roast on a rotisserie and everything else on the rack, covered it and let the meal cook.

Then, we went inside for a drink of cold soda. The girl was really impressed with my cooking ability plus the fact that I took the time to help her out. Of course, I was happy to help … that's what I do … I try to do everything that I can to help females. Mom would be proud.

The girl really intrigued me. She was tall, thin and had a very 'narrow' build. Her shoulders and hips were not very wide, yet she had fairly large breasts. How does that happen? I don't know but I am happy it happens.

When she brought me the soda, I was leaning with my backside against the counter. She leaned against me with a big smile and handed me the glass. I could tell she was looking for a kiss, so I obliged her. UMMMMM! She was a great kisser. As we kissed, she started to press her pelvis against mine and gyrate. "Tony … you always know what I need," she said.

Thinking I knew where she was coming from, I replied, "I try to please." I gave her a small kiss on the lips and asked, "Can you show me where you sleep?"

"Sure!" She replied with a gleaming smile. She took off her apron and with just her two-piece bathing suit on she led me upstairs to her bedroom. We stood next to her bed kissing. I cupped her butt cheeks and softly caressed them. She appeared to like what I was doing and she pressed her body against me.

We laid down on top of the covers of her neatly made bed and I started to massage her back with both hands as we continued to kiss passionately. Next, I unhooked her top and slid one hand under it … she did not stop me, so I slid my hand around front to cup her breast. She leaned away from me to give me more room. Her breast was solid, with a soft exterior, with a tiny, taut nipple. I lifted her top up and replaced my hand with my lips. At first, I just circled the nipple with my tongue. Then, slowly I increased the size of the circles and ultimately, I sucked the nipple into my mouth.

Simultaneously, my free hand caressed its way down her tummy and between her legs. At first, I just applied some soft pressure with my fingers and a soft caress. Then, she reached down and unhooked her bottom from each side, opening it up completely. I could see a thin, neatly coiffured landing strip of hair leading to her love lips. I slid my middle finger down over the hair and directly between her labia. She gasped. After several very dry strokes, I brought my finger to my mouth for some saliva, then directly back between her lips. The saliva was the perfect lubricant and my finger moved frictionless up, down and around. (It is very important not to continue to rub anyone's skin when it is dry … the skin can become irritated and sore. Therefore, some sort of lubricant is required when the skin is dry.)

She reached down with one hand and tried to get it under the waistband of my bathing suit which was too tight, so she just started to rub my manhood through the fabric of the suit. We continued for a while, then she asked, "Let's put it in."

"In a minute," I mumbled. As I moved down to put my head between her legs. With my hands, I spread her legs as my tongue parted her moist love lips. After several strokes, up and down my tongue began to circle her clitoris. She really responded by grabbing the sheets with both hands and moaning rather loudly. I effortlessly pushed my finger into her very wet vagina and as I did, I slipped the tip of my tongue ever so gently, under the skin covering her clit (the Hood). As I moved the tip of my tongue back and forth, she started to orgasm … violently. She started to almost scream with pleasure, so she held the pillow tightly against her mouth to muffle the sound. It was exciting to me to get this kind of response … I really enjoy giving a gal pleasure like this, but I was not used to having the girl scream … it really turned me on!

"Oh … Tony, that was really incredible!" She was panting and sweating profusely. She reached down for my head and brought my face to hers for a passionate, thankful kiss. She seemed oblivious to the fact that my lips were covered with her love juice. As we kissed, I tried to continue to stroke her clit but she squeezed her legs together and turned her pelvis to dissuade me (her clit was probably too sensitive to touch at that moment). She reached down and started to tug at my bathing suit … trying to remove it. I obliged her by sliding it off. When she saw my enormous erection, she gasped, "Ohhhh … Tonnnny … how beautiful!" I blushed.

Then, she took my erection in both hands and started to stroke the head back and forth across her nipples … it felt too good! After driving me wild for a while, she put my stiff rod between her breasts, pushed them together around my erection and she started to bounce up and down … the softness of her breasts and her enthusiasm for what she was doing could not have been more sensual … it was every guy's dream … of course, it almost made me climax and I had to stop her by saying, "That is fantastic!" As I pulled my erection away from her … just in time. "Let me put on a condom." Then, I frantically grabbed my bathing suit to get a condom and get it on … I thought I would burst!

When I turned, she was lying on the bed with an approving smile on her face. She quickly spread her legs and I positioned myself between them (the missionary position). She was very tight but well lubricated. I pushed into her very slowly and she started to squeal and moan, loudly again. #31 had to hold the pillow against her mouth to muffle the sound … but it was still pretty loud. I lifted her legs up and started to pump slowly in and out … #31 screamed with pleasure every time I pushed in.

Then, I decided to try it with #31 on her side, so I put one leg down and straddled it, while I lifted the other leg straight up, without disengaging from her vagina (the split leg position). It felt like I could penetrate #31 much deeper, and #31 screamed into the pillow, "Yes Tony … Yes Tony … Yes Tony … Yes Tony!"

I reached over and started to caress her breasts with one hand and caress her butt cheeks with the other. We were getting hotter and hotter! Then, I got the idea to slid my finger down her butt crack. I first moistened my finger tip with a copious amount of saliva, then I slid it down #31's butt crack. As my finger made its descent, #31 pushed her pelvis more and more forward, so that I penetrated her far more than I would think possible. When my finger arrived at her butt hole, #31 pulled her head out of the pillow, looked me in the eye and said, "No! I don't do that!"

It had its desired effect though. That is, even if a girl does not like 'anal', just touching or approaching to touch their butt hole makes them hotter. Plus, it has the same effect on me. The closer I get to the butt hole, the hotter I get.

This case was no exception and touching her butt hole brought both of us to the point of no return. I started to pump very quickly and #31 rocked into each of my thrusts. #31 started to climax seconds before me. I loved this position, because I love the feeling of my scrotum sliding back and forth along her smooth, soft inner thigh … it makes me even hotter! My orgasm was incredibly powerful, and long.

I kept stroking slower and slower until we were both done. Then, #31 put the leg that was sticking up flat on the bed and reached for my head so that she could bring my face to hers and we started to kiss passionately again. We kissed until my erection started to subside and I was afraid we might get 'leakage' from the condom. So, I pulled out and started to clean up. #31 immediately started to kiss and caress my neck and shoulders, saying, "WOW … Tony … that was FANTASTIC!" Her voice and her hands were now extremely soft and delicate. As I dressed, #31 could not take her hands off me. She continued to compliment me and caress me … it was extremely nice and I appreciated it.

Finally, I said, "You better get dressed and we better check on the supper … the other girls should be here any time now."

That brought #31 back to reality and she replied, "You're right … but I really enjoyed that!"

"So did I!"

We checked the food on the grill … it was cooking just right.

Then, I hurried down to the beach and arrived just in time to help carry everything back to #30's cottage.

While #30 and the aunt prepared dinner, I went back to the beach, which was now sparsely populated, to take a dip, cool off and stow my stuff.

******

At dinner #30 asked what I had done all day. I said, "Mostly laid on my blanket … there were so many people on the beach it was almost impossible to walk to the water."

#30 laughed and said, "Yes, there were a lot of people out there today."

After dinner, I took off for the arcade. I wasn't there long before #31 showed up, all happy and smiley. She was looking mighty good. Wearing a small bright blue halter top and short white shorts. She was looking for me.

"Tony … you are a genius," she yelled across the arcade. As she reached me, her face was beaming as she said, "The dinner was a big success! All of the girls loved it and I told them it was your idea."

"I shouldn't get all of the credit … you did most of the work … I only helped a little."

"No … you should get all of the credit … you were magnificent this afternoon!" She said rather loudly.

I laughed and replied, "You know, it takes two to tango."

#31 snuggled right up to me, front side to front side. Pushed her pelvis against mine and said, very softly, "I would like to tango again … right now!"

Her body was warm, soft and she smelled great! "Let's go for a walk outside," I said. #31 agreed and with her clinging to me, we started to walk toward the beach. "Where would you like to go?" I asked.

#31 replied, "We can't go to the cottage, several of the girls got too much sun today and they are not going out tonight."

"I have a place on the beach that we can go, if you would like."

"I'd love it!" #31 answered.

When we reached the water's edge, we started to kiss. #31 sucked my tongue out of my mouth, was rubbing up against me as she ran her fingers through my hair and caressed my neck and shoulders. She was really wound up and ready to go.

#31 asked, "Is your place far from here?"

"Not far," I replied. She couldn't wait to do it again. So, I led her to my place between the boats. It was a dark, clear night with just the light of the moon … very romantic … but I don't think that #31 noticed … she was really hot!

We both lay on our sides on the big beach towel and resumed kissing. #31 reached down and started to stroke my manhood. Then she asked, "Will you be able to do it again … after what we did this afternoon?"

I chuckled and answered, "I believe so … I am usually ready to go again in ten minutes." #31 looked impressed and happy as she started to be the aggressor. Again, she sucked my tongue into her mouth while she pulled down my fly. Then, she reached into my boxers for the one thing she needed from me. It only took a few strokes, skin on skin for me to produce an excellent erection. I untied her halter top, pushed it up and burrowed beneath with my lips. #31's breasts were red hot with passion and she gasped as I sucked her nipple into my mouth and flicked at it with the tip of my tongue. #31 let go of my pulsing rod, just long enough to push her shorts off. Then, she tried to unbuckle my belt, to get my jeans off. I took the hint and stopped groping her breasts to remove my pants.

"Let's put it in," #31 said immediately. She may have been the same laidback girl that I had sex with this afternoon but tonight she was a possessed love goddess, who wouldn't be denied!

"Ok … in a minute." Then, my lips went back to work and her breasts and my hand between her legs. Her labia were on fire! It couldn't be wetter or more inviting. #31 was stroking my stiff shaft like a pro (in other words, with enthusiasm). I decided to go along with the flow. Therefore, I put a condom on and positioned myself between #31's legs. As I moved forward to enter her, she pulled her knees up toward her chest. I could see her love canal open up in the dim moon light and it was glistening from her love juice. I slid right in and put her feet against my chest … I grabbed her knees and as I spread her knees apart, I pushed into her (what a view) … as I withdrew, I pushed her knees back together (the butterfly position).

Ever so slowly, I pushed my stiff rod into her love canal, feeling her tightening and loosening her love canal; I started to tighten and loosen the muscles of my shaft in unison with #31. She started to moan … "That's it, that's great!"

Once I fully penetrated her, I pulled out until the crown on the head of my love rod was at her G-spot. Then, without moving anything else, I started to tighten and loosen the muscles of my shaft, slowly at first, then faster and faster. Within minutes #31's body started to convulse, she pulled her knees tight against her chest and I could see her face tighten in what looked like pain but was really intense pleasure. It was difficult to resist the impulse to stroke in and out, but I continued to just tighten and loosen the muscles of my shaft … and #31 continued to orgasm for quite a while.

As #31's climax came to an end, she spread her knees further apart and I lowered my head to kiss her. Fortunately, my tongue was firmly attached or #31 would have sucked it completely off! Then, she grabbed my butt cheeks and pulled me into her extremely hot, wet, still pulsing vagina. #31 stopped kissing me and asked, "Did you climax?"

I said, "No."

She smiled and said, "Great! … now I want it hard, I want it fast and I want it deep!"

She didn't have to ask me twice for I started to thrust … harder and faster … all the way in and all the way out. It felt amazing to me, and I could see by the smile on her face that the feeling was mutual. Without missing a stroke, I bent over to kiss her and as our lips met, I sucked the air from her lungs into mine … she moaned and instantly started to climax again. I could feel her love canal tighten and grab my penis and start to secrete even more of her love juice. This encouraged me to climax as well.

When we were done, we were both exhausted.

#31 told me that she had never had such wonderful, magnificent sex … she didn't always have a climax with other fellas and never had more than one climax in a night. With me, she had had the longest most powerful orgasms and she had multiple orgasms … a total of four powerful orgasms in one day … with that said, she pulled my face to hers and gave me a long passionate kiss.

Then, we put our clothes back on and walked back to her cottage … kissing from time to time.

At her cottage, we kissed goodnight, and I was on my way back to #19's cottage.

******

As I approached #19's cottage, I could see #30 sitting in a chair on the screened-in porch, reading a book and drinking (whisky and ginger ale) by the light of the table lamp.

When I entered the porch, #30 seemed very happy to see me. She said that she was home alone with only the small children. Her sister had gotten all dressed up and had gone out to find a man.

#30 asked me how my night had been going and I told her that I had spent my time in the arcade with friends. I noticed that day's newspaper on the other chair, so I sat down to read the paper.

About 20 minutes passed and #19 came in, said she was beat and went up to her bedroom.

When the clothes dryer in the kitchen stopped, #30 put down her book and went into the kitchen and returned with a basket of beach towels, which she dumped onto the daybed. Then she put the basket on the chair she had been sitting in and as she folded each towel, she put it into the basket. When she was done, #30 smiled at me, said goodnight and headed for her bedroom (I wondered if she was preparing to come down later).

I went into the first-floor bathroom to wash off my lower extremities, just in case. Then, with the lights off on the porch, I stripped down to my shorts and turned down the daybed and I laid on my back with my hands behind my head … waiting to see if, when, #30 would come down to visit me.

I laid there for about 45 minutes, just letting the cool night air wash over my body before #19's aunt came in. I could smell her perfume as soon as she walked in the door.

She asked, "Are you up?"

I replied, "Yes."

As she walked toward me, I could see that she was wearing high heels (which she took off at the door), a tight blue short skirt, a small pale yellow halter top (to show off her assets), and bright red lipstick. She looked gorgeous!

She kneeled down on the floor next to my pillow—gosh, she smelled good!—and she asked me how I was doing. I replied, "Great!"

She frowned and said, "I had a terrible night … after listening to my sister boast, all day, about her session with you last night, I went to the three bars in town tonight and couldn't find even one, single, decent looking guy, to satisfy my itch for an orgasm … I haven't had one in the last six months and my sister is bragging that she had 3 with you last night … do you think you could help a suffering girl out?"

I replied, "I would be happy to try."

The aunt smiled widely, stood up, took a beach towel from the basket and went into the cottage and in minutes returned, wrapped in the beach towel. Still with the big red smile, as she approached me, she removed the beach towel and let it drop to the floor.

Voila … at 27, she still had a magnificent body! She was shorter than #30, but more athletic, smaller breasts (but still outstanding), a flat tummy and spectacular legs, with a small brown V of pubic hair … now I was smiling widely. I couldn't resist whispering, "You are beautiful … from head to toe!"

She kneeled down next to my bed and as she learned forward to give me a short kiss, she reached back to my groin to fondle my semi-erect penis. Then, she turned, still on her knees and pushed my boxers down, to fully expose my now stiff erection. She grasped the shaft and gave it a slight squeeze, then she looked back into my eyes and whispered, "My, you are … a big boy!"

I chuckled and replied, "All the better to please you!"

She opened up her pocketbook that she had left next to my bed and removed a condom and a small bottle of lube oil, which she put on the edge of the bed. Then, she pulled my boxers off, lifted up my erection and covered the head with her mouth. She circled the head with her tongue several times, then she slowly lowered her head … sucking my love stick further and further in … I was ecstatic!

Then she gripped my shaft tightly with her lips and as she brought her head up, she teasingly wagged her tongue back and forth across the underside of my erection … FANTASTIC!

Then, she took the bottle of lube oil and poured a line of (cold) oil along my shaft. Next, she poured a copious quantity of the lube oil into her hand and rubbed it around on her labia … in an instant she was straddling me and lowering her labia down onto my erection. As she slid forward, she looked down at me and said, "My sister said this was fabulous!"

I was speechless … I reached up to fondle her breasts … she leaned forward to help in that regard. I could feel her erect clitoris as she sort of slipped it back and forth across the tip of my erection … she said, "Oooooh yeeess … that is going to do it!"

I could feel her knees squeezing in against my sides, so I started to squeeze her nipples between my thumbs and index fingers … she slid even further up my erection until the head caught the top of her love lips and as she pressed down, with renewed strength … she moved back and forth in very short quick strokes in a tugging motion … I reached down and gabbed the cheeks of her butt and spread them apart and she lowered herself down to kiss me … I immediately sucked the air from her lungs and held it … she started to orgasm … then she sucked the air back into her lungs, held it, before I sucked the air back into my lungs … she never stopped rubbing/tugging against the tip of my erection … I could feel her stomach tightening and loosing as her body convulsed … finally I felt her body relax. She broke suction with my lips and whispered gently, "That … was outstanding … even better than my sister said!"

I just smiled and as she laid on top of me … resting. I started to caress her luscious butt and the soft, smooth skin on her back … she moaned.

Finally, she pushed herself up into a seated position, slid back and forth a few times, then, she slid all the way back off my erection, which popped up like a spring as she slid off … we both chuckled. She reached over and picked up the condom, opened the package and put the condom onto my stiffer than ever erection (I almost came).

Next, she lifted herself up onto her feet, held my erection straight up and lowered her, incredibly wet, love canal down, down, down onto my love stick. All the time, looking straight up and moaning, "Yes … yes … yes!"

I pushed up into her, as well and she leaned forward to support herself with her arms … she made several long thrusts, before she shortened her thrusts with the head of my penis against her G-spot … I reached up to fondle her breasts and simultaneously I started to tighten and loosen the muscles in my penis, which made it enlarge and contract against her special spot. #32 said, "You are doing it again!"

"What?" was my reply.

"Just the right thing," she said. Then she started to pump back and forth wildly, as her face contorted, her abdomen tightened and loosened in rhythmic convulsions, while her vagina grabbed my erection tightly as she continued to pump in and out violently!

I don't know how I held off from ejaculating … except that I had just had fantastic sex hours before.

When #32's body started to relax, she asked, "Did you come?"

I replied, "Not yet."

She whispered, "Great!"

Then she reversed her position, facing my feet and took my engorged erection and slid it back into her very moist, very warm vagina (the reverse cowboy position). Very similar to the cowboy position, but with an entirely different feeling and an entirely different view.

She started to sway in and out and moan. Soon she leaned forward and supported the upper part of her body with her arms, between my legs. I don't think my erection could bend any farther without breaking. I reached out to caress and spread #32's buttocks apart and I noticed that as she rotated her hips forward, her butt hole opened up and closed as she slid back … it looked like she was winking at me. This got my attention … so I slid my thumb down her butt crack and sort of circled her butt hole. "Ooooooh yes," #32 moaned … so I continued moving my thumb up the crack and back down and around her butt hole. I noticed the lube oil bottle laying on the bed … so I picked it up and poured some down her butt crack … now my thumb slid effortlessly up down and around her butt hole … with my thumb covering her butt hole, I poured more of the oil down her crack and as the oil reached my thumb, I pushed it gently into #32' butt hole. #32 really seemed to be enjoying what I was doing because as she gyrated forward and back, her vagina was gripping my love stick tighter and tighter and she was moaning. She asked, "Can you slip your finger in?"

I replied, "I can try." I was getting more and more excited … not to mention that #32's continual pumping and grinding was driving me wild. I think I would have climaxed if I wasn't distracted by playing with #32's butt hole. So, I gently slipped the tip of my middle finger down #32's crack and when it reached the desired destination, I poured more oil down her crack and as it reached my finger, I sort of tried to push the oil into her anus. I noticed that #32 was holding her breath. Then I poured a little more oil down the crack and as I was sort of working the oil in with the tip of my finger, #32 pushed back, intentionally and my finger slipped in to the first knuckle ... #32 froze for a moment ... then I poured more oil down the crack and pulled my finger almost out and when the oil reached my finger I started to slide my oily finger in, as #32 pushed back simultaneously so that my finger slipped in all the way.

"I love that!" #32 moaned and then she started to slide up my erection all the way to the head (and almost off my finger). Then, back down and fully onto my finger.

#32 started to pump faster and harder and I could feel her vagina and her rectum tightening and loosening as #32 began her third (most powerful) orgasm and with all this stimulation, I climaxed with her ... finally! I had, probably, the longest and my most powerful orgasm of my life ... WOW!

When #32's body started to relax, she extricated her body from mine ... turned over and laid on top of me ... chest to chest and face to face, with her face showing extreme excitement, as she looked me in the eye and asked, "Do you know how to do anal?"

I replied, "I believe so."

#32's smile widened as she asked, "Do you have another condom?"

I replied, "Yes."

She said, "Then let's do it ... I've got to have it!" With that said, #32 climbed off me and picked up the beach towel that she had dropped on the floor earlier and she laid it on the bed when I got up to grab several tissues to remove my used condom. Then, I went over to my slacks, which were on the chair where I had read the newspaper, and retrieved a condom. When I turned around, #32 was right next to me, holding her pocketbook open to pull out a bottle (to my surprise) of 'anal lube'! She whispered, "This is really very slippery!"

#32 handed me the bottle, then, she climbed back onto the bed (on top of the beach towel) on all fours, doggy style ... I knelt behind her and as I started to work the cold anal lube into her butt hole with my middle finger, #32 was right, this lubricant was much thicker and much slipperier than the love oil. #32 began to wiggle her buttocks as I applied more and more of the lube with my middle finger. I reached around with my other hand to manipulate her clitoris ... which I circled with the tip of my finger (she was quite moist). #32 moaned favorably. I worked my middle finger all the way into #32's butt hole and as I did, she pushed backward. I applied more and more of the Anal Lube each time pushing my middle finger all the way in … I noticed that #32 stopped breathing each time I pushed my finger all the way in and it became easier as her anal muscles relaxed. I continued to stroke her clitoris and this time, as I pulled my finger out, I said, "Let's try two fingers."

#32 replied enthusiastically, "Good!"

I put my index finger and middle fingers together and started to work them in with even more lube and #32 turned her head around toward me and smiled in approval. I was pushing my fingers in and simultaneously sliding my finger upwards over her clit … then as I pulled my fingers outwards, I would slide my finger down past #32's clit. She said, "Ok, I am ready!"

It had been a while since I ejaculated and given my manipulations, I was semi-hard. I opened the package and slipped the condom on as I could feel my penis enlarging with enthusiasm. I put copious amounts of the anal lube on my erection, then put the tip against #32's butt hole. I said, "Take a deep breath, then as you push your hips backward, push out like you are trying to poop." #32 pushed backward and her butt hole opened and the head of my erection slipped right in. I said, "Take a few deep breaths and push back again when you're ready." She did and voila, I slid several more inches into her extremely hot anal canal. "Stop there … take several more breaths and then slowly pull out a bit … then in slowly, at your pace."

She did and as her muscles relaxed more and more #32 picked up the pace and I started to pump in and out as well. I couldn't hold off, given the tightness and the warmth and I climaxed. When I was done, I pulled out, got some tissues, and removed my condom.

#32 picked up the beach towel from the floor and wiped the lubricant from her butt and down her thighs … then, she turned toward me and gently wiped the lubricant off my stomach groin and thighs … it felt great! She said, "Can you go again?" as she fondled my scrotum and my penis.

I said, "Of course."

Given my reply, #32 sort of rotated toward me (still on all fours) and took my semi-hard penis into her mouth and started to expertly fellate me, with maximum enthusiasm, while ever so gently massaging my scrotum.

It didn't take long for me to reach maximum stiffness. I hated to have to stop #32 long enough to take a condom out of my backpack and slide it onto my ever-hardening erection.

Meanwhile, #32 turned over and laid on her back with her knees bent and spread apart. I knelt between her thighs, lifted up her feet and put them on my chest, then, pulled her knees apart as I entered her extremely moist love canal … then, as I pulled out, I pushed her knees together … then apart as I pushed all the way in, I looked into her eyes and said, "This is the butterfly position."

She replied, "I love it … now go fast and hard … I am ready to come again!"

So, I started to pump in and out as fast and hard as I could and #32 reached over and grabbed the sheets with both hands and her body started to convulse again … over and over … she arched her body (in pleasure) as I continued to pump fast and hard until #32's body relaxed completely. She looked me in the eye and said, "That was outstanding … you … are magnificent … did you come again?"

I just shook my head, no.

#32 said, "Good, lay here."

So, we changed positions … me lying on my back, on top of the beach towel, and #32 kneeling between my legs. Then, to my complete surprise, #32 removed my condom and replaced it with her mouth … she circled the head with her tongue, stopping underneath where the foreskin is attached to the head and flicking her tongue back and forth and up and down … all the while she had pulled the skin surrounding my erection down and tight (not too tight which would hurt) … I moaned. Next, she started to flick her tongue back and forth on the underside of my hardened shaft … all the way to the base, then, gently down the middle of my scrotum and several times around a testicle … then back up to the head which she started to suck as she started to pump her hand up and down in unison with her mouth. She purposely covered my shaft with her saliva … then pushed my shaft more and more into her mouth and ultimately into her throat, as she took all of my erection into her mouth. She started to pump her head up and all the way down and I warned her, "I am about to come!" To give her time to remove her mouth.

But #32 pushed her head all the way down … sucking my shaft … I think she tried to say, "That's ok." The vibrations in her throat as she tried to speak reverberated in my shaft and caused me to orgasm immediately. My orgasm didn't last long and I don't think I ejaculated a lot since I had just orgasmed a short time before.

Then, #32, without ever taking my member out of her mouth, pulled her head up sucking out leftover ejaculate and when she reached the head, she brought her hand up tightly to squeeze any of my love juice up into her sucking mouth. As she removed her mouth from my member, she reached down for the beach towel on the floor and spit my love juice into the towel; she sort of wiped her tongue and the inside of her mouth off with the towel.

Then, she laid down on her side resting against me. #32 put her hands on each side of my face and gave me a big, wet, salty, French kiss. She said, "That was the most outstanding sex of my life … I have been with many men and married for several years, but I have never had two orgasms in one session and I have never had pleasurable anal sex until tonight … with you … you are an expert!"

I told her, "If you are going to have anal sex in the future, you really should do an enema until clear, to avoid what could be a mess."

"You see … you really are an expert!" She smiled, gave me another short kiss (no tongue), got up, took a clean beach towel from the basket and wrapped it around her body. Then she picked up the beach towel from the floor and the one on the bed as I got up to put on my undershorts. #32 picked up her pocketbook and clothes and on her way off the porch, she said, "I will put these dirty towels in the wash."

After I heard #32 go up the stairs, I went into the first-floor bathroom to pee. Then, I headed to my daybed. I was exhausted.

I lay on my bed thinking how lucky I was and as I tried to relive the details of what had just happened, I fell asleep.

******

The next morning, I got up with the sun, got dressed and went directly to the beach to set up my spot. Then, I stopped at the donut shop to get three coffees and eat a Boston Cream donut. I bought a newspaper and headed back to #19's cottage to deliver the coffees and have breakfast.

#30 and #32 were in the kitchen giggling as I came in the door. I asked, "How is everyone this morning?"

#30 said, "Great."

But #32 said, "I'm tired and sore … I didn't get much sleep last night!"

I said, "You can probably catch up with your sleep on the beach today."

Then, the three of us and the small children had breakfast. #19 came down late and just had a glass of OJ.

Ultimately, I carried the cooler and everything down to the beach and set it all up, before heading to my place on the beach.

I followed my recommendation, to sleep on the beach. I formed the sand beneath my towel into a pillow, laid my head back and dozed off in minutes.

When I awoke, I was refreshed. It was already lunch time. So, I walked down to get a hamburger, fries and an iced tea. Then, I took a dip to cool off and headed back to my spot on the beach.

As I approached my spot, I noticed a rather tall, thin, attractive, blonde girl, talking to #20 (the umbrella girl). I walked over to be introduced. #20 graciously told the blonde that I was the king of the beach and continued to say that the blonde was her best friend and lives up the street. #20 went on to say that the blonde was the best volleyball player in the state.

The blond was very attractive, had a thin athletic body with smallish breasts. She was wearing what I would call 'a string bikini'. It consisted of a very small triangle of blue material covering her groin and another small triangle on her backside, tied together with a blue cord (the front barely covered her pubic area) and there were two more tiny triangles of material covering her nipples, again tied together with a blue cord around her back and another blue cord going around her neck. She had an excellent tan and a very flat, muscular tummy. When the blonde decided to leave, she asked me if I would like to walk her home … of course, walking is my second favorite thing to do.

Little did I know that the blonde lived near the main road, several blocks past #19's cottage. As we walked, the blonde explained that she had already accepted a full scholarship to a big-time west coast college.

I mentioned what a nice tan she had and she told me that her backyard was very private so that she would lay out, on a chaise lounge, nude several hours each day, an hour on each side. The result was that she had an even tan everywhere.

"I'd like to see that!" I replied.

"Wait until we get to my house," she answered.

When we finally arrived at her house, she explained that her parents both had full-time jobs and did not get home until after 5:00pm (which meant that we had plenty of time to do whatever we wanted … I know what I wanted).

In the kitchen, the blonde gave me a beer and leaned in to give me a very nice, soft kiss. I reached around and gently cupped her, mostly naked, butt cheeks and pulled her tightly against my body and deposited a long, wet, French kiss on her.

She moaned, then she said, "Follow me."

We went directly to her bedroom, where she untied and removed her bikini top and bottom. I was sitting on the edge of her bed. She proudly said, "You asked to see my tan!"

I replied, "My eyesight isn't all that good … I am going to need a much closer look."

She walked over and stopped between my legs and an inch from my nose. She was 100% correct … she was tan everywhere … even her armpits. Her nipples directly lined up with my mouth. So, I cupped her now naked butt and pulled her toward me, so that I could circle one taut nipple while gently rubbing the other between my thumb and index finger.

The blonde moaned and leaned into me and after a while she ran her fingers through my hair (I love that). Then she pulled my head back from suckling her nipple and bent over to give me a long passionate kiss. Then, she said, "Loose the bathing suit!"

When I stood up to remove my bathing suit, the blonde lay on the edge of the bed with her feet hanging over the edge. I took out a condom but wasn't physically ready to put it on, so I put it on top of my bathing suit on the floor.

In her present position, it could only mean that she wanted me to perform cunnilingus. (Cunnilingus is the oral stimulation of the female genitalia. Most women highly enjoy it as a form of oral sex.) I was happy to oblige. As I approached and kneeled down next to the bed, the blonde bent her knees and spread them widely.

I started by gently kissing and massaging her inner thighs … she moaned. Next, as I kissed my way toward her vagina, she put one hand down there and with a finger on each side, she spread her labia to expose her clitoris and vaginal canal (she sure knew exactly what she wanted … that is good … I am not a mind reader … but I am a lip reader and her lips are saying; kiss me, lick me, caress me). So, I took the moist tip of my tongue and slid it up one side of her labia around her clitoris and down the other side. Then, I did it again and again … she started to gently gyrate her hips … that meant to me that she was enjoying what I was doing.

Then I started to circle her clitoris, around and around and around, before I slid my tongue down the middle to her love hole. Then, up and down with the tip of my togue … she spread her legs further apart and her lips were becoming more and more moist from her own lubrication. Time for my finger. I started to slid the tip of my middle finger up and down and around her love hole and I was licking and sucking her clitoris into my mouth … my wet finger slid up into her vagina … slowly sliding all the way in. On the way out I stopped at her G-spot and started to tap it with the pad of my finger, while simultaneously sucking her clitoris in and out of my lips in unison to the tapping. She was sort of rocking forward and back to my rhythm. She whispered, through clenched teeth, "You are going to make me come!"

I just continued my manipulations while she pulled her knees to her chest and her body started to convulse (the muscles in her abdomen tightened and relaxed). She was rocking violently … pushing against my finger. Her body finally relaxed and she lifted her head up and said, "That was magnificent … you are an expert!"

I chuckled and replied, "The girls at home call me the Sexpert."

She smiled and told me to stand up.

As luck would have it, my groin lined up with her mouth. With one hand, she took my semi-hard penis into her wet mouth … with her other hand she began pumping my manhood up and down … vigorously. She licked, and flicked and sucked on the head … driving me crazy! I had to pull away, so I could bend over. pick up and put on my condom. I asked her to move up more on the mattress and lay on her side … she did. I lifted her top leg up, straddled her bottom leg and slid up her soft, tanned inner thigh and entered her extremely moist love canal (the split leg position) … she gasped. I held her long leg against my chest as I pushed deeply into her … it felt heavenly. She moaned in enjoyment … she had a broad smile on her face, I think she was enjoying it as much as me! I pumped in and out several times … then, I pulled out until the crown around the base of my engorged penis head met #33's G-spot … at that point I moved in and out slowly … in very short jerking motions … so that I was continually stroking #33's special spot.

#33 murmured, "You … are … driving … me … crazy!" She started to orgasm. It was long and powerful. I pumped all the way in and out several times, before returning to her special spot. It drove her wild!

I was just getting warmed up … I hadn't climaxed. When her body started to relax, I asked #33 to turn over onto her stomach … as #33 did, she slipped a pillow under her hips and spread her legs wide. I entered her again. The lying dog position—the female lies face down on the bed with her legs straight and hips slightly raised (she can place a pillow under her hips). The male partner enters her vagina from behind. When on her stomach, #33's legs were closer together, which in turn created a snugger fit for my penis … and she was tight!

I squeezed her buttocks and pulled the cheeks apart while pumping in and out. It felt great to me and she seemed to really enjoy it, since she was moaning and pushing her hips upward to meet my inward thrusts. I decided to lift her thighs up toward my waist. (The wheelbarrow position #33 laid flat on her stomach and spread her legs wide. I knelt between her legs and lifted up #33's pelvis to enter her. She supported herself with her arms). Then I began pumping, faster and faster … deeper and deeper. I could feel her body start to convulse and her vagina started to gush even more lubricant. I couldn't hold off any longer and I climaxed with her … we both had long powerful pleasurable orgasms.

When we were done, we were both out of breath. I pulled out, grabbed several tissues from her nightstand and removed my condom. Then I laid down on my side next to #33. She turned toward me, put her hand on my cheek and brought my face toward hers for a long, wet, salty French kiss. When the kiss was over, she kept her face very close and whispered, "I can see why they call you the Sexpert … you are the best lover ever … I am generally lucky to have one orgasm and you gave me three, fantastic orgasms … thank you!" And then she gave me another tender French kiss, as she ran her fingers through my hair.

I said, "I enjoyed it as much as you did!" We laid there, relaxing for a while. Then, I got up, got dressed, stopped in the bathroom to relieve myself and headed back to the beach, to help #30 and #32 carry everything back to their cottage.

******

#32 whipped up a wonderful spaghetti and meatball dinner and after helping with the dishes, I changed my clothes and #19 and I went out to the arcade.

Actually, I was not sure where #19 went, but I hurried down to the beach to put my beach towel between several boats. Then, I headed over to the arcade.

Guess who I ran into? #33, wearing a red and white striped halter top and white shorts, with her long blonde hair in two braids which she wound around her head (like Heidi). She looked outstanding!

She said, "My parents went out to my uncle's house, about 60 miles away, for a surprise birthday party and they won't return until very late … I can't stop thinking about what a wonderful time we had this afternoon and I am looking forward to a double header this evening … especially given the fact that I am leaving in the morning with my mom to attend an all-girls volleyball camp for the next four weeks!"

I asked. "Today is Monday and tomorrow is Tuesday … isn't that an unusual day to start a camp?"

#33 laughed and replied, "The fella that runs this camp runs another camp on the west coast, which just finished yesterday afternoon. He and his counselors fly out in the evening, set up the camp today and we start tomorrow."

"Well, I would hate to disappoint you … let's go!"

As we walked, arm in arm, all the way back to #33's house, it was dark and we stopped frequently to kiss … it was romantic in the moonlight.

When we reached #33's house, the lights were on. She didn't like to come home to a dark house. When we went into the kitchen, #33 asked me if I would like a drink, she said, "But not a beer, my mom noticed that two beers were missing and gave me hell, so, I can make you a mixed drink … how about a rum and coke?"

"Sounds good!"

#33 took out two tall glasses, added ice, then she poured three fingers of rum and filled the glasses with coke. I took a drink … it was strong and very refreshing. We walked to #33's bedroom. The bed had been turned down and a beach towel had been placed down the center. There was just a soft white table light illuminating the room.

"How should we begin?" she asked.

"How about with a kiss … then we can undress and lay down on the bed," I replied.

We came together, wrapped our arms around each other and kissed passionately. Then she; stepped back, removed her halter and shorts and other than her stud earrings and the nail polish on her toes, she was naked. It only took a moment for me to strip off my T shirt and shorts.

#33 led me to her bed and I noticed there was a hardcover book on her pillow. It was a book showing sexual positions. On the left page, it had a full-size picture of a couple in a sexual position and on the right-hand page, it had the name, a description of how to get into that position and then the advantages of using said position. There were a number of small pieces of paper sticking out from the edges of the book and I noticed there were numbers on them.

#33 informed me that she had looked through the book and made selections of the positions she would like to try … then sequenced them. Interesting!

My partner suggested that we begin with the 69 position. Me on the bottom and her on the top. I was only too pleased to comply.

It wasn't long before I was all charged up, so I had to, grudgingly, ask #33 to discontinue what she was doing and sit up. She got up and turned around, to straddle my face in the other direction, so that she could better control the pressure and position of my tongue … all the better to please her.

#33 soon had a strong clitoral climax … great!

Then, as she referred to her book, I put a condom on, she said, "Next, we will do the End-to-End Position," and she showed me the picture. In this position, I sat with my legs bent, leaning back against a pile of pillows. Then, #33 did the same and then she inched toward the me, putting her legs over mine with her feet on the bed, until we made contact.

#33 then grinds and pumps as she wishes. This was a relaxing position … not very aggressive. After a while, I sat up more and fondled #33's breasts … she smiled in enjoyment, then I took one hand and after putting some saliva on the pad of my thumb, I started to rub it around and around #33's clitoris as I squeezed her nipple between my thumb and index finger of my other hand … she seemed to really enjoy it. I could feel that #33 was using the head of my erection to stroke her G-spot and shortly she climaxed for the 2nd time. Hurrah!

Then she picked up the book and said, "Let's try the Criss Cross." In this position, I entered her from the missionary position, then I slide my chest and legs off #33's body, so that my pelvis was in the same location but my body formed an "X" with #33.

I didn't see any great advantage to this position and I don't think that #33 did either, for very soon she said, "Now let's try the Drop in the Bucket." She showed me the picture; in this position, she laid on her back (on the floor) with her legs raised and folded over so that her ankles were on either side of her head and her vagina was pointed toward the ceiling, then I squatted and dipped my penis in and out of #33's vagina.

So, #33 slid off the bed on her back, until her head and neck were on the floor and her back was resting against the side of the bed (I think she must have practiced this position earlier), then, she lowered her legs until her feet were on the floor … she was bent in half.

I straddled her body facing away from the bed, to enter her, I had to raise up on my toes to put my erection down into her very wet, hot vagina. Then, by squatting, I could penetrate her rather deeply … and by raising myself with my legs, I could withdraw. I loved this position and #33 did as well, she was grunting and yelping, "Wow … Wow … Wow!" Then, she climaxed (for the 3rd time) and the tight contractions of her vagina caused me to climax with her.

We both had very strong orgasms in this position.

#33 asked, "You didn't come, did you?"

"Yes, I did! And it was great!"

#33 breathlessly replied, "I know!"

When she had righted herself, she said, "I so wanted to finish in the split leg position … that is my favorite position!"

I wouldn't want to disappoint her. So, I said, "Give me ten minutes and let me change my condom and I will be ready to go." #33 smiled happily. I instructed her to lay on the edge of the bed and pull her knees up. I removed my used condom, then knelt between #33's knees and started to lick around her clitoris, then up and down to her love canal … she loved it … she was moaning … she reached forward to pull my face tighter against her. I regained my erection and when I stopped to put on a fresh condom, #33 moaned in displeasure.

When I resumed my tongue manipulations. I noticed how wet #33 was. As my tongue started its' decent toward her love canal, #33 pulled her knees up and rotated her hips upward, which brought my tongue directly to her butt hole (I think purposely). So, I rotated the tip of my tongue around and over and slightly into her anus (this is referred to as rimming). A few times all the way up, around her clitoris and back down around her butt hole and #33 was ready to explode … she urgently said, "Put it in NOW!"

I instructed her to slide up on the bed and turn onto her side. She bent her top leg so that I could staddle her bottom leg … then, I lifted her top leg straight up against my chest and slid ever so deeply into her. She gasped in pleasure. I started to stroke very deeply in and out and I could see the wide smile on her face change as her face began to contort and her body convulsed in pleasure (for the 4th time), as she had a clitoral G-spot and an A-spot orgasm. (The A-spot is otherwise known as the Anterior Fornix Erogenous Zone (AFE) and is located about four to five inches inside the vagina. Lesser known then the G-spot, this deep spot is just above the cervix.) As #33's body began to relax, she looked me in the eye and said, "That … was the strongest and best orgasm of all time!"

I pulled completely out of her and sat on the edge of the bed to remove my condom. #33 stood up and said, "Wait, you didn't come, did you?"

"No."

#33 then came over, between my legs, and pushed me back flat on the bed, with my feet still on the floor. She knelt between my legs, grabbed my still semi-erect penis, and started to pump viciously, up and down. It felt great, until she stopped … reached for the bottle of baby oil on the table (evidently, #33 would rub baby oil on her body to improve her tanning) and she poured it onto my manhood. Then, as she resumed the masturbation of my erect member … she slowly spread the oil around with her hand, before resuming her strong pumping up and down. It felt marvelous and before long I was ready to explode. I whispered, "Don't stop … I am about to come!"

I could see the sense of completion on her face as she put her mouth down over the head of my erection and started to suck … with vigor, while she continued the tight, strong pumping … voila … I began to climax … in her mouth … she pulled the skin all the way down tight and held it there as she continued to suck all of my ejaculate into her mouth. When my orgasm was complete, #33 stood up, swallowed what was in her mouth and then laid down on top of me, I could see her sweep her tongue over her teeth, to remove any residue, Then, she gave me the most passionate French kiss … it was extremely salty, but extremely enjoyable!

We laid there in that position for a while … me softly stroking #33's back … kissing on and off … she was running her fingers through my hair … it was delightful and restful … which we both needed.

Then, I said, "I better get going."

We got up and as I was putting on my bathing suit, #33 kissed me and emphatically said, "Thank you... that was great... I am going to take a shower... hope you have a great summer!"

******

It was getting late, but I had to walk all the way back to the beach to retrieve my towel and put it back, but first I decided that I should take a dip in the ocean to wash off my face and body and to lower my swim trunks, to wash off the oil and all of the other lubricants. Then, I rushed up to #19's cottage … I was exhausted.

#30 and #32 were waiting for me and #19 on the screened-in porch. They saw that I was wet and asked if I had been swimming. I told them it was a hot night and I took a dip to cool off.

They must have washed all of the beach towels and folded them on the daybed. So, I took a towel and my boxer shorts, went into the bathroom, removed my bathing suit and dried off. Then, I went back out to the porch and sat on the daybed next to the basket of towels.

#30 had a frown on her face as she asked, "Where is #19?"

I replied, "I lost track of her … I went in one direction and she went in the other direction."

Soon, a fancy sports car pulled up and #19 got out and came onto the porch. Her mom was furious and told her that she wanted to talk with her in her room!

After they left, #32 got up, picked up the basket of towels and put it on the side chair, she smiled at me, said goodnight and went up the stairs, presumably to bed. I shut off the table lamp, turned down the bed and laid down … physically exhausted. I began to wonder if #30 or #32, or both would come down to use me as a dildo and I fell fast asleep in about two minutes.

I awoke to a warm soft hand on the side of my face. #30's face was about 2 inches from mine and she was whispering, "Are you up?"

I must have slept for two hours or so. I replied, "Yeah … sure."

She looked excited to tell me that her sister had gone out after lunch and bought several enema kits, more condoms and a large bottle of anal lube … Great! #30 went on to say that her sister had talked all day about what wonderful anal sex you guys had and that you are really an expert (I am the

Sexpert)! #30 went on to tell me that she had to wait until #19 went to sleep, so that she could do the enema (until clear), then take a shower.

"First," she whispered, "we need to get warned up!"

Then, she took off her robe … she was completely naked. Next, she removed my undershorts and, ever so gently, she started to fondle my extremely sensitive testicles with one hand and stroke my manhood with the other. Quickly, I sprang into action. #30 poured some love oil all along my now bulging erection. Then, she straddled my hips and lowered her love lips onto it. #30 slid back and forth, increasing and decreasing her speed and pressure. I took the opportunity to reach up and caress her large, beautiful breasts. Finally, her body froze and shook. I could feel that she was having an orgasm.

When her convulsions were finished, #30 climbed off me and took a condom from her robe. I took the opportunity to sit on the edge of the bed. I took the condom from #30 and asked her to lie on the bed on her side. Then, after putting the condom on, I straddled her lower leg and lifted her upper leg up against my chest … as I entered her (in the split leg position) … she gasped and as I pushed in further, she smiled and said, "That is wonderful!" It was!

I slipped my hands up and down her thigh, as I tried to make contact with her clitoris, G-spot and A-spot as I slipped in and out of her love canal. It worked, for after a while I could see #30's face contort while she went into the throws of her orgasm … I continued pumping fast and deep.

Concerned, #30 asked, "You didn't come, did you?"

"No."

"Ok … good, let's prepare to do anal." Then she got up, put a beach towel on the bed, took out the bottle of anal lube and got on the bed on all fours.

I positioned myself behind her and I said, "At any point, if it hurts or you want to stop, just say … stop." I poured a copious amount of the anal lube down her butt crack and sort of worked it into her rectum with my index finger. #30 seemed to be enjoying what I was doing. I reached around and tried to massage her clitoris, with my other hand, as I poured more lube down her crack and pushed it into her butt hole. #30 was pushing her hips back, so I switched to my thumb … which went right in, so I decided to try two fingers. I added more lube on my fingers and said, "Let's try this … take a deep breath and hold it." As I, gently, pushed the two fingers in, #30 gasped and held her breath

… slowly, I pushed them in a little more and a little more … when I felt the muscle relax, I said, "Let's try the real thing!"

#30 nodded … I covered my erection with a lot of the lube, especially on the tip. Then, as I inched closer, I positioned the tip of my erection against #30's anus and I said, "Take a deep breath … then push your hips back and try to push out like you're pooping." I didn't move as the head of my erection entered #30. I said, "Take a few more deep breaths and then push back some more." This time I slid in a few more inches and stopped, I asked, "How are you doing?"

#30 replied … through clenched teeth, "Great!"

Slowly, I pulled out several inches and then in … her rectum was very tight at first but slowly the muscles relaxed and #30 was pumping fast and hard; after she tired, she said, "I am going to turn over and I want you to make me climax, again."

I pulled out and as I took off the used condom and put on a fresh condom, #30 laid on her back, pulled up her knees and spread her legs … I entered her and she put her ankles on my shoulders (the folded in half position). I pushed, harder and faster than normally, having the feeling that is what #30 desired. I leaned way forward, pushing her slippery thighs (slippery from the anal lube dripping down) toward her head and #30 reached forward to grab my head and pull me toward her waiting lips and as she kissed me passionately, I sucked the air out of her lungs and held it for several seconds … she started to climax and so did I … but I continued to pump harder and harder … we both had strong orgasms.

As our bodies relaxed, I leaned back and withdrew from her. Then, I got up and removed my condom and wrapped it in several tissues. #30 got up and used the towel from the bed to wipe the lube from her butt Then, she wrapped the towel around her waist and put her robe back on. Then, she approached me and gave me a hug, as she whispered in my ear, "That was outstanding! I have never enjoyed a moment of anal sex with any man … until just now. You were delicate and patient and the anal was sex great! Not to mention the mind-blowing orgasms … Thank you!"

Actually, I was embarrassed. I am sure that I blushed, which wasn't noticeable in the limelight. When #30 left, I picked up my undershorts, went into the bathroom, washed my hands and groin, and put my undershorts on.

When I returned to my daybed, I was really beat and I fell asleep quickly.

I arose early the next morning, half rested. I quickly dressed in my bathing suit and a black T-shirt and headed for the beach to set up my spot.

Then, over to the donut shop for a coffee and a Boston Cream donut. As I sat there, looking down the street, two girls came out of the grocery store each carrying a paper bag full of groceries. I couldn't allow that, so I got up, went down the street and told the girls that I would be happy to carry their groceries for them. They sort of blushed but were pleased. They both smiled broadly and happily handed me their packages.

They were both very pretty and they were the same size (about 5'4") and they both had the same brown, shoulder-length hair and they both had exactly the same black bikinis. I had to ask if they were twins … they both giggled and told me that they were just best friends. As we walked to their cottage, they explained that they were the president and treasurer of their sorority. The treasurer was responsible for cooking breakfast for the sorority and the president was responsible for dinner, that evening … the ingredients for the meals were in the bags.

When we reached their cottage, they invited me in for breakfast which the treasurer whipped up quickly … I had pancakes and bacon, as well as having the opportunity of meeting the rest of their sorority sisters … mostly in their baby doll pajamas!

Once I had finished breakfast, I had to excuse myself (to hurry back and carry #30's stuff to the beach), but I told the girls where my spot on the beach was and said we would meet up later.

I had to hustle to the donut shop, pick up two coffees and get to #30's before they left for the beach. Fortunately, they were just piling everything up in the front yard.

#32 had to carry her youngest for some reason, so #19, reluctantly, had to carry one of the beach chairs … I carried everything else.

Once I set up everything on the beach, #19 stayed with her family while I returned to my spot on the beach. The weather was still very warm and I was extremely physically tired. So, I laid down in the shade of the umbrella, covered my face with my T-shirt and quicky fell fast asleep.

When I awoke, several hours later, the sorority president was sitting on one side and the treasurer on the other side of me on my blanket. I sat right up and said, "Good morning!"

They laughed and told me that it was after lunch (good, I had needed the sleep). The girls said that they were going to head back to their cottage for a cold drink and would I like to join them?

"Of course … I am very thirsty!"

As we walked, the president held my hand and the treasurer held my other hand. The president said, "All of the girls should have had lunch and be back at the beach."

The treasurer looked over to the president with a devilish look on her face and replied, "Good … we will have the place to ourselves!"

When we reached their cottage, we went into the kitchen and we each took a soda bottle from the refrigerator. It was refreshing.

The girls asked if I would like to see their room?

Of course, I would!

When we reached their bedroom, the president held the door open while we walked in. The treasurer walked over to the bureau and turned on a radio which played classical music. The president closed the door and locked it. Then she said, "Let's take our bathing suits off first … then climb onto the bed." I stripped off my bathing suit and dropped it next to the foot of the bed. I watched as the president and treasurer met in the middle of the room and shared a passionate kiss … that turned me on! Then, they removed each other's bikini tops, dropped them on the floor and then fondled each other's breasts, which were very ample. Next, they removed each other's bikini bottoms and dropped them on the floor.

They hugged and kissed once more, before turning toward me and walking toward the bed. As the treasurer turned down the bed, the president got a big beach towel and placed it in the middle of the mattress … she looked at me and said, "The treasurer is a gusher (I hoped that was a good thing)."

Then, we met in the middle of the bed, kneeling on the towel. One attractive, naked girl on each side of me. The president told me that they don't do anal. I was sitting back on my calves and they both were kneeling straight up which made all of our heads at the same height. Before I had the chance, the president kissed the treasurer right in front of me.

I said, "That's hot!" They stopped kissing each other, giggled and the president gave me a long, wet delightful French kiss. When she stopped, I turned toward the treasurer and she slid her hand up my back, into my hair and pulled my head toward her as she gave me an equally lovely French kiss. When we completed our kiss, I said, "You are a great kisser," as I looked directly into her eyes. I didn't know the effect it would have on the president, for she now had to outdo her girlfriend, so she started to kiss me way more aggressively … great!

We went back and forth, one girl trying to outdo the other in a kissing contest, before I noticed that the treasurer was fondling the president's breasts. Good idea. I started fondling one of the breasts of the girl that I was kissing at the time. When I dropped my hand down to the treasurer's crotch, the president started to fondle my semi-erect penis … it didn't take long for me to reach full protuberance … I think the president was impressed. I said, "Why don't you girls lay down on the side of the bed and make yourself comfortable?"

The three of us climbed off the bed and the President repositioned the beach towel lengthways along the side of the mattress with a third of the towel hanging over the edge. Then, the girls laid down on the bed, side by side, with their legs hanging over from the knees down. I knelt down between the President's legs, which she spread apart for me. As I brought my head down to orally stimulate the President, the Treasurer turned on her side and began kissing and fondling the President's breasts. As my head bobbed up and down, licking away, I noticed that the Treasurer would rub her palm around and around on the President's nipples, which made the President moan (I will have to try that).

Meanwhile, I would rotate the tip of my tongue around and around the President's clit, occasionally running my tongue directly over her clitoris. Then, I would slide my tongue down, and slightly into her vagina, then back up and around her clitoris again. As she became wet from her own lubricant, I slipped my middle finger into her love canal … she slowly ground her hips into the mattress. The Treasurer started to lick and suck the President's nipples (watching that really turned me on)! As I circled her clit with my tongue, I pushed my middle finger in, palm up, and began gently stroking the President's G-spot while I made my lips look like fish lips and I sucked her clitoris into my mouth. When I ran my tongue under the hood covering her clitoris, she arched her body and began to convulse. She brought her thighs tightly against my head and arched her body as the waves of pleasure washed over her body. When her orgasm was finished, I said, "Ok … the Treasurer is next!" Then, I moved sideways to the next set of legs and she turned onto her back.

By now the Treasurer was quite moist. As I started to work my tongue between the Treasurer's labia the President turned on her side and started to kiss and fondle the Treasurer's breasts. I noticed that she cupped the underneath of the breast, stoked it gently and lifted it up … the Treasurer moaned in delight. Then, as the President slid her hand up, she spread her index and middle fingers apart and slid the Treasurer's nipple between them … then, she squeezed her fingers together … to tweak the nipple (luckily, I was watching how women like to get pleasured). I slipped my middle finger into the Treasurer's love canal and began tapping my finger against her G-spot, as I made fish lips and sucked her erect clitoris into my mouth, then, as I ran my tongue under the hood covering her clitoris, the Treasurer said, "You are driving me wild!"

Moments later, her body arched up and her thighs closed tightly against the sides of my head and I could feel her body start to convulse. At the same time, I felt a large amount of her lubricant wash down over my fingers … it was different … much thicker than her normal lubricant … off-white, not clear and as each wave of pleasure washed through her body, she would secrete more of this love fluid. I guess she was gushing. I continued my manipulations until her body physically relaxed.

At that point, the President said, to me, "OK … now it's your turn!"

I replied to the President, "Oh no … this time it is your turn again."

"Really?" she said and then she started to laugh.

Then, as I picked up my bathing suit to take out a condom and reposition myself between the President's legs, the Treasurer got up off the bed, walked around me to get some tissues from the nightstand and wipe the residue from between her legs. I slipped the condom onto my rock-hard erection, lifted up and spread the President's legs, while lowering my mouth down onto her clitoris. She was still quite moist.

The Treasurer, interestingly, got back onto the bed and straddled the President's head, facing toward me while lowering her clitoris down onto the President's waiting mouth … my goodness … that was HOT!

I wanted to get the President ready for intercourse quickly. So, I started to lick left and right over the President's clit … then as I slid my tongue down toward her love canal, I pushed back on her thighs and my tongue slipped all the way down to her butt hole, which I circled twice before returning to her clit. After several trips from clit to butt, I had the sense that she was ready. I wasn't sure what position to use, since I didn't want to interrupt what the President was doing to the Treasurer.

So, I put one foot each side of the President's hips, squatted down and positioned my erection directly in front of the President's love canal (with a little forward pressure) … instinctively the President spread her legs apart and my manhood went slip, sliding in … all the way in (this position is referred to as the Roman Stallion)! It felt excruciatingly fantastic to me and I think the feeling was mutual for #34 stopped licking and she stopped breathing … I pulled out slowly … then wham … back in. (It was soooo easy to move in or out … unobstructed … and felt soooo good … this was without a doubt, the best position that I have ever tried.) I leaned forward, supporting my upper body by placing my hands on the mattress. The Treasurer leaned forward, positioning her clitoris directly over #34's tongue and she kissed me … I took this opportunity to suck the air from her lungs (while still pumping in and out), I held her breath in my lungs, then let her suck the air back into her lungs … both girls were moaning loudly. I must be doing something right.

I pumped faster and faster as #34 orgasmed (although there were only two parts of our bodies that were touching (my penis and her vagina), I could feel the intense pleasure that she was experiencing. I had to hold back my own orgasm, to save myself for the Treasurer … (fortunately, I had been somewhat desensitized by the incredible amount of sex that I had had recently). #34's body wildly rocked, arched, convulsed, she moaned and even screamed, as the waves of pleasure engulfed her … fantastic!

When #34's body finally relaxed, the Treasurer repositioned herself back onto the side of the bed (picking a dry spot), next to #34. Then, as I withdrew from #34, she spurted out, "That was unquestionably the most powerful orgasm that I have ever had … without a doubt! You will have to do the Treasurer in the same position."

With that said, #34 straddled the Treasurer's head and I knelt down between the Treasurer's legs to get her ready again. She was incredibly wet from what #34 had been doing. So, I sucked in the Treasurer's clit and stroked it side to side with my tongue. Then I lifted and pushed her legs back as I slid my tongue down … given the response I received from #34, I slid my tongue all the way down and around her anus … then back up to her clit. She moaned with pleasure as I went down, around and up again … she was ready! I put a foot on each side of her hips and pressed my bulging manhood against the opening of her love canal. When she spread her legs, I slipped right in … all the way … even farther in than with #34 … everyone's body is different. I started to pump slowly at first, then faster and faster. Since I was leaning forward, #34 reached out and started to French-kiss me appreciatively. Soon, I could feel #35 start to gush … I couldn't hold back any further and I started to explode … we both had long strong orgasms … FANTASTIC!

I do not think that having sex could ever be more pleasurable than what we had just had.

#34 climbed off #35's face and laid down in the middle of the bed. #35 and I joined her. We were all panting and sweating. We laid there about 15 minutes, without touching or talking.

Then, I sat up and said, "I have got to get going … I have an errand to run."

Both girls gave me a delicate goodbye kiss, then I got up, put my bathing suit on and headed down to the beach … leaving #34 and #35 in the bed.

******

When I reached the beach, I was sweating, hot and covered in love juices. So, I dove into the water and swam the last 100 yards back to where #30's spot on the beach was.

#30 and #32 were surprised to see me coming out of the water and walking up the beach toward them, dripping wet. I asked, "Have you girls had enough for the day?"

#32 threw me a towel and replied, "More than enough!" Then #30 got up out of her chair to gather all of the beach toys and put them into a large canvas bag that she put over her shoulder. #32 picked up both beach chairs and the two women corralled the small children and headed for their cottage.

I put the cooler in the sand and pulled the plug to drain out the water. Then, I folded and piled up all the beach towels on top of the cooler. Next, I picked up the blanket, shook off the loose sand, folded it and put it on top of the cooler. Finally, I put the plug back into the cooler, took the umbrella down and put it into its' carrying case. Then, with the umbrella case over my shoulder, I picked up the cooler and followed the clan back to their cottage.

Each afternoon we would go to the back of the cottage, where #30 would turn on the hose and wash the sand off each child, #31 would then dry them with a towel and shoo them in the back door. I would hang the blanket over the clothesline and secure it with several clothespins. #30 would then wash #32's feet off and she would take the pile of towels into the cottage and put then into the washer, while I would lift up the cooler so that #30 could wash the sand off it. Next #30 washed off my feet, then she held the cooler so that I could dry my feet and then I washed off her feet and I took the cooler into the kitchen, while #30 dried her feet and came in. Next, the moms took their children upstairs to remove their bathing suits and put their PJs on, so they would be ready for bed after supper.

I retrieved my outfit for the evening and I took a well-deserved shower … nothing feels better than to feel the water washing over your body when you return from the beach.

Then, as the women prepared supper, I headed down to the beach to remove my stuff from the beach … there were only a few people on the beach.

When I returned, the moms were just putting the supper on the table … hot dogs and beans … it hit the spot!

About midway through dinner, #19 came in and ran upstairs to change. She came back down looking better than ever … while we were having dessert (vanilla ice cream with chocolate sauce). #30 made a plate for #19 and put it aside, then #32 put all of the dishes and pans in the sink.

As soon as #19 finished her dinner, she grabbed my hand, pulled me up and said, "Let's go … they are waiting for us at the arcade." In other words, some guy in a car was waiting for her at the arcade.

******

When we got to the arcade, #19 jumped into a flashy red sports car and they drove away.

Inside I came across #34 and #35. I said, "I am surprised that you can still walk!"

#34 replied, "Both sets of my lips are smiling tonight!" We all got a good laugh from that.

The most beautiful girl that I ever saw just walked in the door. Wearing a yellow halter and shorts. I had to excuse myself and went directly over to her, to welcome her to the arcade. She had an engaging personality … beautiful lips with sparkling white teeth … gorgeous!

I asked her if she was new to the beach. She told me that they were there for the month. She was looking for help … her brother had chipped a tooth at lunch and her parents took him to their hometown dentist about two hours away and they will stay at their home tonight, so that her father can water the lawn … so she was all alone … her dinner was in a cabinet and somehow the cabinet door was stuck and when she pulled on the handle, it came off … boohoo! She went on to say that she didn't want to break a nail fixing it (she had beautifully manicured fingernails). So, I asked if I could be of any assistance. She took my hand and said, "Come with me."

We left the arcade and walked quite a distance to her cottage, which was right on the beach and fairly new. It must have been very expensive to rent for a month.

On the way she told me that she was a sought-after model, she and her mother had to leave early the next day for her to attend a photo shoot (for the rest of the week), for the fall line of clothes, for a big-time department store.

I believed everything she told me. She was tall, thin, had a great body, the most beautiful face and hair that I had ever seen … gorgeous!

When we entered the cottage, the furniture, carpets, tile floors were beautiful, but the cabinet door was stuck. I asked if she had a screwdriver and she said there was one in the drawer. I took out a flat-bladed screwdriver and wedged the cabinet door open … voila!

The model was extremely pleased. She offered me a beer, which I took. Then she went into the cabinet that I had opened and took out a container. She opened the container and scooped several portions into a blender containing water. She mixed up a green, thick potion, poured it into a tall glass and drank it … that was her dinner! Ugh!

I found the screw that held the handle on the door on the bottom of the cabinet and I put the handle back on the door and really tightened the screw.

The model opened up a bottle of champagne, poured it into two flutes and handed me one. She toasted me, "To my hero … my repairman!"

We were standing in the kitchen leaning against the counter. I started to feel the effects of the champagne after the second glass, so I said, "Let's get off our feet," meaning let's go sit in the living room. The model misunderstood me and took the bottle of champagne and told me to follow her (she appeared a bit tipsy too). Well, she led me to her bedroom, put the bottle and her glass on the nightstand, turned down the bed, plopped in and asked, "Will this be comfortable enough?"

I laid down on my side next to her, marveling in her beauty. I said, "You have the most beautiful face that I have ever seen … your teeth are sparkling white and your lips look perfect for kissing!" With that said I leaned in and gave her a soft, short kiss … the model pulled my head toward her face and opened those beautiful lips and we kissed passionately. She was a squealer, which she did throughout our kiss.

The beauty said, "When we met, I had a tingling feeling that you would be a great kisser."

"Really … where was this feeling?" I asked.

The model took my hand and put it on her crotch.

I asked, "Was it sort of an itchy feeling … that needs to be scratched?"

"Exactly!" She smiled.

I went back to kissing her, but since my hand was already between her legs, I decided to start a soft massage down there. The model squealed even more and even louder. She sat up and took off, what looked like expensive, short pants. What blew my mind was that she had no underwear on … very sexy! While she was upright, I reached over and untied her halter top on her back. She reached up under her hair and untied the halter and removed her halter top. "The view keeps improving," I uttered.

She laid back, smiled and said, "Your turn." She didn't need to tell me twice … I sprung up, removed my pants, underwear and T-shirt in a blink of an eye. I watched her check me out … from top to bottom … I was fairly muscular, well-tanned but the part she was staring at never got to see the sun … I had a semi-erection which was pretty good-sized. I think she was impressed.

The model asked, "Do you have a condom?"

I took a condom from my jeans and tossed it onto the bed. "You bet!"

I laid back down, next to this beauty. We started to kiss much more aggressively. I put my finger down and between her labia, which was dry. So, I licked my finger to wet it, then back down to slip between her labia. The model was moaning as she pushed my head down to her breasts. I licked around and around her nipple, before sucking it into my mouth, while flicking my tongue back and forth across her nipple. The model went, "Oooooooo … mmmmmm!"

I continued to stoke my finger across the model's clitoris and down into her love canal … she was becoming wetter and wetter. Then she pushed my head down to where my finger was and spread her legs. (She was not afraid to show me what she wanted … good.)

I started to lick around and around her clitoris, I sucked her clit into my mouth and ran my tongue under the hood that protected the clit, she said, "OH … MY … GOD!" And she was grinding her hips into the mattress. She was getting very turned on. I pushed my middle finger into her wet vagina (palm up) and when the tip of finger brushed across her special spot, I asked, "Is this where your itch is?" No answer, but soon her legs tightened up and her hips were wiggling … then she arched her body as she climaxed.

Once she relaxed, she asked me to lie down and she started to suck and stroke my penis until it was rock hard, as though she owed me … which she didn't. Very quickly, I said, "I'm ready!" I put the condom on and she straddled me in the cowboy position. She was the type of girl that liked to be in control … fine with me. I enjoyed looking at this gorgeous creature, completely nude, bouncing up and down in my lap, as much as the fantastic pleasure that I was feeling from her hips grinding her vagina up and down my swollen manhood. #36 did not have great stamina and in a short time, she ran out of gas. I said, "Lie down." (I wanted to try the Roman stallion position that I so much enjoyed this afternoon.)

So, once #36 was on her back, I quickly straddled her hips … standing up. I then squatted down, leaning forward on my outstretched arms and hands, placing the tip of my erection at the door way to her vagina (the Roman Stallion position), with a little pressure, I asked, "Spread your legs!" When she did, my manhood slid in … in … in … as far in as it was possible to go. #36 gasped loudly … followed by, "OH MY GOD! That is soooo good!"

Yes, it was. It couldn't have felt any better. I slid out and in, over and over again, until we both had incredibly long, intense orgasms … magnificent!

Exhausted, I laid beside #36, who was also gasping for air. She turned onto her side and gently kissed my face all over. She told me that she seldom was lucky enough to orgasm once with any fella … but I just gave her two fantastic orgasms … with ease. I said, "My aim is to please." She smiled.

#36 said, "I would follow you to the ends of the earth … but I have to leave for my photo shoot first thing in the morning!"

I sat up and said, "I better get going so that you can get a good night's sleep." Then I sat up, pulled several tissues from the box on the nightstand, removed my condom and dropped it into the trash container next to the bed.

When I got up and dressed, #36 came over to me and gave me a very tight hug and a long, passionate goodbye kiss. Then she said that she was going to take a shower … I almost asked if she would like me to wash her back … but I really needed to get back to #19's cottage … Oh well!

******

When I got back, #32 was sitting in her PJs and robe on the porch, reading a book. #30 had gone to bed. #32 said, "She didn't get much sleep last night," then she smiled. #32 then told me that she had saved time by doing her enema, which she had just completed … TMI.

I picked up the newspaper and sat in the other chair and we both read until #19 came in. #32 told her, kiddingly, that we were just going to send out a search party for her. #19 laughed and went up to bed and #32 followed her.

I went into the bathroom. Washed my face, hands and groin, put on my boxer shorts and went back to the porch. I moved the basket of clean, folded towels from my daybed to the side chair, turned down the bed and laid a large beach towel down the middle of the bed. Then I laid down on my back (waiting for company).

An hour later, #32 paid me a visit; she slid back and forth on my erection, for her first orgasm … then cowgirl for her second orgasm … then anal, which worked out extremely well after her enema. Then, I decided to try out what I was now calling my signature move, the Roman Stallion position!

I asked #32 to lie on her back on the bed. #32 looked surprised as I stood over her on the bed, with one foot on each side of her hips. I squatted down and leaned forward to support myself with my arms and hands. I asked #32 to spread her legs and my erection slid as far in as possible … #32 gasped, then moaned, indicating her pleasure. I pulled mostly out then all the way in, over and over. Finally, I could feel her entire body tighten up … her breathing stopped … I continued to pump in and out faster and faster … the tightness in her vagina pushed me over the edge … and we both had very strong simultaneous orgasms.

I laid next to #32 on my side on the narrow bed. We were both still panting. #32 whispered in my ear. "I have had intercourse with many men … I have been married … and I thought I had done it in every position … but I have never done it like that and I have never had a more wonderful orgasm … my entire body had a climax … you are really terrific!" Then, she held my head with both hands and gave me a long, wet, sexy, French kiss!

When I got up to grab some tissues and remove my condom, #32 jumped up, grabbed the towel from the bed and used it to wipe her groin and thighs off. Next, she put on her baby doll PJ top and robe. She softly whispered, "Goodnight," and with the towel in her hand disappeared up the stairs.

I took a quick trip into the bathroom to wash myself off and put my boxer shorts back on. When I laid down, I fell asleep immediately.

******

On Wednesday, I woke up, fairly refreshed, put my bathing suit and T-shirt on and headed down to the beach, to set up my spot. The weather continued to be hot, this day seemed to be the hottest!

At the donut shop, it was a quiet morning … no girls shopping. I had two Boston Cream donuts and a large coffee. Then, I took two more coffees and headed back to #19's cottage.

#30 and #32 were always pleased to see me … maybe it was because I brought them coffee. #30 was doing the cooking, making pancakes, bacon and eggs. I had the pancakes and some bacon. #32 sat next to me and said, "You need to keep your energy up."

After lugging all of the beach stuff down to the beach and setting them up, I headed off to my spot on the beach.

I took off my T-shirt, laid down on my blanket, using my rolled-up beach towel as my pillow, thinking how lucky I had been to be able to stay another week. I dozed off and awoke about noon. Fortunately, I noticed, out of the corner of my eye, a girl trotting along the water's edge. She had a shiny silver two-piece bathing suit but what really caught my eye was that her blonde hair glistened like gold as the sun shone on her.

I was not sure how far she went past me, but when I saw her coming back, I got up and went down to the edge of the water and I stood directly in her path. She was pretty, tall and lean. She was smiling as she ran around me. I started

194

to run and quickly caught up to her. Trotting next to her, I asked, "Why are you running during the hottest part of the day?"

Her reply was, "I like to sweat."

We continued to trot about a mile down the beach (way past #36's cottage), to a completely residential area, devoid of any stores or restaurants, etc. When we reached the beach where her cottage was, she said, "Now we cool off," and she ran into the water and dived in … I followed behind.

When I stood up, she splashed me. She was only a couple of inches shorter than me. The waves were a little larger than normal, so we tried to body surf in them … we were successful a few times but, in any event, we cooled off.

When we got out of the water, she asked me if I could go for a cold beer. I told her that a beer would be perfect! We walked up to her blanket and she picked up a beach towel to quickly dry her body and her hair. There were not many people on the beach, because it was a private beach, to be used by the people that stayed in the adjacent cottages.

Soon, this girl's hair was glistening again in the sun. I had to compliment her. I said, "You have the most beautiful hair … it looks like gold."

Her reply was, "Everybody compliments me … I guess that I am lucky."

I didn't see a cooler, so I asked, "And the beer?"

She told me, "I live in the second cottage … let's go."

As we took the short walk to her cottage, she told me that she was a serious volleyball player and she was getting in shape to go to a volleyball camp on Saturday for the week.

I told her that I had met another serious female volleyball player on Monday. "She lives down here, near where I met you, and she went to a volleyball camp on Tuesday, for four weeks."

"Really!" She asked. "She is the best volleyball player in the state … her team beat ours for the state championship. She will be a senor this year and I am going to be a junior. I am sure that I will be attending a different camp."

As we walked up to the front door to her cottage, she told me that her parents owned this cottage and the next five cottages. Her parents worked about 45 minutes away. So, she kept an eye on the other cottages during the day … great!

I was hotter than ever, after jogging and swimming, the cold beer really hit the spot. I noticed that after taking a couple of beers from the refrigerator, she replaced them with a couple of warm ones from a cabinet.

She led me back to the porch (where the Venetian blinds were down to prevent the sun from heating up the porch). I sat in a large wicker chair and she sat in a swivel rocker. I told her about my school and my job. She told me about her town, but mostly she talked about her volleyball team.

When we finished our beers, she sprang up, went into the kitchen and came back with two more ice-cold beers. The conversation was pleasant and relaxing and the beer really hit the spot.

When we finished our second beer, she sprang up again and went into the kitchen to retrieve two more cold beers. She came back all smiley and as she approached me with the beers, she said, "I can't believe that you haven't tried to take advantage of me."

I replied in a term she would understand, "The ball is in your court."

She handed me a beer and plopped down onto my lap, put her arm around my neck and pulled my face toward hers for a delightful kiss … great! I had the feeling that she was getting a little buzzed … I know I was. When we stopped kissing, we both took another long drink of our beers. I put my beer and her beer on the adjacent table, to free up our hands. Then, we kissed more aggressively … our tongues darting back and forth from mouth to mouth. I was caressing her back with both hands, not sure if I should move one hand to the front. She was running her fingers through my hair and on my neck … she was driving me crazy!

We were sitting in an awkward position, so, without breaking suction from our mouths she repositioned herself … straddling me on her knees … She leaned in to kiss me and now, while she ran one hand through my hair, the other softly caressed my neck … but the best part was that in this position she could rub/grind her mons veneris against my ever-enlarging manhood.

As we kissed more and more passionately, I untied the top of her bathing suit and slipped my hand under the front, first softly caressing the underneath of her breast while slightly lifting it … she murmured, "Mmmmmm!"

Then, I slipped the palm of my hand over her stiffened nipple and she moaned, over and over, "Mmmmm … MMMmm … MMMMM!"

I decided, as we were kissing, to suck the air out of her lungs and into mine … then hold it … before allowing her to breathe back in … it was a very sexy move! She sat up straight in my lap, lifted up her top and being tall her breasts were directly in front of my face … so, leaving the palm of my hand sliding over one nipple, I covered her other nipple with my lips … I sucked her cool, salty nipple into my mouth and ran my tongue back and forth around and over it. I could tell that she was really enjoying what I was doing and I know I was too!

She bent her head down and whispered in my ear, "Do you have a condom?"

Since my mouth was currently full of her breast, my muffled response was, "Yes!"

She got up, grabbed my hand as she pulled me up out of the chair, she told me to follow her. With her bathing suit top flopping around and my fully erect penis bulging in my bathing suit … we rushed directly to her bedroom. While I took a moment to extract a condom from my bathing suit pocket, she turned down her bed, removed her bathing suit and dove onto the bed with outstretched arms, waiting for me. In an instant, I removed my bathing suit and joined her. As we began kissing, I slid my hand down over her toned tummy, to the hot spot between her legs. She was extremely moist as I slipped my middle finger between her labia and around her clitoris … she held her breath as my finger went softly around and around and over her clitoris. She reached over and started to stoke my erection, which was turning me on. I slid my finger down and into her very wet love canal and found and rubbed her G-spot … with my other arm I pulled her into me as I sucked the air from her lungs into mine and held it … she orgasmed immediately! I continued to hold her tightly, stoke her special spot and kiss her throughout her complete orgasm.

When her body relaxed, she panted, "Wow … are you good!" Then, she asked, "Are you all ready to go?"

"Sure!"

She told me to put my condom on … then I straddled one of her legs as she turned on her side and put her other leg straight up in the air. I pulled her thigh toward my chest and entered her slippery love canal (the split leg position … one of my favorites). #37 stopped breathing and moaned. I slid out and all the way in several times and she was rocking toward me as I slipped in and away as I pulled outward. I positioned the ridge around the head of my penis, at her G-spot and moved forward and back only one-half inch at a time … staying at #37's special spot … #37 loved it and soon began to orgasm … I then started to pump in and out fast … and we both orgasmed together. As her body began to relax, #37 said, "I was wrong … you're not good … you're … GREAT!"

I just put her leg down, leaned forward and kissed her.

We were both sweating profusely, so, I suggested we go for a dip in the ocean. #37 thought that was a lovely idea.

After diving into the cool water and body surfing a few waves, I bid #37 farewell and good luck at camp.

******

I didn't have the energy to run back about a mile and a half. So, I walked fast and as I would get hot from the afternoon sun, I would dive back into the water and swim a bit. When I arrived at #19's place on the beach, #32 was sitting by the water making sand castles with the three youngsters. #30 was sitting in a beach chair reading a book. I guess I was about an hour early, so I laid down on their blanket and took a nap. Too soon, I was awakened to help pack up for the trip back to the cottage.

By the time I had taken a great shower and had gotten dressed, dinner was ready. #30 had prepared a ziti and meatball feast … yum! #19 ate one meatball, no dessert! #19 and I left for the arcade holding hands and as we approached the arcade, #19 jumped into the red sports car and off she went.

I rushed down to get my beach towel from #20's seat and lay it between two turned over boats on the beach. Then, back to the arcade to mingle with my friends (mostly girlfriends).

When I entered the arcade, I soon came across #34 and #35 with a third, rather plump, sorority sister. They were all giggly. They said that they missed me the night before, since I darted off so fast. I explained that the girl that I left with was home alone and had an emergency that I had to repair.

In any event, #34 and #35 had to run off to conduct some sorority business and they asked if I would entertain their sorority sister in the meantime. I would be delighted! After her girlfriends left, I asked her if she would like to go for a walk. This girl had an extremely nice personality, a cute face and while she wasn't physically the type of girl that I was attracted to, I thoroughly enjoyed talking with her. We strolled down near the water's edge and talked for an hour or so. I asked if she would like to sit down and she said she would. So, we walked down to where the boats were tipped over on the beach and we sat down, fairly close together.

We continued to have an easy, interesting conversation. She leaned in once or twice, I think for a kiss, but I didn't pick up on her signals. Finally, she stood up between my legs, put her very soft and tender hands on each side of my face and whispered, "I find you extremely attractive!" Then, she bent over and gave me one of the most delightful kisses of all time. Her perfume was intoxicating, her lips were incredibly soft and sexy. I returned her kiss with a longer, more passionate kiss … with tongues darting back and forth … she pressed one of her knees in to caress my groin … very effectively!

It was very romantic, with the waves crashing in the moonlight.

I asked, "Would you like to lay down?"

She smiled broadly and replied, "I thought you would never ask!"

So, I led her over, hand in hand, several rows, to where my beach towel was. Once we laid down, she reached over and pulled my face toward hers and savagely started to kiss me again. At the same time, she brought her knee up and began to rub up and down along my manhood. Again, it was very effective. I put my hand on her large soft breast and felt it through her blouse and her bra. She quicky took the hand that was tenderly massaging the back of my neck and she unzipped the front of her blouse and unsnapped her bra from between the cups (how convenient). I spread the bra cups wide to marvel at her large breasts … with large nipples, surrounded by very large areolas … outstanding!

I couldn't wait, I just had to cup and caress her incredibly soft breasts. As I rubbed the bottom and lifted one breast, I brought my mouth down and circled her nipple with my togue … she moaned and pushed my head down against her chest … I was having a great time. And so was her knee … it was expert at rubbing over my manhood and inflaming my desire. Unfortunately, I had to push that leg away and push up her skirt to reach her labia, which to my complete surprise … she wasn't wearing any underwear … WOW … that is very sexy! My finger slipped right in between the softest, most plush labia lips that I had ever felt and as it stroked and circled her clitoris, she masterfully directed my head from breast to breast and nipple to nipple. While I was enamored with her breasts, she was enamored with my finger, which had made its way to her G-spot and was titillating her senses. Her thighs came together tightly and she pressed my head into her chest, while she experienced her orgasm … she moaned and moved in such sexy ways.

I removed my Bermuda shorts and boxers, put a condom on and straddled her hips, with my feet and supported my upper body with my arms and hands on the beach towel. I squatted down with my erection between her thighs and said, "Spread your legs!"

As she complied, my erection entered her incredibly soft love canal (the roman stallion position). Slipped all the way in and I could see #38 biting her lip … WOW, this position felt phenomenal! Without missing a beat, I lowered my head and started to kiss #38 passionately … soon, I sucked all of the air from her lungs and held it until she began to orgasm … she reached down between my legs and softly started to caress my scrotum … causing me to climax with her … WOW, was she good! I continued to kiss her and she continued to caress my scrotum, well after our bodies relaxed … it felt soooo good!

Before my erection subsided too much, I had to pull out, lay on the towel and remove my condom. Fortunately, I had several tissues in my pocket for such an occasion.

While I put my boxers and Bermuda shorts back on, #38 snapped her bra in place, pushed down her skirt and zipped up her blouse. Neither one of us spoke a word. I looked over at #38 and I could tell she was about to cry. I asked, "Are you all right?" I didn't think I had hurt her.

Her reply was, "This has been the night of my life!"

"You are right … it has been fantastic!" I replied. We did not rush off … I leaned in, put my hand on the side of her face and kissed her gently … long, slow and sensual! Then we got up and sat down on a boat and talked for a while, before I put my arm around her shoulders and walked her back to her cottage, where I gave her a goodnight kiss.

******

Then, I hustled back to the boats to retrieve my towel and returned it to #20's bench. When I returned to #19's cottage, both moms were sitting in the chairs on the porch. They always seemed happy to see me and not so much for #19.

I went into the kitchen and drank two bottles of water. I was incredibly thirsty. I wondered if I was dehydrating myself, ejaculating so often?

When #19 finally came home, she notified the three of us that she was going to spend the entire day with us tomorrow! WOW!

The two moms followed #19 up the stairs. I shut off the lamp and changed into my boxer shorts. Then, I laid on my back with my hands behind my head wondering if #30, #32, or both would come to visit me.

I didn't have to wait long before I heard the floor in the doorway squeak. It was #30, she was smiling as she approached me. She bent over and whispered in my ear, "I decided to forgo the anal sex tonight!"

She sure did not have to apologize to me.

She settled for sliding back and forth on my erection, until she had an orgasm. Riding cowboy, then reverse cowboy for us both to orgasm, finally she got up put her robe on and went upstairs. Wham, bam, thank you Mam!

The next morning, #19 got up early and made breakfast for everyone. Then she told us that she was planning on making lunch and dinner.

I volunteered to make breakfast tomorrow.

#19 helped by carrying both beach chairs down to the beach. When everything was set up, #19 took my hand and led me back to my spot on the beach and we laid down on the blanket, where she informed me that she had broken up with her boyfriend. She said that he was a jerk. She told me that her ex-boyfriend thought he could do anything he wanted, because he had tons of money, since his father owned several car dealerships.

After a while, #19's eyes became wide, like bulging out, and she requested that we head back to her cottage. When we arrived at the cottage, #19 told me that she was going into the kitchen to get a couple of cold beers … great! While she was gone, I dropped the mini-blinds down along the front and side of the porch (for some privacy) … we always needed to keep the end of the porch toward the beach open, to watch for her mom or aunt, who may be coming back for something.

#19 came back to the porch carrying the two bottles of beer and she had a devilish look in her eyes … mmmm. She had me sit in the chair that faced the beach and she kneeled on the floor, between my legs. After taking several drinks from her bottle of beer, she put the bottle down on the floor next to her and reached up and pulled my bathing suit off … I took a drink of my beer and went right along with her.

She took my placid penis and started to stroke it with one hand and caress and fondle my scrotum with the other, her hands were ice-cold from holding the two beer bottles … nonetheless it had the desired effect and I became aroused. As I sat there drinking my beer, #19 went to work stroking and sucking on my ever-enlarging erection. #19 had both of her hands around and pumping my manhood as she looked up into my eyes, with saliva dripping down her chin and said, "This is what I have missed! My boyfriend doesn't have half of what you've got!"

Then she resumed sucking, licking and pumping ... with renewed enthusiasm ... until I said, "If you don't stop, I am going to come!"

#19 continued, for some reason unthwarted ... her hands tightened some and she began to pump faster and suck, twice as hard ... I just sat back and thoroughly enjoyed it as I ejaculated into her mouth ... #19 continued pumping and sucking until I was drained of all of my love juice. Then, she leaned back and took a long drink of her beer, with a look of accomplishment in her face!

Then, as she stood up to sit in my lap, I asked, "What did I do to deserve that?"

#19 replied, "You have been there for me, my mom and my aunt for the last two weeks ... thanks!"

WOW!

It was getting close to lunch time so #19 jumped up and said she needed to make the sandwiches for lunch. #19 was pleased that I volunteered to help. While she made three salami, provolone cheese, tomato, and lettuce sandwiches with mayo, for the adults ... she directed me to make three peanut butter and banana sandwiches for the children ... and cut the crust off them. Quickly, she packaged the sandwiches into baggies and loaded them into a canvas beach bag for the trip down to the beach.

The moms were both very happy to see us and were just about to go back to the cottage to make lunch. #32 got up, put a cover-up on and darted over to the bar. She returned with two very large cups of frozen mudslides, with straws stuck in the middle ... one for her and one for #30.

Everyone enjoyed their sandwiches (although the moms seemed to enjoy their mudslides even more)! #19 ate a container of yogurt.

While the moms sat next to each other in their beach chairs, #19, the three children and I sat on the blanket in a semi-circle facing them. #30 announced that there was going to be cartoons and a full-length spy movie on the beach, after supper and we were all invited to attend ... sounded good!

Once lunch was finished, #19 collected all of the debris and tossed it in a trash container on the beach. Then, she grabbed my hand, pulled me up and announced that we had to take a walk for exercise.

Actually, we circled around and headed back to her cottage. I turned down my daybed and turned the pillow on its' side against the arm on the end ... so we could look down the street toward the beach. We kissed for a while, before I said, "It's my turn to return the favor!" Then, I started my descent down her body, kissing my way down her world-class tummy, tonguing her belly button, removing her bikini bottom and kneeling between her legs. I brought my tongue down and parted her labia, before licking and sucking on her clitoris.

When she was well lubricated, I introduced my middle finger to her love canal. Slowly entering, before pushing further and further in. #19 moaned with pleasure. After a few stokes in and out, my finger tip stopped on her special spot, which I tapped over and over, while I simultaneously sucked in and pushed out her clitoris, it didn't take long for my manipulations to take effect for her body began to convulse and her body bucked in pleasure. As #19's body begun to relax she whispered, "I haven't had one of those in a while!"

While I removed my bathing suit and extracted a condom from my its' pocket, #19 sat up and began to suck and stroke my semi-rigid erection to full protuberance … great! I had to remove her head to put the condom on, before she straddled my body (reverse cowboy) and lowered her love canal onto my swollen member (I am sure she chose this position so the she could watch for her mom or auntie). Well, it suited me … my view was delightful and #19 slid back and forth, wiggling and squirming … moaning in extreme pleasure … finally, I wetted my middle finger in my mouth and slid it down her butt crack and over her butt hole … #19 squealed and sped up her rocking motion … I continued stroking, then, I grabbed her butt cheeks and pulled them gently apart and as I felt her vagina start to grip my erection tighter, I began to orgasm with her … It was great!

#19 then, sat on the edge of the bed, put her bikini bottom back on and bolted off, inside the cottage. After removing my condom and stuffing it into several tissues, I put my bathing suit back on and went into the kitchen to find #19 with a very large cooking dish that she had just put a layer of uncooked rice in and was strategically layering chicken legs, breasts and wings into. I dashed out the back door to hide my tissue-wrapped condom well down in the trash can. On my return to the kitchen, #19 was covering the chicken with several cans of cream of celery soup. She covered it, slid it into the oven and turned the temperature up to 325 degrees. I asked, "Why didn't you cook the rice first?"

She laughed, "The rice will cook in the soup juice and from the chicken." What do I know … I am not a cook … I am the Sexpert!

#19 took out a bunch of string beans and filled a pot about halfway up with water. She put the pot on the table, then retrieved two cutting boards and two knives. She showed me how to cut the ends off the beans and throw them into the pot. It went by quickly. #19 then put the pot on the stove with a cover but didn't turn the stove on … it was too early.

When we got back to the porch, we kissed for a while but not too long, #19 didn't want us to get carried away again. We put the mini-blinds back up and headed back to the beach … #19 told her mom that she had put the dinner in the oven. Her mom was very mellow … I think she had more than one of those frozen mudslides!

Then #19 dashed down the beach and into the water … me right behind her. She ended up in shoulder-deep water … I could tell that she was pulling her bikini bottom down, to sort of wash off her crotch … I asked, "Can I be of any help?"

She blushed and replied, "Certainly not … with my mom 100 feet away."

So, I did the same thing … I pushed my bathing suit down and washed off my genitals … then, with my back to the beach, I bent over and washed off my face.

#19 and I frolicked in the water, until we saw #30 and #32 stand up and start to pick up and organize everything … for the trek back to the cabin. We ran up the beach and helped.

When we got back to the cottage, the house was filled with the aroma of the chicken baking! If you were not hungry, you would be, just from the smell.

While everyone else was changing their clothes to go to the movies, I ran down to the beach to stow my blanket, towel and umbrella, then back to the cottage to change my clothes for the evening.

Dinner was just being served and it was fantastic. The chicken was sooooo tasteful and it just fell off the bone and amazingly the rice was perfectly cooked and was delicious!

I decided to announce that I would cook breakfast in the morning. #30 said, "I didn't know that you could cook."

I laughed and replied, "I can't cook … the only thing that I can cook is German pancakes … which I learned to cook when I was on a camping trip with the boy scouts."

After the dishes were all washed and dried, #30 put a bunch of cold sodas and water in a large canvas bag, we corralled the children and headed for the beach.

To our surprise, a huge movie screen was set up on the sand and there were no seats for the audience, most people sat on towels or blankets. I said, "Hold on … I have a blanket!" So, I ran over to #20's seat and retrieved the blanket and laid it out on the sand for everyone to sit or lay on it. #32 had run off to purchase several more of the large, frozen mudslide drinks for #30 and #32.

As dusk rolled over the beach, the cartoons started. At first it was difficult to see the characters on the screen, but as it got darker, the picture became very clear. They showed several cartoons before the feature movie. Shortly into the movie, all three children were asleep. The movie was excellent but at the end, the children had to be carried home. The moms carried the little girls and I carried the boy and #19 carried my blanket and the empty canvas bag.

It was late when we arrived at the cottage, so, we put the children in their beds and then we all went to bed. Each night I lay in bed wondering just who will come to join me; #30, #32, #19 or all three!

Well, it was #32's turn to 'entertain' me tonight, she tiptoed through the doorway and over next to my bed, wearing just the top to her baby doll pajamas … she was gorgeous! She bent over and informed me that she didn't bother to do the enema tonight. That was fine with me.

So, she took off her top, pulled down my shorts, fondled my manhood until I was firmly erect. Then, she squirted lube oil up and down the shaft and finally she straddled me so that she could rub her clit, back and forth on my shaft until she made herself orgasm. Then, she asked, "Can we do it with you on top … like the other night?"

"Sure!" I think she was referring to the Roman Stallion position. So, she laid down, when I sat on the edge of the bed putting my condom on. Then, I positioned myself between #32's legs, with my erection pressing slightly against the entrance to 32's love canal … she spread her legs and as usual I slid right in, further and further, until I was all the way in, #32 moaned, "Yeeessss!"

I slid effortlessly, in and out and every single time I got all the way in, #32 would moan, "Yeeessss!"

I pumped faster and faster … I could feel her body starting to stiffen … #32 stretched her neck up to kiss me while reaching behind me to grab the cheeks of my butt and squeeze. I sucked the air out of #32's lungs and held it while we both had explosive orgasms … fantastic! Then, as I sat on the edge of the bed, #32 got up, put on her sheer top, took her lube bottle and went back upstairs.

I had to pee, so, I went into the bathroom, washed off my groin, put on my boxer shorts and returned to bed … I fell asleep quickly.

******

The next morning, Friday, was going to be my last full day at the beach … boohoo!

I sprang up, put on my bathing suit and T-shirt. Remembered to take my blanket and I went down and set up my spot, for the last time. Then, I quickly walked up to the grocery store, bought a loaf of Wonder Bread and stopped at the donut shop for a coffee and a warm honey-dipped donut. Then, I ordered two more coffees and carried them and the loaf of bread back to #30's cottage.

Everyone was up and coming down for breakfast … great!

I took out a large bowl and started to mix up a large batch of pancakes … then, I put a large skillet on the stove and rubbed a pat of butter on the bottom. Everyone watched me as I put a piece of bread in the bowl with the pancake batter, completely covered the bread with batter … then, into the skillet. I was able to fit three pieces of bread into the skillet at one time … which was perfect, for I had one for each child … their moms, buttered, cut and covered the 'German pancakes' with maple syrup and the kids loved it! Soon, the next batch was ready for the moms … two for #32 and one for #30 … they loved the pancakes as well! The next batch, #30 had one and I had two, plus I finished the last batch of three … um, um, good!

I washed the dishes, while #19 dried and #30 got everything together to go to the beach. We set up the beach for the moms, then #19 and I departed … heading back to my spot … but as we were getting close, we noticed #19's ex-boyfriend's flashy red car at the edge of the beach and the ex-boyfriend not far away. He was waving for #19 to come to him. They spoke for a few minutes before #19 climbed into the sports car and they drove away.

I just sat on my blanket for a few minutes before I decided to take a walk down the beach. The sand was hot so I walked in ankle-deep water. When I got to the second private beach, I noticed a group of girls, standing in a circle, in waist-deep water, playing 'keep the ball up' with a multicolored beach ball. The girls all seemed to be quite fit. Someone hit the ball too hard and it flew out of the circle and landed at my feet. I picked it up and intended to toss it back to the girls in the circle, but one of the girls was walking toward me, with a smile I handed her the ball. She politely asked me if I would like to join them … who wouldn't?

For the next 30 minutes, we played an intense game of 'keep the ball up'. The girls were all sweaty from the game, so I suggested that we form a line, paralleling the beach … then stand about 6 feet apart, all facing in the same direction and put their hands on their knees … the last person in line then starts to leap-frog over each girl … leaving someone else to be the last person in line, so they start to leap-frog … on and on. You keep leap-frogging each girl until you have leap-frogged every one, then you stand 6 feet apart and bend over while the remainder of the line leap-frogs over you. We went way down several beaches and back. When we were done, everyone was tired and they decided to go up on the beach and sit on a big circle on their blankets (they had placed four blankets together in a big square).

The girls were all talking and giggling. I spoke mainly to the girl that I had handed the ball to initially. The girl that I was talking to told me that this group was a gymnastic team. They had won the state championship and their sponsor had paid for their cottage for the week!

One of the girls opened a cooler and passed out sandwiches and cold bottles of water to everyone … including me! As we ate, the other girls told me that the girl that I was talking to was the best gymnast in the state. She had won the all-around and had the top score in dance.

I asked her, "Are you a good dancer?" She blushed and told me that her mother had put her in jazz, ballet and tap dance lessons … since she was six years old. I guess she was a dancer.

I told her there was a big dance that night, with a great band at the bar on the beach. They had a bop contest and I needed a partner … I asked if she would help me out? She, and by the screams of the other girls, would be delighted to dance with me.

When we finished eating, the gymnast informed me that we had never danced together and that we should head to their cottage to practice. So, she took my hand and led me up the street to her cottage. She was short (5'2") and had a solid compact body. She had tapes of all kinds of songs and asked if I knew what song the band might play, for the dance contest.

I said, "Rock Around the Clock and At the Hop are probably favorites."

She looked through her tapes and came up with Rock Around the Clock. She put it on and I told her that what I do is a triangle (most people call it the Lindy Hop).

I demonstrated very slowly. Then, I took her hand and we slowly went over the moves. She was a natural and learned the steps quickly. I told her that it would look good as we picked up speed and added a bit of bounce to the dance.

She put on the song and we were bopping to the music in no time … she was a quick learner. When, I told her that I intended to do several splits during the dance her face lit up. I told her that we could dance down into a squat, from which I would jump up and land in a split, then we would resume dancing for a while before she would dance down into a squat and I would jump over her and land in a split. She suggested that she could do a hand stand, then spread her legs and I could jump through and land in a split … perfect … she demonstrated what she intended on doing … WOW was she good! Finally, to end the dance, she suggested that she do a backflip and land on two feet (which she did right in front of me) and then both of us would do a split simultaneously next to each other … what a wonderful idea!

I took her in my arms and kissed her. She asked, "What have you been waiting for?" And she returned the kiss much more passionately and with a lot of tongue. We laid down on her bed and continued kissing. Somehow, she worked her way on top of me. I caressed her back while she ground her hips masterfully against my manhood, until I had a solid erection. I unhooked the back of her top and moved the front so that she could put her nipple in my mouth; as I licked and sucked on one nipple, I rotated my palm over her other nipple … she very softly squealed in pleasure. She whispered in my ear, "Do you have a condom?"

"Yes!" I replied.

Then, I went back to nibbling on one nipple, squeezing the other nipple and she went back to squealing in pleasure … great! After a few minutes, my little gymnast rolled off me onto the mattress, so she could remove her bathing suit and I stood up to remove my bathing suit and to take a condom out of the pocket. I grabbed her by the ankles and pulled her over to the edge of the bed, I kneeled between her legs and started to run the tip of my tongue up and down her labia looking for the opening. She pulled her knees up and spread her legs apart and, voila, I had complete access!

I started with just the tip of my tongue, slowly circling her clitoris and then sliding down and around her love canal, then up to the clit, around and around. As she became moist, I started to slid the tip of my finger up and down, from just beneath her clitoris down and around her love canal. She was continually squealing, louder and louder! I slid my finger into her love canal and found her G-Spot, softly, slowly I started to rotated the tip of my finger over and around, her special spot. Very soon her knees tightened around my head and she was shaking violently … she stopped breathing and her entire body contorted … I continued my manipulations until her body relaxed … she said, as she was panting, "Wow … that was great!" She sat up, reached both hands out and pulled my face to hers, for a big, passionate French kiss, completely undaunted that my tongue and lips were coated with her love juices.

She told me to lie down … then, she picked up the condom package from the mattress, opened it and removed the condom. With one tiny hand she stroked my erection several times (to achieve the desired stiffness), then she rolled the condom onto it, like a pro, plus it felt great! Quickly she straddled my hips, standing over me, she asked, "Can you put your knees up?"

"Sure." I bent my legs and put my feet on the mattress. My gymnast put a hand on each knee and lowered her body down onto my fully erect manhood (cowboy style). With her hands on my knees #39 slid up and down, with her back against my thighs. The view was fantastic and the feeling was too! Basically, she controlled the speed and the depth (I have found that many times, small women choose to be on top, so that they can control the depth of penetration … to prevent many males from jamming it in painfully). I reached forward with my right hand and stroked my thumb up, down over and around #39's clitoris … it drove her wild … she pumped faster … I could feel her lubricating more and more. Finally, I moved my thumb, just above her clitoris and pulled the hood up off her clitoris and she began to orgasm as she squealed, "OOOOooooooooooo!"

When her body relaxed, #39 slid her body up until my still engorged erection pulled completely out of her … it sprang back against my abdomen with a *Thwack*! #39 laid on her side next to me, smiling, she asked, "You didn't orgasm, did you?"

"No."

#39 reach over and grabbed several tissues from the nightstand, removed my condom and wrapped it in the tissues. Then, she grabbed several more tissues and put them on my chest. She slid the tip of her finger around and around where the foreskin connects to the head of my penis … great … then slowly down to my scrotum … which she gently caressed … then back up, several times … finally she wrapped her powerful hand around my erection and she started to pump … slowly at first … then faster and faster. All this time, #39 was continually whispering in my ear; how much she enjoyed her two orgasms, how powerful they were, how large my erection was, how good it made her feel, how it filled her up … on and on … it was incredibly sensual and made me hotter … her masterful manipulation brought me to the edge of orgasm … as I put the tissues over the tip of my penis, without missing a beat, #39 covered my mouth with hers and kissed me passionately … Fantastic! #39 continued to kiss me until my erection completely subsided. She whispered in my ear, "We make a great couple!"

I agreed. We both put on our bathing suits and headed back to the beach, holding hands. We hung out with the rest of her teammates, went in the water and played a long game of 'keep up' with the beach ball.

When they started to form a leap-frog line, I decided that I needed to head back to #30's spot on the beach to help with the last trek home.

******

I could tell that #30 and #32 were sad that today was their last day at the beach. When we arrived at their cottage, #32 ordered two pizzas for dinner. In the meantime, I showered and dressed, to be ready for the dance contest. The pizza was very good.

I went down to the beach … there wasn't anyone on the beach … for the last time, I took down and returned my umbrella and sand chair to where #20 rented them from. I put a note on the bottom of #20's empty bench saying, "Thank you for everything!"

I folded up my blanket and beach towel and brought them back to #19's cottage for cleaning. Then, I hurried back to get ready for the dance contest. #38 and I had agreed that we wouldn't dance fast together, until the contest. When I arrived, #38 and her team were already there. #38 looked very plain.

She was wearing white sneakers, white short pants and a thin, black, long-sleeved cardigan sweater.

I asked #39 to dance to 'Love Me Tender'. I asked her if she was going to be warm, wearing the long-sleeved sweater. She told me not to worry and that she was going to take it off for the contest … fine! I danced, slow, with several of #39's teammates. Then, I circulated around the room saying, "Hi and bye!" to those I knew.

When the dance contest was announced, I met #39 at the center of the floor. She had removed her black sweater and was wearing a skinny, sequined halter top, which reflected light in every direction … I darn near needed sunglasses to look at her … Perfect!

The band started to play 'Rock Around the Clock' and I took #39's hand and we started to dance to the beat of the music. Soon, I let go of her hand, jumped up and I did a split … unbeknownst to me #39 also did a split, landing right next to me. Several of the couples dancing around us stopped to watch us. We both jumped up and regained our dancing moves. Shortly we danced down into a squatting position … then I jumped up and over #39, landing in a split … #39 jumped up and over me, landing in a split. Those couples that were watching us and several others, screamed, stopped dancing and watched us. We popped up and started dancing again, but shortly #39 did a hand stand, spread her legs and I jumped through her legs and landed in a split … a larger crowd grew around us … screaming and clapping … I jumped up and we continued to dance … shortly we were coming to the end of the dance, so on que, #39 did a back flip, landed on both feet and simultaneously we did splits, right next to each other … the crowd erupted … screaming and clapping! I could not have found a better dance partner than #39!

The band leader said into the microphone, "Is there any question who won the contest?"

The crowd on the dance floor replied in unison, "No!"

The band leader asked the two of us to go up on the stage with him, as we walked to the center of the stage, the Band Leader announced that I had won the Dance Contest the previous week, which made me the King of the Dance Floor, the only person to win twice during the summer! The Band Leader said that he had never seen a better couple on the dance floor. He asked us how long we had been dancing together? We explained that we had just met that afternoon. The audience screamed!

We were like celebrities, when we went back down onto the dance floor. We danced with others and we danced together, but we didn't do any more splits.

I asked #39 if she would like to take a walk on the beach with me … unfortunately, several of her teammates decided to join us. We went back into the hall and danced several more times before the team decided to go back to their cottage … I walked hand in hand with #39, and the remainder of the team … when we arrived at their cottage, #39 and I stayed outside while the others went inside. I thanked #39 for being such a great dancer and for dancing with me. We kissed good-bye and then I headed back to #19s cottage.

******

The moms stayed up late; cleaning and folding all of the clothes and towels and packing all of the groceries from the cabinets, etc. #30's husband would be there at 10:30am, the next morning.

I got up when the moms were trying to wake and dress the youngsters. I ran over to the donut shop and bought a dozen, freshly made donuts and three coffees. The moms really appreciated it! Each kid had one, the moms had two each and I ate the rest. #19 had a yogurt.

We had everything piled up on the curb when #19's dad pulled up in a gigantic, 9 passenger van, wearing a face mask. He didn't get out (concerned that he would still be allergic to the 'beach air'). So, I packed everything into the back of the van, except for my backpack. While the moms herded the three small ones into the third row of seats. #30 sat up front, while #19 sat on one side in the second row, #32 in the middle and me on the other side. As soon as I closed the door #19s father sped off!

Once we were on a major highway #19's dad removed his mask. I don't think he was enthused about having to drop me off, but it really wasn't much out of his way, As I walked away from the van #30 put her window down and reminded me that they could … use … me again next year.

My parents were very happy to have me back home!

THE END

PostScript

Fortunately, you haven't come to the end of Tony's exploits. In his next book (The Sexpert II), follow Tony through his junior and senior years, graduation and beyond.

Of course, Tony will explore many more sexual positions and techniques. As well as entertaining multiple women at one time.

Tony continually learns what women like, while telling us what men like.

So, continue your education and enjoyment reading *The Sexpert II*.

Appendix

Sexual Positions

The Missionary Position: The female lies on her back with her legs spread and her knees bent slightly. The male lies between her legs and guides his penis into her vagina, supporting his body weight with his arms or elbows.

Doggy Style or Rear Entry: In this position, the female kneels on all fours, supporting herself with her hands and knees. The male crouches behind her and enters her vagina from behind.

The Lying Dog: The female lies face down on the bed with legs straight and hips slightly raised. (She can place a pillow under her hips.) Her partner enters her vagina from behind. When on her stomach, the female's legs will be closer together, which in turn creates a snugger fit for her partner's penis.

The Squatting Dog: Similar to Doggy Style or Lying Dog—the female lies face down on the bed with legs straight and hips slightly raised. (She can place a pillow under her hips.) The male then straddles the female, putting one foot on each side of her hips. The male then squats and enters the female.

Cowgirl: In this sex position, the male lies on his back, and the female faces him and kneels, straddling his pelvis and guiding his penis into her vagina. She can then sit up or lie down on him.

Reverse Cowgirl: The male lies on his back on the bed while the female sits astride him, facing her partner's feet, and slips the penis into her vagina.

The Corkscrew: Leaning forward, the female lies on the edge of the bed, resting on her hip and forearm while her partner enters her vagina from behind.

The Butterfly: The female lies flat on her back at the edge of the bed, then lifts her legs, spreads them apart, bends them at the knee and places her feet flat on the bed. The male stands at the edge of the bed, between the female's legs. The male enters her vagina and the female places her feet on the male's chest. Then, as the male trusts in, he spreads her knees … as he withdraws, he pushes her knees together.

Side by Side: The male and female lie on their sides, facing each other. The female lifts her top leg so the male can insert his penis. She can then wrap the leg around his waist or across his leg.

Face to Face: In this position, the male sits on the edge of a bed, or in a comfortable seated position, while the female climbs onto his lap, face to face, wrapping her legs behind him.

Split Leg: The female lies on her right side as the male straddles her right leg. The male then pulls his partner's left leg up and around his left side, or straight up against his chest and enters her vagina.

Reverse Split Leg: The female lays on her stomach and slides one leg forward, the male can straddle her other leg and slide all the way to the A-Spot as he thrusts.

Coital Alignment Technique (CAT): If you want to rock rather than thrust, roll with CAT. This position is similar to missionary; the main difference is that the male pushes the base of his penis so that it lines up with the clitoris and the two body parts make contact. Once they do, the couple rock back and forth and maintain constant contact.

Plowing the Field: The female lies flat on her stomach and spreads her legs wide. The male stands between the female's legs and lifts up the female's pelvis to enter her. The female supports herself with her arms and can grip the male's waist with her thighs.

End to End: The male sits, legs bent, leaning back on his hands and forearms. The female does the same and then they inch toward until they make contact.

Standing Upright: Standing, facing each other, on one foot the female wraps her other leg around the male's waist while the male helps to support the female. It is safest for the male to lean against a wall.

Criss Cross: The male enters the female from the missionary position, then the male slides his chest and legs off the female's body, so the male's pelvis is in the same location but his body forms an "X" with the female.

Edge of the Bed: The male stands next to the bed (facing the bed) and the female lies on the bed with their hips and booty toward the edge.

Drop in the Bucket: The female lies on her back (usually on the floor) with her legs raised and folded over so that her ankles are on either side of her head, while the male squats and dips his penis in and out of her vagina.

Reverse Face-to-Face: The male sits on the edge of the bed and the female sits on him, facing away, while leaning back on the male. The male can keep his legs together or spread apart.

Tabletop: The female lays face up on a table while the male stands on the floor and enters her while she is lying at the edge of the table, counter, or maybe even a bed.

The Roman Stallion: The female lies on her back, face up. The male straddles the female placing one foot on each side of her hips, while facing her. Then as the male leans forward to support himself with his hands and arms, he squats down positioning his erection in front of the female's vagina, waiting for the female to spread her legs, before he enters her (the farther the female spreads her legs, the better).

Face-Off: The man should kneel with his back straight. His partner then straddles him, lowering herself onto his erect penis and wrapping her legs around him in a tight embrace.

Folded in Half: The female lies on her back with their legs spread apart, or "spread eagle." She lifts her legs up and back toward her head. Her partner kneels in front and penetrates, holding her legs for support.

The 69 Position: A series of sex positions where two people perform oral sex on each other at the same time. It gets its name because the body positions of the two people involved look like the numbers 6 and 9.

Definitions

Areola: The human areola is the pigmented area on the breast around the nipple.

The A-Spot: The A-Spot, otherwise known as the Anterior Fornix Erogenous Zone (AFE), is located about four to five inches inside the vagina. Lesser known then the G-Spot, the Deep Spot is just above the cervix.

Clitoris: The clitoris is an erectile tissue of the females, located at the junction of the inner lips of vulva and immediately above the external opening of the urethra.

Cunnilingus: When a man has oral sex with a woman. He licks her sex organs with his lips and tongue.

Dildo: A sex toy that you can put into the mouth, anus, or vagina. While they are most times meant to feel like a penis, they don't have to look like one. They come in all different materials, shapes, and sizes. Some dildos are curved in order to stimulate the prostate or the g-spot.

- There are many different kinds of dildos. You can find ones that are: Made to look like a penis with testicles
- Made to be strapped on with a harness
- Meant for two partners to use at once, called double-sided or double-penetration dildos
- Vibrating dildos
- Made with a suction base to adhere to a surface
- Glass or metal dildos

Hymen: The hymen is a thin membrane of tissue that surrounds and narrows the vaginal opening. It may be torn or ruptured by sexual activity or by exercise.

Labia: The labia are part of the female genitalia; they are the major externally visible portions of the vulva. In humans, there are two pairs of labia:

the labia majora (or the outer labia) are larger and thicker, while the labia minora are folds of skin between the outer labia. The labia surrounds and protects the clitoris and the openings of the vagina and the urethra.

Mons Veneris: The mound of fatty tissue covering the pubic area in women.

Perineum: The area between the anus and the scrotum or the vulva.

Rimming: When one partner runs the tip of their tongue (or licks) their partners anus. The anus is the opening where the gastrointestinal tract ends and exits the body.

Scrotum: The pouch on the outside of the body that in males contains the testicles.

Vagina: The vagina is an elastic, muscular canal with a soft, flexible lining that provides lubrication and sensation. The vagina connects the uterus to the outside world. The vagina receives the penis during sexual intercourse.